A Death of
One's Own

A Death of One's Own

Literature, Law, and the Right to Die

✦

Jared Stark

NORTHWESTERN UNIVERSITY PRESS
EVANSTON, ILLINOIS

Northwestern University Press
www.nupress.northwestern.edu

Printed in the United States of America

10   9   8   7   6   5   4   3   2   1

Library of Congress Cataloging-in-Publication Data

Names: Stark, Jared Louis, author.
Title: A death of one's own : literature, law, and the right to die / Jared Stark.
Description: Evanston, Illinois : Northwestern University Press, 2018. I Includes
    bibliographical references and index.
Identifiers: LCCN 2017041791I ISBN 9780810136779 (cloth : alk. paper) I ISBN
    9780810136762 (pbk. : alk. paper) I ISBN 9780810136786 (ebook)
Subjects: LCSH: Suicide in literature. I Euthanasia in literature. I Right to die—
    Law and legislation. I Right to die—Moral and ethical aspects. I Law and
    literature.
Classification: LCC PN56.S744 S73 2018 I DDC 809.933548—dc23 LC record
    available at https://lccn.loc.gov/2017041791

For my parents

Here lies the water—good. Here stands the man—good. If the man go to this water and drown himself, it is, will he nill he, he goes; mark you that. But if the water come to him and drown him, he drowns not himself.

—Gravedigger, *Hamlet*

It would not make much sense to say that one may not kill oneself by walking into the sea, but may sit on the beach until submerged by the incoming tide.

—Justice Antonin Scalia, *Cruzan v. Director,*
Missouri Department of Health

CONTENTS

ACKNOWLEDGMENTS

The winding path this work has taken has given me the opportunity to learn from and be inspired by a great many people. The ideas and arguments explored here bear the mark of countless rich, provocative, and often difficult conversations with friends, colleagues, and students too numerous to name. It is a great pleasure, however, to recognize some of those without whose support this book would not have been possible.

Michael Levine has been a vital, sustaining presence, unstinting with his intellectual creativity and commitment from the earliest stages of this project. I have been continually nurtured and challenged by Alexander García Düttmann's ardent rigor, Emily Sun's incisive wisdom, and Anupama Rao's compassionate brilliance. Their comments and incitements have contributed significantly to my writing and thought. Ulrich Baer, Alessia Ricciardi, Carolyn Johnston, Davina Lopez, and Johannah Rodgers have been truly wonderful readers and interlocutors whose erudition and insight have been decisive at key moments. The teaching and work of Shoshana Felman, Geoffrey Hartman ז״ל, and especially Cathy Caruth have provided formative models of scholarly engagement.

Among the many friends and colleagues who have shared my vocation at Eckerd College, Cornell University, and New York University are Nathan Andersen, Constantina Rhodes, Julie Empric, Leonard Block, Jewel Spears Brooker, Douglas Mao, Martin Harries, Stefan Helmreich, Heather Paxson, Neil Saccamano, and Natalie Melas. Their warmth, knowledge, and discernment have touched this work in crucial ways. For their invaluable encouragement and confidence at critical junctures, I thank as well Wayne Koestenbaum, Denis Hollier, Vera Kutzinski, Marianne Hirsch, Avital Ronell, Peggy Kamuf, Margaret Higonnet, Cynthia Chase, and John MacKay. Jennifer Ballengee and David Kelman have embodied the promise of intellectual community.

Northwestern University Press has shepherded this project from manuscript to publication with responsive and unwavering care. My gratitude extends to the entire staff, in particular Gianna Moser, J.D. Wilson, Marianne Jankowski, and Anne Gendler. The thoughtful and beautiful reports submitted by Elisabeth Weber and Melissa Zeiger offered astute guidance for the final revisions of the manuscript. Joanne Rudof, Agnieszka Makles, and John Benjamin provided expert research assistance.

Family and lifelong friends have breathed this project along with me, with forbearance and boundless generosity of spirit. Andres Batista, Catherine

Dana, Sheryll Solis Neville, Eugenia Gomez-Escobar, Anne-Christine Habbard, and Christopher Yu have been constant companions across time and distance. Elaine Golin has been an essential part of my narrative. I am forever enriched by the love and friendship of Rachel Stark and Ryan Lilienthal. Noah, Evan, Jacob, Frankie, and Charlie are pure joy. Armando Solis has been my partner at every turn and in every way, immeasurably, my perfect solution. My parents, Ellen and Albert Stark, never cease to amaze me with their unfailing enthusiasm, contagious vitality, and uplifting presence; I dedicate this book to them.

Institutional support from Eckerd College, Dean of Faculty Suzan Harrison, and the Lloyd W. Chapin Faculty Fellowship Program has been instrumental in completing this work. Additional appreciation is due to the American Council for Learned Societies and the Cornell University Society for the Humanities for generous fellowship grants, as well as to the Institute for Comparative Literature and Society at Columbia University.

Several portions of this book appeared, in vastly different form, in the following journals, whose permission to include here I acknowledge: a short section of the introduction as my contribution to "Forum: Responses to Carolyn G. Heilbrun's Guest Column," *PMLA* 119 (2004): 339–41; part of chapter 2 in "The Price of Authenticity: Modernism and Suicide in Baudelaire's 'La Corde,' " *Modernism/Modernity* 14, no. 3 (2007): 499–506, copyright © 2007 John Hopkins University Press; and part of chapter 3 in "Suicide after Auschwitz," *The Yale Journal of Criticism* 14, no. 1 (2001): 93–114, copyright © 2001 Yale University and Johns Hopkins University Press. I also thank Editorial Planeta for permission to publish my translation of lines from Ramón Sampedro's poem, "¿Y cómo hablo de amor si estoy muerto?" in *Cartas desde el infierno* (Barcelona: Planeta, 2005): 23–24.

Bill Jacobson's tender, patient eye has long been a source of awe and consolation. I am deeply grateful for permission to reproduce his work on the cover of this book.

A Death of
One's Own

Introduction

Once follow the misleading ring of the night bell—and it
cannot be made good, not ever.
        —Franz Kafka, "A Country Doctor"

Along with Kafka's country doctor, we find ourselves today confronted with a disorienting appeal. Called upon in the midst of a snowstorm to attend to a young man in a distant village, the doctor finds that what is asked of him is not to fulfill his accustomed role of healer. Instead, whispering so that his family cannot hear, the young man issues what has become a familiar if nonetheless troubling entreaty: "Doctor, let me die."[1] This intimate, hardly audible plea finds itself amplified, if also filtered and mediated, by the often hypercharged debates that surround the right to die today. But in its bare simplicity, in its direct address to someone who is not just a doctor but also occupies the place of any other who might hear and respond, the young man's unexpected demand raises the questions that lie at the heart of this book: What does it mean to respond to such an appeal? What does it mean to have one's relationship to another defined by the moment, present or eventual, when he may call upon you, or you upon him, for assistance in dying?

In Kafka's tale, these questions are evidently experienced as new and unsettling ones, as they remain today. The doctor, for his part, does not quite know how to respond. Even when inclined to assent to the patient's request, he can only entertain such a thought, the story tells us, blasphemously or transgressively.[2] To assist the other in dying is an act that goes against the grain of his professional training, as well as broad ethical and cultural norms. Nor is it clear that the patient knows, or can know, exactly what he is asking. For without explicitly retracting his first demand, he later whispers, "Will you save me?"[3] Was the request for help in dying, then, a mistake that now cedes to a renewed desire to live? Or is it precisely through helping him die that the doctor would save the young man?

As readers of Kafka's tale may recall, the landscape and domestic spaces through which the country doctor travels are not easily delineated. His concern for his patient becomes uneasily entangled with his own psychic, hallucinatory drama, such that it becomes uncertain as the story progresses whether he can even maintain the position of doctor. Indeed, before long he finds himself stripped naked and laid down in the bed beside his patient, divested of the secure authority of his profession and vulnerably intimate with the condition of his patient. The call of the night bell and the strange appeal that it heralds thus expose the country doctor to a vertiginous existence in which the ethical compass that once may have oriented his practice and his life can no longer be trusted. "Let me die," it would seem, announces a definitive rupture from the past. Once he responds to the distressing call to offer assistance in dying, there is no clear path: "it cannot be made good, not ever."[4]

Although the right to die has been the subject of extensive inquiry in legal scholarship, biomedical ethics, public policy, philosophy, and cultural history, it has received little sustained attention in literary studies. In conversation with these fields, *A Death of One's Own* explores the ways that literary writing, and literary reading, bear witness to the radically new and unsettling experience of modern death confronted paradigmatically by Kafka's country doctor and his patient—an experience that would reportedly lead Kafka himself to issue a similar paradoxical demand at the end of his life to his own physician and friend, Dr. Robert Klopstock: "Kill me, or else you are a murderer."[5] Kafka's paradox suggests that in a world where natural death seems to be vanishing, and where death increasingly entails forms of decision and participation, new modes of thought and a new language are needed. In this book, I therefore turn to literary encounters with modern death in order to probe and sound out what the right to die means—what it means for the ways life and death are imagined, for ethical relations to others, for the idea of what it means to be human. My aim is not to formulate policy or advocate a particular position, but instead to open and explore spaces of reflection across and between various understandings of modern death and the vexing personal and collective questions it raises. As Kafka's country doctor observes, "To write prescriptions is easy, but to come to an understanding with people is hard."[6]

Because the right to die arises first and foremost as a juridical question, *A Death of One's Own* focuses on the ways that literature reflects on the discourse of the right to die as it appears in the law, and more specifically the European and American legal discourse where the right to die has been most influentially adjudicated. At the same time, the questions raised by the right to die touch upon the limits of the law and open it consequentially to the medical, aesthetic, philosophical, historical, and political concerns that both shape and are shaped by juridical conceptions of the right to die. The premise of this book is that literary encounters with modern death can both deepen and reframe the questions that animate discussions of the right to die in law, medicine, and political and social thought. What can we understand, for instance, about living wills by thinking about them not only as legal instruments but also as autobiographical acts? What do we learn about the frequently occurring metaphor of death as a last act or chapter in a life when it is seen through the lens of modernist models of (and challenges to) authorship and authority? What happens to the ambiguous—some say "useless"—notion of death with dignity when viewed through the prism of the literary testimony of writers who attempt to give voice to an experience of radical indignity?[7]

Rather than present a survey or a thematic study, A Death of One's Own identifies and analyzes the three overlapping but distinct arguments that commonly serve as the basis for claims to the right to die. According to the first, the subject of chapter 1, the right to die is an exercise of personal autonomy. One claims the right to die, in this light, on the basis of self-ownership, of the right to establish by and for oneself the proper or legitimate form of one's own death. It is simply out of respect for my personal autonomy, for my right to decide for myself, that others are enjoined to affirm my right to die and assist my death. According to the second argument, which I take up in chapter 2, death is a moment of self-authorship, which is also to say a moment of completion and, as such, of transformation. It is the moment when the story of my life comes into view as a biographical, narrative whole. To exercise the right to die, in this light, is to exercise the right to create my own image, to be the author of my life by planning and participating in my death. According to this argument, the right to die embodies, in U.S. Supreme Court Justice Stevens's words, "the individual's interest in choosing a final chapter that accords with her life story."[8] The third and final argument addressed in this book is the notion that the right to die enacts what has come to be called a death with dignity. To a degree, the idea of dignity overlaps considerably with the other two arguments addressed in this book. One might say, for instance, that the right to a death with dignity, particularly when framed as "personal dignity," is nothing other than the right to act autonomously and to be respected as an autonomous agent.[9] One might alternatively claim that it is nothing other than the right to design for oneself a final image of the self as a dignified self, in the sense of noble, honorable, or distinguished. But dignity, particularly as it shoulders the legacy of Kant, pertains not simply to individual action or to a particular style of dying. It implicates, in its Kantian and related inflections, the image of the human as such. To die with dignity, in this light, is to affirm or seek to affirm a certain idea of the human: to die not as oneself alone, but as an embodiment of human dignity.

These three arguments—personal autonomy, self-authorship, and death with dignity—have played a critical role in marshaling resistance to the bureaucracy, or biocracy, of modern medicine and its often depersonalizing technologies—what the physician and writer Atul Gawande calls "an experiment in social engineering, putting our fates in the hands of people valued more for their technical prowess than for their understanding of human needs."[10] As Gawande and others frequently note, modern medicine is also powerfully structured by the economics of health care, which can incentivize both expensive life-prolonging procedures and efforts to reduce costs by limiting medical options. It may well be the case, then, that the right to die and its recognition by the state are ultimately matters of fundamental freedom. But the texts and contexts explored in this book also suggest, or remind us, that freedom and death cannot be easily aligned, that we ought not overlook the paradoxical nature of a demand for freedom that destroys the conditions of possibility for freedom.

As I examine the normative forms of arguments for the right to die, then, I am also concerned with the ways that the appeal for the right to die, considered as a literary event, interrupts and potentially reconfigures the discourses that ground and frame its production and reception. Even as it seems to instantiate the arguments used to justify it—as it seems to promise and enact autonomy, self-authorship, or human dignity—the appeal for the right to die also attests to something new and singular about modern death, as well as to the strange modernity (or the strangeness of a modernity) in which such an appeal becomes necessary in the first place. Each chapter in this book therefore sets literary texts in relation to normative discourses, in and beyond the law, that frame the right to die.

To appreciate the force, scope, and eventually the limits of these normative arguments also means to inquire into the historical and conceptual conditions on which they are grounded, and which precede the attempts to adjudicate the right to die that began most dramatically and publicly in the 1970s. Thus the literary texts that call my attention, by writers including Rainer Maria Rilke, Herman Melville, Honoré de Balzac, and Charles Baudelaire, as well as critical and testimonial writings by figures including Walter Benjamin, Hannah Arendt, and Jean Améry—ranging, then, from early nineteenth-century to post–World War II Europe and the United States—do not have medically assisted death as their explicit theme. Yet as they variously attest to the advent of modern death, they also, in ways that may only become recognizable today, enact the appeal for the right to die in ways that lay bare and put in question the inner logics of the arguments that commonly ground this appeal, even as they expose their readers to new ways of giving voice and responding to it.

Before turning to these arguments for the right to die, however, this introductory chapter sets out to provide a more specific background for my inquiry. The first part of the introduction reflects broadly on the role of literature with respect to the time of modern death. The second part examines how a paradigmatic encounter with modern death in Rilke's novel, *The Notebooks of Malte Laurids Brigge*, elicits the central questions at issue in each of the main chapters of this book. Finally, the last part offers a preliminary discussion of the ethical concerns raised in this book.

I. Literature and the Right to Die

The Conversation

Over the last several decades, as the right to die has emerged as an increasingly pressing legal, political, and cultural question, it has also become apparent that we lack adequate conceptual resources and an apposite vocabulary to do justice to the experience of modern death. Confronted with the demand for physician aid in dying, the norms embodied in the Hippocratic Oath—its general imperative to "keep [the sick] from harm" as well as its specific commitment not to "give deadly drug to anybody if asked for it"[11]—come to appear feeble and insufficient, even outdated. Conventional juridical paradigms appear similarly unsatisfactory when faced with a plaintiff who asserts that her life interests are best served by her death. As a standard legal textbook notes, the very term "the right to die" can be misleading and controversial, and yet "handy substitutes for the phrase *the right to die* do not easily suggest themselves."[12] U.S. courts have correspondingly demonstrated uncertainty about which precedents and categories to invoke. In what is still the last word in U.S. federal law on the issue, the U.S. Supreme Court decision in *Washington v. Glucksberg* (1997), the majority opinion based its reasoning substantially on long-standing common law that criminalizes assisting or encouraging another's suicide. But as a number of concurring justices noted, this framework may no longer be appropriate, even if they could not clearly articulate an alternative approach.[13] Similarly, within the legal framework of human rights that has been at issue in European cases, the notion of a "right to die" hovers uneasily around the established "right to life," returning courts again and again to the perplexing question of whether death is or is not a part of "life."

These dilemmas are not confined to the clinic and the courtroom. In a culture that is often characterized as sequestering death from view and cloaking it in silence, it becomes a task and a challenge to develop a way of speaking about the end of life. Symptomatic of such efforts, for instance, is the Conversation Project, a nonprofit organization "dedicated to helping people talk about their wishes for end-of-life." Even as this effort seeks to "make these difficult conversations easier," its very name attests to the lack of a more precise term. "The conversation" becomes instead a mystified catchword with all the marks of a commercial slogan. "We've had the conversation. Have you?"[14]

But is this a conversation that one can ever *have had*, that can ever be put definitely into the past? Is it possible to come to an understanding, individually and collectively, about the moment of death, of my death—about an experience that cannot be called an experience, a moment that cannot be joined into a sequence of like moments? How does the enigma of modern dying, its resistance to received paradigms, affect and transform ethical being?

Against the background of attempts to regulate, adjudicate, and formalize the medical, legal, and social understanding of modern death, perhaps there is something to be said for turning to the "infinite conversation" of literature—to literature considered as a form of language, dialogue, and thought that both generates new ways of naming and speaking, new ways of relating to the real, and at the same time perpetually calls meaning, including its own meaning, into question.[15] If literature (and literary modes of reading texts that do not necessarily identify themselves as literary) might bring to light something about modern death that otherwise would remain invisible and unspoken, to approach modern death through the language of literature is to remain attuned to the impasse at the heart of any attempt to grasp the nature of death. "'Death,'" J. Hillis Miller reminds us, "is a catachresis for what can never be named properly."[16] Literature, in making visible and explicit the figurative nature of language, may remind us of what remains unnamable, of what resists understanding. What the encounter with literature also insists, however, is that the mystery, negativity, or unknowability of death cannot have the last word. To call meaning into question radically means to also call into question the very claim to meaninglessness, the insistence on impasse, the silence of death. If literature is an infinite conversation, this is because it insists on maintaining a conversation even when there seems to be no reply, or perhaps especially so.

What, then, does it mean to have a conversation about or with death? In the era of modern death, this conversation distills itself around the question of the right to die. What does it mean to issue an appeal for the right to die, and what does it mean to respond to such an appeal? What does it mean to live in a space and time that, on the one hand, is characterized by startling and even unprecedented forms of vulnerability, and that, on the other, seems to deprive me of my death, a world where the very meaning of death—and the meaning that is said to derive from death—seem to be vanishing or to have vanished? What does it mean to have "the conversation" not according to any recommended script or packaged formula, without the support of a downloaded pamphlet or checklist, but instead in a way that openly and without predetermined answers ponders the experience of living and dying in a world in which this conversation has become increasingly compulsory?

The Time of Postnatural Death

These questions may be usefully situated in relation to the cultural history of death, which was most influentially charted by the French historian Philippe Ariès in his 1977 magnum opus *The Hour of Our Death*. For Ariès, the late nineteenth and early twentieth centuries witness an epochal transformation in conceptions of death and dying, ushering in what he calls the age of "invisible death" of late or post-Enlightenment modernity.[17] He argues that the "traditional model" of death, which remained fundamentally unaltered for the better part of a millennium, undergoes a radical rupture.[18] Whereas death previously was made visible through forms of communal ritual and mourning, in the age of the invisible death it becomes a dirty secret cloaked in the technocratic veil of the hospital. As Ariès notes, this medicalization of death produces "an absolutely new type of dying," characterized by new definitions as well as a new temporality of death.[19] In place of the "old signs" legible to the layman, such as cessation of respiration or of the heartbeat, death is "subdivided" into various technical definitions (cerebral death, brain stem death, cardiopulmonary death) requiring expertise for their identification and classification. Technology also allows the doctor to manipulate the duration of death, "from the few hours it once was, to several days, weeks, months, or even years."[20]

For Ariès, these medical interventions issue from the denial of death as a "natural and necessary phenomenon"[21] and its discursive reconfiguration as "an accident of illness that must be brought under control."[22] No longer imagined as a form of fate, as an external necessity, or as a sheer force of nature, death becomes subject to the medical, legal, and administrative technologies that dispossess me of my death, that render it invisible, to the point that Ariès can suggest that in the age of invisible death, "death no longer belongs to the dying man."[23]

But this medicalization of death, in ways that are not and perhaps could not have been grasped in Ariès's 1977 study, does not simply transfer authority from nature to a medical technocracy. Rather, as death is severed from its traditional link with fate or nature, the era of the invisible death overlaps with and increasingly yields to new forms of visibility produced by what I will call the time of postnatural death.[24] In the time of postnatural death, natural and necessary death seems to have vanished or to be in the process of vanishing. "The timing of death—once a matter of fate—is now a matter of human choice," reported the U.S. Congress's Office of Technology Assessment more than a quarter-century ago.[25] Or as the bioethicist and Hastings Center founder Daniel Callahan puts it, "It is human choice, not nature, which now ends most lives."[26]

To say that the timing of death is now a matter of human choice does not mean that death has become optional—or at least, it does not seem to have come to this, even as investment in longevity research and the quest for a "god pill" grows.[27] Yet a number of new medical technologies, as they attenuate and disrupt the image of fate or nature, announce the time of postnatural death. Transplantation, parabiosis, cloning, cryonics, and cybernetics name but some of the ways that a new relation to death is being enacted. If understood as symptoms of the age of invisible death, these technologies appear as attempts to deny the course of nature, in that each seeks to interfere with the necessity of death, to prolong life beyond supposedly natural limits. And yet they also call into question the very criteria used to identify such limits. Experimental treatments (vaccinations, bypasses, etc.) become standard practice, and what once counted as "extraordinary measures" or science-fiction fantasies come to appear today as ordinary and self-evident forms of care.[28] The seemingly outlandish projects of the self-named "immortalists"— most closely associated with cryonic suspension and reanimation—or "healthspanners"—who seek to extend life through biotechnology—soon make their way into the pages of the most respected medical journals.[29] On the one hand, then, life-extension technologies might be understood as interfering with a natural or necessary process or even as crimes against the law of nature, which countervailing institutions—legal, bioethical, religious—might then seek to safeguard. But on the other hand, such technologies, actual or imagined, disrupt the distinction between what is and what is not a form of interference. They erase or blur the line where nature would have set its limit and so undermine any standard according to which a transgression could be judged as such. Rather than suppress natural death, these technologies herald its denaturalization.

Mainstream bioethics, which shares deep affinities with the sociological perspective of Ariès, tends to resist or elide this denaturalization of death. Leon Kass, chair of the President's Council on Bioethics under George W. Bush from 2001 to 2005, for instance, is acutely aware of the ways in which modern technologies redefine death. "Recently, this necessity [of dying] seems to have become something of a question," he writes. "Slowing the aging process could yield powers to retard senescence, preserve youthfulness, and prolong life, perhaps indefinitely."[30] Yet the required response to these extraordinary developments, he argues, is to renounce voluntarily the pursuit of medical or other death-control technologies. We ought not "covet a prolonged life."[31]

The substitution of moral agency for necessity in Kass's argument—rather than resign oneself to mortality, it becomes a moral duty to enforce it—points, however, to a more profound rift than he allows. Can a deliberate decision not to seek a longer life take the place of mortality defined according to its inescapability and externality? Although such a decision may seek to mimic a necessary death, at the same time this mimicry lays bare the conditions of postnatural death. Thus as life-extension technologies become increasingly available, they fundamentally alter what it means to die. For as death becomes a matter of choice, what was once considered a "normal" or "natural" death is increasingly traversed by the forms of agency, choice, and decision—otherwise put, by the question of suicide.

Within the European and American legal and cultural traditions that are the focus of this study, as I explore later in more detail, suicide has principally been understood as an attempt to evade a natural or proper death. Instead of waiting patiently for a death prescribed and legitimated by nature, God, or the law, suicide prematurely steals death from its legitimate executor. Sinfully, criminally, or simply erroneously, the suicide dies not the death he was meant to die, but instead the wrong death. It will be important at moments throughout this book to attend to the ways that suicide has been and continues to be interpreted along the conventional lines laid out by religion, philosophy, and law as well as by modern diagnostic approaches including medicine, psychology, and sociology. These approaches to suicide continue to perceive it as a form of wrong and wrongful death, although the responsibility for this wrong may be attributed not only to the individual person but also to other causes. In debates concerning the right to die, this distinction between natural and unnatural death has translated into the legal—and for some, moral—distinction between authorized medical practices, such as forgoing or withdrawing treatment, that are said to "allo[w] nature to take its course," and criminalized practices such as assisted suicide that are said to produce death by "artificial" means.[32] As the distinction between natural and unnatural death erodes, however, the formerly critical distinction between suicide and death also collapses. The demand for the "right to die," in this light, signals a crisis in the idea of a proper or legitimate death: one commits suicide because death does not come to pass when it is supposed to come to pass or because one can no longer perceive what the right or natural time to die ought to be. Rather than a denial of death, suicide becomes death's accomplice, its refuge in a world that seeks to eliminate death.

What Ariès and Kass see as the disappearance and dispossession of death thus also generate new modes of engaging death ethically and imaginatively. The question, What does it mean to die? and the question, What does it mean to commit suicide? converge to become one and the same question. The central questions of this book can therefore be restated as follows: What does it mean to think of suicide as a way to die, and, conversely, to think of death as a form of suicide? What does it mean to imagine and represent a death as something that arrives not as necessity but in the form of a "choice"? What does it mean to think of death, in the first place, as something that "belongs" or ceases to belong to the dying? Who are we, or who do we become, in the time of postnatural death?

These questions acquired increasing visibility in the 1970s, which normally serve as the starting point for discussions of the right to die. Often cited as a landmark event bringing the right to die to broad public attention in the United States and abroad was the legal and political battle over the fate of Karen Ann Quinlan, whose parents won the right to remove their comatose daughter from life support in a March 31, 1976, decision by the New Jersey Supreme Court. In identifying and discussing the normative forms of the principal arguments for the right to die, I therefore draw mainly on texts and examples from the recent past, from the Quinlan case through current debates on assisted suicide. But the cultural, historical, and conceptual questions that interest me emerge already in compelling—and, I argue, far-reaching—ways in the earlier moments that are central to each chapter, two of which focus on the nineteenth century and one on the Holocaust and its aftermath. These earlier texts and contexts, I suggest, not only shed light on the underlying conditions and assumptions that inform contemporary debates, but also provide resources for imagining different possible futures for the right to die.

If the dominant paradigm in these earlier moments is what Ariès calls "the invisible death" or "death denied," texts such as Melville's "Bartleby, the Scrivener," Balzac's *La Peau de chagrin*, and the Holocaust testimony of Jean Améry bear witness to the ways in which the time of postnatural death perforates and overlaps with the age of invisible death without entirely displacing it. They attest to the ways that modernity does not merely deny death but instead produces a new and specifically modern image of death. Where the age of invisible death medicalizes dying, treating it as a symptom or failure subject to technical management, the time of postnatural death transforms death into a question that evades medical control and requires each of us to participate, in highly mediated but continually renegotiated ways, in defining what death will mean and how it will take place. When we issue or hear a demand for the right to die, when we sign or witness a living will, when we engage vicariously or actively in the legal, political, and media clamor that surrounds the bodies of Karen Ann Quinlan or Nancy Cruzan, of Ramón Sampedro or Diane Pretty, of Eluana Englaro or Terri Schiavo, of Craig Ewert or Brittany Maynard or Jahi McMath, death becomes visible anew. What is exposed, however, is not simply the natural and necessary death of the traditional model. Instead, we encounter something that we might still call "death" but that remains to be imagined.

II. Death and Modernity

Malte's Vision

The connection this book draws between literature and the right to die may, for some readers, inevitably evoke Maurice Blanchot's 1949 essay, "Literature and the Right to Death." Blanchot's essay, written soon after the end of the Second World War and occasioned by the literary and political debates of postwar France, does not have in mind the question of the right to die in the contemporary sense of the phrase, that is, as it arises with increasing urgency and visibility in late twentieth- and early twenty-first-century bioethics. Nonetheless, one might note the uncanny resonance in the time of postnatural death of Blanchot's image of the writer, and of literature more generally, hovering unremittingly between a demand for radical autonomy— what Blanchot calls a demand for the right to death—and the necessary dependence of the work of literature on existing frames of reference and recognition, leading to what he calls the impossibility of dying. The appeal for the right to die, in this light, is a quintessential literary event, also suspended between freedom and dependence, autonomy and recognition.[33]

As relevant to this book as Blanchot's theoretical reflections on literature and the right to death, however, is his concern with the specific historical emergence of modern death and its implications. He is not alone in finding the paradigmatic image of modern death in the only novel written by the poet Rainer Maria Rilke, *The Notebooks of Malte Laurids Brigge*, published in 1910 and rooted in Rilke's experience in Paris in 1902 and 1903.[34] It is from this novel that *A Death of One's Own* draws its title.[35] By way of introduction, I turn to Rilke's novel so as to open some of the major questions and themes that animate this study.

Rilke's novel seems, in many ways, to mirror Ariès's characterization of modernity as the age of invisible death. Malte, the impoverished Danish aristocrat whose fictional journal comprises the novel, finds himself in modern Paris on the far side of a radical transformation in the image of death. He can recall the dramatic death of his grandfather, Chamberlain Brigge, at the ancestral estate of Ulsgaard. The Chamberlain dies, as in Ariès's typical scene of traditional death, in the same room where his mother had died, surrounded by his household retinue and commanding the attention of the entire village. But Malte, the grandson, finds himself in the modern city where death has been relegated to the hospital—where, indeed, the city itself appears to him as a necropolis made up of nothing but hospitals. "Here, then, is where people come to live; I'd have thought it more a place to die in," the novel begins. "I have been out. I saw hospitals."[36]

But Rilke's novel challenges Ariès's account of modern death in several crucial ways, and in so doing raises the critical questions concerning postnatural death that organize the present study. In a discussion of Ariès, Jacques Derrida points out the limits of the historiography of death. One who sets out to compose a history of death, he writes, "knows, thinks he knows, or grants to himself the unquestioned knowledge of what death is, of what being-dead means; consequently, he grants to himself all the criteriology that will allow him to identify, recognize, select, or delimit the objects of his inquiry or the thematic field of his anthropologico-historical knowledge."[37] By contrast, it is the very enigma of modern death, its unrecognizability and its resistance to assimilation to existing categories, that emerges in the literary space of Rilke's novel. As Malte envisions the modern world as a necropolis, his vision also provides a preliminary mapping of the major questions addressed in this book. What does modern death mean for the thought of autonomy? How does it affect the experience of art? And what does it mean for the image of the human?

Death, Sovereignty, and the Literary Imagination

Malte's vision of Paris as a modern necropolis centers on the major Parisian hospital, the Hôtel Dieu, which he sees as a place of death: "If anyone thought of taking me to the Hôtel Dieu, I should indubitably die there."[38] This vision of modern death arises not inside the hospital but on the square that separates the Cathedral of Notre Dame from the Hôtel Dieu, namely, the Place du Parvis Notre Dame. Implicit in the choice of this site is the historical function of the Place du Parvis Notre Dame as a symbolic locus of sovereign power. Under the ancien régime, it was there that convicted criminals would be made to kneel before the "Ladder of Justice" and seek absolution, while after the Revolution they would be put on display in stocks. By Malte's time, under the Third Republic, the Parvis de Notre Dame was designated and marked as the zero point for all national roads and played a key role in state funerals and other civic displays: it becomes the geographical emblem of "the sacred center of power."[39]

Rilke's novel thus implicitly links Malte's vision of modern death to a certain conception of the law, in which the law and death are mutually constitutive. The law of nature, the law that every man must die, serves as the very model of legal authority and necessity, just as the law in its essential form is grounded in the power to kill. What Malte witnesses at this site, however, is a crisis in this structure of sovereignty, which I have associated with postnatural death, and to which I return with specific reference to the legal structure of the right to die in chapter 1.

In the *Notebooks*, this crisis manifests itself at first as a mere displacement of sovereign power from one side of the square to the other. "It is hardly possible," Malte laments, "to view the façade of the cathedral of Paris without the risk of being run over by one of the many vehicles speeding as fast as they can go across the square to the Hôtel."[40] As Malte contemplates the Hôtel Dieu, his partial translation of its proper name into German—"*Gottes Hôtel*" or "God's own Hôtel" in Hulse's English translation—recalls its origins as a subsidiary of the church, which established the hospital in the seventh century and administered its operations for centuries. Malte notes that at its origins the hospital would have been a modest operation compared to its current prominence. "In the days of King Clovis," he writes, slightly exaggerating, since the hospital was not established until 150 years after the death of Clovis in 511, "people were already dying in some of the beds. Now they die in five hundred and fifty-nine of them."[41] The church, representing divine and royal authority, is thus marginalized and overtaken by the vast medical institution, which by the early twentieth century had become part of an extensive state-managed system. Indeed, after demolition of the original building and the construction of a new facility beginning in 1867 under Haussmann, the hospital had come to occupy a physical footprint nearly three times that of the cathedral. At the site where criminals condemned to death were once paraded before the public with ropes around their necks, where the power over death was once invested in the sovereign as the representative of divine justice, now the traffic of ambulances, so frenetic that it would cut off the carriage of "even the Duke of Sagan," marks the transfer of the power over death to the impersonal forces of a medical and state bureaucracy. The traditional authority of church and state (embodied in the figure of the Duke) yields to the hospital.

The relocation of sovereign power from the church to the hospital witnessed by Malte could be understood as paradigmatic of the advent of modernity. It echoes Ariès's characterization of modern, medicalized death, as well as, for instance, Michel Foucault's classic account of modernity as marked by a redefinition of sovereign power, from "the right to kill" invested in the figure of the king, to the "power to let live" and to "manage life" invested in the bureaucratic governmentality of late modernity. Yet Malte's vision does not simply endorse this sociological account revolving around the transfer of institutional power, for he implicates himself and his own imaginative power in this scene. Not only does he imagine the Hôtel Dieu as the site of his own possible death; he is fixated as well on the ambulances speeding across the square:

> It is worth noting that these fiendish little carriages have immensely stimulating frosted-glass windows behind which one can picture the most extraordinary agonies: for this, the imagination of a concierge suffices. But if one is possessed of greater imaginative resources, and strikes out in other directions, there need be no limit to speculation.[42]

In one sense, the frosted-glass windows of the ambulances, hiding the dying from sight on their journey to the fatal hospital, might provide an especially apt emblem for the age of invisible death, particularly as they turn the viewer's gaze away from the façade of the cathedral and *its* famous stained-glass windows. Yet, beyond and in opposition to the vicarious interest that Malte associates with a stereotypical concierge, these ambulances inspire the imagination to wander in other, new directions, and to experience a radical freedom to speculate to the point of limitlessness (*geradzu unbegrenzt*).

This radical freedom, a freedom that would not be subject to any law, situates the literary imagination in the time of postnatural death, understood as a time when the law of natural death is suspended or interrupted. It opens a freedom to imagine death in a new way. Whereas the law-bound imagination of the concierge attempts to see *through* the frosted glass windows so as to reveal what they hide, the free imagination, which does not remain focused on the enclosed space of the ambulance but rather wanders in other directions, is empowered by the translucent opacity of the windows, that is, by witnessing death *in its very invisibility*.

Thus the *Notebooks*, as Blanchot also suggests, gives a different meaning to the idea of the invisible death. Blanchot, in fact, uses the phrase "invisible death" in connection with the *Notebooks*, in a work that predates Ariès's by two decades.[43] Rilke's novel, he suggests, evinces a "desire 'not to see death.' " But this invisibility of death acquires a diametrically opposed meaning for him. It could be, he notes, anticipating Ariès's characterization of the age of invisible death, a form of denial, a sign of "fear of seeing it, elusiveness and flight."[44] But Blanchot favors an alternative understanding. The refusal to see death, he argues, may indicate instead a radical recognition of death, since death, he writes, is itself the "source of invisibility."[45] In this light, it would be the very idea that death is hidden or denied that would itself constitute a form of denial, in that the idea of hiddenness implies the possibility of uncovering death and making it visible.

If the *Notebooks*, by contrast, bears witness to the invisibility of death, it does so, Blanchot suggests, by exercising the writer's freedom through negation. "This book is mysterious because it turns around a hidden center which the author was unable to approach," Blanchot writes. "This center is the death of Malte, or the instant of his collapse."[46] Unlike, for instance, Goethe's *The Sorrows of Young Werther*, which reports the protagonist's death in the editorial voice that closes the novel, Rilke's novel pursues the structural consequences of the form of the fictional journal to its end: Malte cannot report his own death and so this event must remain invisible, but also, as the novel's unlocatable "hidden center," ubiquitous. We might also compare the *Notebooks* to Tolstoy's "The Death of Ivan Ilych," which, for Ariès, quintessentially illustrates the advent of modern death.[47] For Ariès, Tolstoy's text reveals the characteristics of invisible death most fully when Ivan himself comes to participate in "the lie . . . that he was only sick." Yet Tolstoy's story preserves the ability of the author to see and know the death that is concealed from his protagonist. The text ends confidently in the omniscient voice of a third-person narrator: "He drew in a breath, stopped in the midst of a sigh, stretched out, and died."[48]

The rejection of realism and of the position of objective narrator, which might indicate modernism of form in Rilke's novel in that they render the novel permanently fragmentary, are thus owed to the novel's attempt to bear witness to modern death in its invisibility. The power of the novel comes to reside in its ability not to represent the unknown or to reveal the hidden, but rather to transmit the very experience of confronting opacity. Thus, in what we might call a gesture of literary suicide, the novel does not write its own central scene.[49] It leaves Malte's death invisible, and in so doing, becomes, as it were, another frosted-glass window in which a reader might imagine the time of postnatural death "with no limit to speculation."

The Art of Death in the Age of the Commodity

The crisis of sovereignty that Malte discovers in the scene of modern death thus opens the question of the literary imagination. And yet this imagination, as the impoverished writer Malte is all too aware, cannot be disjoined from the historical conditions in which it is embedded. Thus, alongside the closed ambulances that excite the imagination, he records the operations of a commerce in death: "I have also seen open hackney carriages arriving, hired cabs with the tops folded down, making the trip for the standard fare of two francs per hour of death."[50] How can the literary imagination, which finds its freedom in the time of postnatural death, operate in this marketplace of death?

This question, to which I return in chapter 2 as it concerns the image of modern death in Balzac and Baudelaire, lies at the heart of Rilke's image of "a death of one's own." Recalling a lost past, the world of traditional death, Malte can evoke "a feeling that formerly it must have been different.

Formerly, people knew (or perhaps they had an intuition) that they bore their death within them like the stone within a fruit. . . . They *had* it, and that conferred a peculiar dignity, and a tranquil pride."[51] The hospital, where modern death takes place, is by contrast "a factory production line, of course, and with such an immense output the quality of individual deaths may vary. But that is neither here nor there; it's quantity not quality that counts." Transformed into a factory of death devoted to efficiency and productivity and without regard for the individual, the hospital loses its traditional meaning as a place of healing and hospitality. It comes to epitomize instead an inhospitable modernity. Malte memorably elaborates on this image:

> Who today cares about a well-made death? No one. Even the rich, who could afford to die in well-appointed style, are lowering their standards and growing indifferent; the wish for a death of one's own is becoming ever more infrequent. Before long it will be just as uncommon as a life of one's own. Dear God, it is all there waiting for us; along we come and find a life ready to wear on the rack, and all we have to do is put it on. You wish to go, or have to, and that too is no trouble: *Voilà votre mort, monsieur.*[52]

The image of "a death of one's own" had already appeared in Rilke's writing in very different form in his 1903 poem "The Book of Poverty and Death," where we find the prayer-like utterance: "O Lord, give to each a death of his own." This poem links such a death to the organic image of fruit: at one moment, death is "like a piece of fruit, / green and sour, refusing to mature," while later what the poem calls "the large death" is said to be "the fruit around which all revolves."[53] In the *Notebooks*, however, the organic metaphor of the fruit, which links death to ideas of natural necessity, gives way to the quintessentially modern image of industrial production and commodification.

Malte thus seems to set two images of death in opposition to each other. Whereas the organic metaphor imagined death as the unique and singular property of each person, the factory and garment metaphors figure death as alienated from the individual. Postnatural death appears in generic, anonymous, and interchangeable form, in the form of a commodity definitively severed from the image of nature. Yet the ambiguity of the notion of "a death of one's own," "*einen eigenen Tod,*" also complicates this distinction. On the one hand, *eigen* may indicate a "proper" death, a death that seems to be fated or waiting for one, and the properness of which would situate it as natural and necessary; this is the meaning it seems to bear in "The Book of Poverty and Death." Yet in the *Notebooks*, where it is bracketed by the conceit of commodified possessions, of the ready-to-wear garment, *eigen* also implies an idea of death as possession, as something that can be bought and sold in the marketplace of modernity. The "death of one's own" that seemed to belong to the lost time of natural death already participates, in other words, in the postnatural logic of possession and commodification. It is only within the time of postnatural death that the very idea of a death of one's own arises, even if it arises only in the form of a lost or disappearing wish.[54]

The denaturalization of death in Rilke appears even more radical if we consider the function of the image in the *Notebooks*. For Malte's caustic elaboration of the image of modern death—as a manufactured item produced in quantity, as a possession or consumer good, and as a ready-to-wear garment which, in turn, he continues, mining a vein of dark humor, might be "a little too large" or "tight at the throat"[55]—not only signals the advent of new images of modern death but also foregrounds their status as images. Indeed, in Malte's vision, even natural death can appear only in terms of a simile, "*like* the stone within the fruit," that seems to denaturalize even the "proper" death and expose its manufactured quality.[56] The image, which seems at first to designate what it pictures, to convey meaning through metaphor, becomes preoccupied with its own operations and so generates a crisis in meaning, an unwillingness or inability to refer to something beyond itself. In this respect, Rilke's novel might be said to allegorize its own image-making operation in that the image it unfolds, the image of the garment, is itself an image of images, a metaphor for metaphoricity as such. "Expression is the dress of thought," as Alexander Pope writes.

Indeed, the particular image Malte manufactures, of death as garment, might remind us that the garment itself appears as the very image of the commodity in Marx's *Capital*, where the example of an overcoat illustrates the nature and function of commodities. As the image of the commodity form as such, what the overcoat figures, in fact, are the ways that the commodity is itself a sort of metaphor for the processes of production that it stands in for and mystifies. To say that death has become a commodity, then, is to say that it is always already an image, that it only becomes visible in and through an image of images.

The image of a death of one's own is thus subject to a paradox: even as it seems to name a form of death that would resist the commodification of death, that would allow one's death (and, as Malte suggests, one's life) to stand out as singular and original, the very image of such a death only becomes visible within the homogenizing logic of commodification.

The Human Catastrophe

To imagine the possession of death, then, also means, in Rilke's novel, to face a dispossession. It is not simply, as a conventional image would have it, that death strips one of all possessions, but that modernity dispossesses one of death itself.

As Blanchot observes, the dispossession of death is decisively linked to the modernity of the crowd, the masses, the modern city. "Malte's anguish has more than a little to do with the anonymous existence of big cities—to that distress which makes vagrants of some, men fallen out of themselves and out of the world, already dead of an unwitting death never to be achieved," he writes.[57] Blanchot here alludes to one of the striking motifs of the novel, Malte's encounters with the *Fortgeworfene*—the outcasts, the vagabonds, the homeless, the untouchables—and his explicit anxiety that he could all too easily join their ranks, that he may all too easily be mistaken for one of them, that he may already be, without knowing it, counted among them.

But if the *Notebooks* thus points backwards to the ways that modern death is crucially linked to the experience of the modern city for authors such as Balzac and Baudelaire (as I will suggest in chapter 2), Rilke's novel also seems to anticipate the catastrophic modernity of the Nazi death camps. Ulrich Baer, for instance, sees in Malte's vision of "the technicalization of existence and of death" a precursor to Paul Celan's post-Holocaust poetry.[58] Giorgio Agamben has similarly suggested that Malte's image of the *Fortgeworfene*, to whom Malte refers as "husks of men" (*Schalen von Menschen*), ties his vision to a genealogy that includes the "husks of men" that Primo Levi sees in the *Muselmänner* of Auschwitz and that he writes of in his final book, *The Drowned and the Saved*.[59] As Sandra Gilbert observes, the image of the hospital-as-Auschwitz casts a long shadow. "Indeed, the more I study the daunting technologies of the contemporary hospital, the more I begin to see why a patient confined in its life-supporting but often depersonalizing realm might, in extremis, associate that space with the life-destroying, always depersonalizing arena of the prison camp. Molly Haskell reports in fact that as he hovered between life and death during his excruciatingly uncomfortable stay in the ICU, her husband, the ordinarily lucid and incisive film critic Andrew Sarris, became 'very confused, insisting that he was in Auschwitz.'"[60]

Malte's vision echoes through accounts of the camps not only in its preoccupation with anonymous death, but also in the image of industrialized death. In what may be the first application of this image to the death camps, and in an image that may be owed to Rilke, the SS physician F. Entress described the systematic murder of Jews in the camps as taking place by "conveyor belt."[61] In Hannah Arendt's writings, the death camps are described as "corpse factories" designed for maximum "productive capacity."[62] Indeed, we might note that the specific image of modern deaths as industrially produced garments prefigures the internal terminology of the camps, where it was forbidden to speak of human corpses, which were instead called, among other terms, *Schmattes*, rags or tattered garments.[63] What appeared as a self-conscious and radically imagined *image* in Rilke's novel is subject, in the language of the camps, to disastrous literalization: genocide takes the form of garbage disposal, in which those who are annihilated cannot even be said properly to have died. It is in this light that we might understand Jean Améry's testimony to "the total collapse of the aesthetic view of death" in Auschwitz.[64] It is not simply that death can no longer be thought of as beautiful, but that the distance between death and the image collapses. Death can no longer excite the imagination. Or, to the extent that modern death for Rilke names the very condition of possibility for the literary imagination, death itself would have died.

This poses a critical ethical problem in the wake of Auschwitz, which I take up in chapter 3. What does it mean to speak of death—and more specifically, of voluntary death—after Auschwitz? What does it mean to appeal for the right to die in a world that has undergone the totalization of death? "He who has been the contemporary of the camps is forever a survivor: death will not make him die," writes Blanchot.[65] In the contemporary discourse of the right to die, the challenge of recovering death as a human experience, of humanizing death, has been most powerfully at issue in the concept of "death with dignity." But dignity, too, emerges damaged from the ashes of the Shoah, as the history of the right to die shows. If death with dignity is to take place in the shadow of Auschwitz, it will have to be on the basis of a new sense of what dignity might or can come to mean.

III. Ethics and Interpretation

Possible but Not Necessary

The study of the right to die has almost uniformly been motivated by the need to support one side or the other in the polarized and often emotionally agonizing debates that have erupted with increasing frequency since at least the early 1960s, but that also have deeper historical roots.[66] With the recent legalization of various forms of medically assisted death—at the time of writing, in seven U.S. jurisdictions, Canada, and several countries in Europe, and under active consideration in thirty U.S. states, in the United Kingdom, Germany, and France—research into the subject has been unsurprisingly enlisted to inform and underwrite political, legal, and medical decision-making. As noted earlier, it is not the aim of the present study to advance a particular position in this debate or to make policy proposals. And yet it is owed to readers who engage with the arguments explored here to state something like a position: that the exercise of a right to die ought to be possible but not necessary—that is, independent of coercion or a sense of duty. If such an unnecessary possibility might form the basic conditions of any right, it is also the case that what is permitted and what is required become, as we shall see, thoroughly entangled when it comes to the claim for the right to die.

On the one hand, then, I agree with Drucilla Cornell that ethical being requires, even presupposes, recognition of a right to die—and, consequently, of assistance in dying—both on the individual and collective level. "We do not choose to be 'ethical'—we can do good, and we can do bad, but it is impossible that we not decide to be in an ethical relation," Cornell writes, evoking the philosophy of Emmanuel Levinas:

> We are always with others, and how we are with others is what shapes us, indeed constitutes us, if I may risk the word. The other presents a demand on us, and never more powerfully than at the hour of her death . . . . We are together in "our dying." And so let us face that, and have that fated togetherness be recognized by the state as a matter of right.[67]

Cornell here posits the law as an institution that would make possible something always already required by an ethical relation that precedes and exceeds governmental authority. The state would merely perform an act of recognition and thus allow an ethical relation that is currently restricted or criminalized in all but a few jurisdictions to fulfill itself freely.

Recognition, however, is not neutral with respect to what is recognized. It splits into at least two moments at odds with each other. "That which is to be recognized does not know what will happen to it and what it will do to that which recognizes. Conversely, that which recognizes does not know what will occur to it and, because of its own response, to that which it recognizes," Alexander García Düttmann observes.[68] One consequence of the structure of recognition, then, is that recognition risks acting as a form of coercion. What seems to be an appeal for recognition may turn out to be (or may also be) an artifact produced by the recognizing agency, called forth by the force of law. What appears to be a demand freely made may secretly (or openly) derive from factors that limit freedom and route "end-of-life options" (as they are called in the recently passed California law) into predetermined channels. What is called autonomy may be fundamentally "bounded and constructed."[69]

Among the factors that might determine what is supposed to be a voluntary decision are those that critics of the right to die routinely but not unjustifiably recite: the danger of economic motivations whereby prohibitive health care costs could make death appear as an attractive or necessary "choice"; the fear of becoming a burden on one's loved ones or other care providers; the internalization of a socially produced image of disability as a form of social death; and the economic or moral incentives for both patients and health care providers to treat the body as a resource for biomaterial. Under such pressures, the right to die can all too easily come to feel like a duty to die. Any defense of the right to die depends on the design of institutions and procedures that safeguard against such discernible abuse. As the philosopher Judith Jarvis Thomson observes, "Many people oppose the legalizing of physician-assisted suicide on the ground that (as they think) there is no way of constraining the practice so as to provide adequate protections for the poor and the weak. They may be right, and if they are, then all bets are off."[70]

The moral, political, and social dilemmas at issue in the right to die have perhaps been most effectively and powerfully addressed in a startling variety of films and television shows. Films such as Michael Haneke's *Amour*,

Valeria Golino's *Miele* (*Honey*), Marco Bellocchio's *Bella addormetata* (*Dormant Beauty*), Denys Arcand's *Les Invasions Barbares* (*The Barbarian Invasions*), and documentaries such as John Zaritsy's *The Suicide Tourist* and Peter Richardson's *How to Die in Oregon* meditate on tensions between personal responses to appeals to the right to die and the legal, institutional, and cultural restrictions that mediate such responses. The short-lived BBC sitcom *Way to Go* and Daniel Stamm's "mockumentary" *A Necessary Death* hold up darkly comic mirrors to the motives that may drive those who assist in suicide, responding to what were often characterized as the fanatical and fame-thirsty activities of Jack Kevorkian, himself the subject of a biopic starring Al Pacino, *You Don't Know Jack*.

Such films suggest that beyond the admitted risks posed by the legalization of assisted death, the question persists as to what takes place when the right to die becomes recognizable in the first place. What does it mean to appeal for assistance in achieving an end that may, in fact, resist intelligibility altogether? What is it that one appeals for, in the end, in the appeal for the right to die? And what does it mean to respond to such a demand? As the explorations conducted throughout this study suggest, the appeal for the right to die persistently, perhaps necessarily, assumes the risk of misrecognition and violence. To sign or execute the prescriptions of a living will, to petition or grant a petition for physician assistance in acquiring lethal medications, to demand or respond to a demand for the right to die with dignity: these actions are haunted by blind spots, by possibly murderous discontinuities that traverse what appears as desire, intention, or decision, and what appear as forms of ethical responsibility. The legitimation of the right to die, in this light, could function iatrogenically: in making a death of one's own seem possible, it might solicit rather than simply allow the demand to die. It may produce an unwelcome temptation.[71] As such, it might not simply acknowledge a preexisting right, but might instead create an obligation to think our own death or the death of the other in a new, and always potentially untimely, way. As the right to die becomes newly possible, then, it also risks becoming newly necessary. The question at the heart of the present work is whether the powerful ethical call of the other at the hour of her death can ever be adequately disentangled from conditions that do not simply wait in a state of ready and responsive vigilance but that may insidiously encourage this call.

The Politics of Suicide

The entanglement of freedom and necessity appears in particularly acute form when the ethical relation to the other is understood, as it must be, as a political relation as well. This became particularly clear to me when I was asked to contribute a text reflecting on the death of the literary scholar and writer Carolyn Heilbrun, who, in October 2003, took her own life at the age of seventy-seven. A prolific and influential critic and the author of a successful series of detective novels under the pseudonym Amanda Cross, Heilbrun had been a professor of English literature at Columbia University from 1960 until her retirement in 1993. According to friends and family, the days leading to her death unfolded without incident, with no immediate event or situation triggering her decision. Alone in her New York City apartment and with her husband away at their country home, thus ensuring he would not be the one to find her body, she took a large dose of barbiturates and tied a plastic bag around her head. The note she left at the scene of her death stated simply, "The journey is over. Love to all." Shortly after Heilbrun's death, I received a message from the editor of the journal of the Modern Language Association, *PMLA*. A week before her death, Heilbrun had submitted an invited guest column to the journal, several months in advance of the deadline. Confronted with the question of how to present this now-posthumous essay, the journal invited a group of scholars to submit responses to Heilbrun's essay.[72] Although the majority of the contributors were friends, colleagues, and former students of Heilbrun, the editor hoped my research on the right to die could shed light on Heilbrun's death. I had never met Heilbrun, but I became a belated witness to her final act.

Heilbrun's writing leaves little doubt that she understood suicide as a fundamental human right. Her book *The Last Gift of Time*, published six years before her death, discusses an unrealized decision to end her life at seventy, and her death at seventy-seven followed a method recommended by right-to-die advocacy organizations such as the Hemlock Society.[73] "I have always believed that, over 70, one should be free to choose one's death," she wrote in an essay published four months before her death.[74] Katha Pollitt, writing in the *New York Times*, acknowledged that many of Heilbrun's friends accepted this view of her death. "For its defenders, rational suicide is more than a way of cutting your losses; it's about freedom and power, the right to shape the arc of your life, to decide when the journey is over."[75] And yet, Pollitt writes, "Why do I feel that something is left out of this happy story? At the memorial service, several eulogists expressed—delicately but with unusual candor—anger, regret and self-blame. I felt that way myself, and I had hardly known her. Weren't we supposed to have gone for coffee in 1996? I should have called. Well, she could have called. It's hard not to see suicide as rejection, as a comment on the failure of others to give you what you need to keep going."[76] Pollitt goes on to suggest that Heilbrun may have suffered from an "undiagnosed depression"—even as she highlights the problematic logic behind this suggestion: "It's often a retroactive diagnosis, though: the evidence of the depression is the suicide itself."[77] Heilbrun's death, then, raised the central ethical question of this study: was it an expression of freedom, or was she driven to take her life by depression—or by a world that had failed her?

There is reason to be suspicious of the sort of "retroactive diagnosis" Pollitt proffers and questions, in which suicide itself is seen as invalidating the autonomy of the deceased. Not only the medical-psychiatric discourse of

depression but also, at least since Durkheim, prevalent sociological interpretations that trace suicide to a range of social conditions—political and
economic factors, family or religious structures, societal attitudes towards
diversity, to name but some common themes in the sociological literature—
commonly deploy this same circular logic. As the historian Lisa Lieberman
observes: "Therapeutic strategies that treat suicide as an illness, medicating
the depression while ignoring the underlying motivations that drive people
to end their own lives, effectively diminish individual responsibility for the
decision to die. In a similar way, sociological explanations . . . serve to make
suicides passive: victims of forces beyond their control." Indeed, according
to Lieberman, this is characteristic of the entire cultural history of suicide:
"Suicide is a statement that cries out to be deciphered, yet the cultural history of self-destruction consists of a series of attempts to evade this truth by
depriving suicide of its broader implications."[78] The interpretive frameworks,
especially in medicine and sociology, that take a therapeutic approach to
suicide, that claim to identify underlying causes and seek to mitigate those
causes, appear in this light as strategies of containment aimed at shutting
down the excessive, unruly autonomy of suicide, its demand to be deciphered
in each and every case on its own terms.

Was Heilbrun's death crying out to be deciphered? At least in one of the
mysteries she penned under the name Amanda Cross, Heilbrun shows a keen
awareness of the political implications of suicide, of its possible interpretation as a protest or lament commenting on social conditions. In *Death in
a Tenured Position*, when Janet Mandelbaum, the first tenured woman in
Harvard's English Department, is found dead of cyanide poisoning, various
theories are proposed. Was she murdered by her ex-husband, Moon, who
was known to possess a stash of cyanide capsules? Or was she the victim
of a crime against women, "murdered," Moon speculates, "because of what
she was and where she was and what she represented"?[79] Clues that others
overlook allow Heilbrun's detective, Kate Fansler, to solve the mystery: a
biography on Janet's desk of Eleanor Marx, known for having translated
Flaubert's *Madame Bovary* into English and who, like the heroine of Flaubert's novel, poisoned herself using cyanide, and a reported conversation
Janet had with a student about Simone Weil, who starved herself to death
in what many interpret as an act of political protest. "Janet was always
a woman of determination. Once she made up her mind, she was not to
be deterred by anyone. No more than Eleanor Marx, or Emma Bovary, or
Simone Weil did she mean to be rescued."[80] Kate's solution to the mystery
overturns the conventions of detective fiction. Whereas the traditional sleuth
sees suicide as the mask of murder, she sees suicide hidden beneath murder
scenarios. The irony of this conclusion is that, as the latest in a series of wom-
en's suicides, Janet's death is all too easily read according to other plots of
victimization. "Janet was murdered all the same," Kate's friend argues. "We
all conspired in it. We isolated her, we gave her no community. Only death

welcomed her."[81] Otherwise irrelevant details—recurring appearances of a dog named Jocasta, a passing comparison of Janet to Hedda Gabler, a name (Mandelbaum, "almond tree") that foretells the "characteristic smell of burnt almonds" associated with cyanide poisoning—become omens framing Janet as the doomed heroine of tragedy or melodrama.[82] The suicide thus ironically justifies Moon's femicide theory.

Kate, herself a professor of English when she is not drawn into detective work, in fact is able to recognize Janet's death as suicide because it conforms to a conventional image of female suicide. She also, however, seems to realize that Janet's fashioning of her death in the mold of Emma Bovary and Eleanor Marx need not signal mere victimization; instead it becomes an expression of agency: "Once she made up her mind, she was not to be deterred by anyone." As the novel concludes with Kate dedicating a memorial lecture to Janet on "the new forms possible to women in making fictions of female destiny,"[83] Janet's death thus becomes something like a performative quotation of the stereotype of the female suicide—an act that recognizes the suicide-inducing oppression of women, but which through that recognition enables new forms of political and cultural agency, emblematized both by Kate's feminist scholarship (which echoes Heilbrun's own literary scholarship) and, taking a step back, by Heilbrun's own reworking of the detective genre.

Heilbrun's late work expands this implied analogy between the politics of feminism and the politics of the right to die: in the same essay where Heilbrun stated her belief that "over 70, one should be free to choose one's death," she also described "life beyond 70" as "an adventure so far largely unacknowledged, unanticipated, unrecorded."[84] A similar argument animated her final essay for *PMLA*, which voiced clear dissatisfaction with cultural expectations of the retired and aging, with the conventional end-of-life plot. Does Heilbrun's death, like Janet Mandelbaum's, thus encode a protest, a complaint against an inhospitable world that has failed to acknowledge and foster viable forms of destiny for the aging, or that has failed, even, to acknowledge fully a right to die? If this interpretation avoids reproducing conventional narratives of victimization, it nonetheless recasts her death in a conventional pattern whereby suicide becomes a means to an end outside itself. For to the extent that Heilbrun's death appears as a political appeal, to the extent that it attests to conditions of injustice or unfreedom, it becomes, however paradoxically, a form of obligation.

Contested Terms

Implicit in the paradox of recognition is the generative and consequential force of naming. Indeed, in few areas of public discourse is the matter of terminology as contentious. Should one speak of "(physician-)assisted suicide" or "(physician-)assisted death"? "Voluntary active (or passive) euthanasia"? "Killing" or "letting die"? "Death with dignity" or "aid in dying"? "Death" or "dying"? "Death" or "end-of-life"? "Life-prolonging" or "death-prolonging" medical technologies? "Hastening death" or "ending life"? Do the medical professionals who undertake to assist suicides remain "physicians"? Or do they become "obiatrists," "marantologists," or "thanatologists"? The genealogy and implications of key terms in this discussion come under explicit consideration in the chapters that follow. But at the same time, I have opted to leave the vocabulary I employ in this work unsettled, at times adopting one alternative, at times another, trusting that context reveals and supplies nuance.

It may be helpful, nonetheless, to situate the phrase "the right to die," which titles this study. "How strange," exclaims the philosopher Hans Jonas, "that we should nowadays speak of a right to die, when throughout the ages all talk about rights has been predicated on the most fundamental of all rights—the right to live."[85]

What is perhaps the first use of the phrase "the right to die" in its modern sense occurred in German debates on euthanasia that began in the 1890s and extended through the first decades of the twentieth century.[86] In what may be its first significant usage in the modern sense, in Adolf Jost's 1895 treatise *Das Recht auf den Tod* (*The Right to Death*), it already encompasses a range of practices with which it has come to be associated, from the refusal of life-prolonging (or, as some right-to-die advocates call them, "death-prolonging") treatments, to taking one's own life (with or without assistance), to death by injection or other direct medical action.

It is perhaps significant that we find the modern use of this phrase occurring first in German, since the German noun *Recht* may ambiguously signify both "right" (which German jurisprudence often glosses as "*subjektives Recht*") and "law" (or "*objektives Recht*"). Indeed, in Jost's treatise, the right to die, on the one hand, ought to be demanded and exercised by the individual, while on the other it is subject to social interests and determinations. This is apparent even from the way in which Jost poses the very question of the right to die: "'Is there a right to die [or a right to death]?' Are there cases, in which the death of an individual is desirable for the individual himself as well as for human society in general?"[87] This joint consideration of individual and social interests, which Jost subjects to a logic of calculation in which a life of suffering is deemed as having less than no value, as having a negative value (*negativen Lebenswerth*), underwrites the movement from right to law, from freedom to duty. When someone exercises the right to die, Jost contends, "he not only rids himself of his suffering, but he also frees human society of a useless burden; with his suicide, he is fulfilling a duty. In the same way, everyone who comes to his aid is carrying out an act of humanity and thereby also indirectly fosters the advancement of the human species in general."[88]

The line from such ideas to the gas chambers is not hard to trace. As I discuss in chapter 3, Jost's ideas were later endorsed by Karl Binding and Alfred Hoche in their 1920 pamphlet, *Die Freigabe der Vernichtung lebensunwerten*

Lebens (*Permission for the Destruction of Life Unworthy of Life*), which in turn provided ideological justification to Nazism. Thus from its first artic-ulations, the notion of the right to die was shadowed by the problem of obligation—as, we shall see, it continues to be today, even when the sense of obligation is not conscripted into a violently imposed program of a state-sponsored death.

Silent Cries

But if the right to die bears with it the possibly irreducible risk of appear-ing as a duty, one must also keep in mind that the movement from right to duty can translate also into an untenable obligation to live. For the one who issues the demand for the right to die, in the words of Ramón Sampedro (the subject of the Spanish film *El mar adentro* [*The Sea Inside*]), may do so from the impossible position of "one who is dead among mortals."[89] He may therefore issue a demand that does not simply conform to the requirements of a recognizing agency but that also, to turn to the other consequence of the structure of recognition, does something to that which recognizes, which itself will have changed in the effort. Thus whereas those to whom he makes his demand imagine death as something yet to come—if to be mortal means to be fated to a future death—Sampedro justifies his demand on the basis of a death that has already taken place and which would merely be ratified by the physical demise for which he requests assistance. He asks for help in dying because he is already dead. But the voice of the dead, as the poem continues, can only be "silent" or "in vain":

> Plastered with excrement, mucus, and madness
> Impertinently they persist in cleaning him up, filled with disgust and rage.
> And it asks to free itself, the cadaver, from among the crazy living,
> but the living do not hear the silent cries of the dead.
>
> And with pathetic cruelty they continue to encourage him:
> tell us, dead one, the story of what you are undergoing;
> it seems that you are one of us, the living,
> at least you look like a human being.
>
> In vain I tell them, no! that I am dead!
> and that I cannot speak in the same way as them
> because it has become absurd to speak in the same way as humans.
> And they don't allow me to be either dead or alive
> these unhinged and deluded madmen.[90]

As the living call upon him to testify, to explain and justify his renuncia-tion of life, they—we—require that he appear as "one of us," that he speak according to the logic of the living. But he cannot speak "in the same way" or "as an equal" (*hablar igual*). For when a cadaver speaks, when it says, "I am dead," logic fails. This is a "vain" or "absurd" utterance, a nonsense language that discredits itself and cannot be heard by the living, that falls on deaf ears. And yet, despite that, it insists on a hearing, it calls upon us to be equal to it, even if this hearing must take place in a language yet to come.

Chapter 1

✦

Preferring Not To

Living Wills, Assisted Suicide, Bartleby

One of the most common and powerful ways that the appeal for the right to die is framed is as a demand for the recognition of personal autonomy, understood as the right to choose the time and manner of one's own death. Borrowed from the political domain, where autonomy describes territorial sovereignty, the claim to personal autonomy ascribes to the individual the right to self-rule, self-determination, and self-ownership. But because the question of a right to die arises only at the moment when one's death comes to depend on another, arguments based on autonomy cannot evade the question of the surrogate—the question, that is, of what happens when the law authorizes itself, a physician, or another acting with its authority to help someone end his or her own life, to serve as the surrogate of his or her suicide. The question of surrogacy is foregrounded most acutely in cases where those whose death is at stake can no longer act for themselves due to physical or other impairment, and where death therefore cannot be accomplished without the action of another. But the question of surrogacy also permeates scenarios where the direct responsibility of another seems less clear. For even if it is only the case that a physician honors a patient's instructions and withholds a potentially life-saving treatment, if he only lets a patient die, this deliberate inaction cannot be simply distinguished from a deliberate action, from killing. Nor can the provision of a lethal drug to be self-administered be easily distinguished from its active administration. For even if the physician (or other assistant), having provided the means of death by prescription, is absent from the actual scene of death, he is nonetheless virtually present as the surrogate of this suicide, which is no longer, of course, simply a suicide. The involvement of the surrogate raises a crucial question about the act and scene of assisted death: namely, to what extent is it the decision and the act of the one who dies? How can one imagine an act of suicide that necessarily involves another?

Laws and policies that legalize and regulate the right to die, or that seek to do so, hope to neutralize the role of the surrogate. The surrogate should

simply be the instrument of the one who dies, carrying out or implementing an autonomous act that, but for a logistical limitation, would have been
accomplished alone. For instance, under the systems of assisted death legal as
of this writing in some U.S. states and some European nations, the physician
is said to act strictly in accordance with the choice and decision of the one to
whom he supplies lethal drugs. Similarly, when persons living under jurisdictions where assisted death is not legal seek assistance in often complicated
travel or relocation projects, those who answer their call are said to support
the decision of the one they assist while remaining themselves strictly neutral.
And yet, as critics of the right to die have noted, the introduction of a surrogate risks undermining autonomy.[1] It may be impossible, that is, to limit
the surrogate to a merely neutral and instrumental position. The surrogate
introduces a representation of the self, a supplement to the self, and as such
transforms what this death means or will have meant. The surrogate introduces or exposes a complexity in the scene of assisted suicide that calls into
question the claim to autonomy.

In this chapter, which is divided into three parts, I consider the implications of legal surrogacy for the argument that the right to die is justified as
an exercise of autonomy. The first part examines what has become a widely
accepted and even encouraged practice, namely, requests for assistance in
dying through the legal instrument of the advance directive or living will,
through which a patient can request to forgo or discontinue life-prolonging
medical treatments and so be allowed to "let die." The second part turns
to the more controversial practice of assisted suicide, in which physicians
provide the direct means (or in some cases, act themselves) to bring about
a patient's death. In considering the legal and rhetorical structure of these
two forms of assistance in dying, I argue that as the law confronts the
scene of death, the rhetorical forms that seek to guarantee autonomy work
instead to undermine the notion of the autonomous self. As a result, they
attest to the implication of the surrogate in a scene that necessarily risks
becoming something other than what it seems or wants to be—in which
what appears to be assistance in suicide may in fact be murder. This risk
haunts the scene of the law, and leads me, in the third part of the chapter, to consider the ways in which a literary encounter with the demand for
the right to die may teach the law something about the role of the surrogate. Whereas the law attempts to regulate or suppress the indeterminate
consequences of the supplementarity of the surrogate, Herman Melville's
story "Bartleby, the Scrivener," I argue, stages the question of what happens
when the law, and the conception of autonomy on which it relies, touches
its own limits. In his faltering attempt to serve as Bartleby's surrogate, the
lawyer-narrator of Melville's tale confronts the appeal for the right to die
as a problem that cannot be adjudicated according to existing legal categories and precedents, but that instead solicits an unprecedented form of
response.

I. Legal Surrogacy and the Living Will

"More Illusory Than Real"

European and North American courts and legislatures have been hesitant to legalize assisted death. Physician-assisted suicide, in which a doctor prescribes a lethal drug to be self-administered by the patient, is permitted at the time of writing in seven U.S. jurisdictions (California, Colorado, Montana, Oregon, Vermont, Washington, and the District of Columbia) and three European countries (Switzerland, the Netherlands, and Luxembourg). Canada, the Netherlands, and Luxembourg additionally permit doctors (and in some cases qualified nurses) to administer lethal drugs directly at the request of a qualified patient, while Belgium permits only this second practice. At the same time and by contrast, the right to refuse or withdraw medical treatment, often called the right to natural death, is broadly accepted. For most European Union member states, this right is affirmed in the European Convention on Human Rights and Biomedicine.[2] In U.S law, this right is based on a series of court decisions and state laws and was effectively nationalized in the Patient Self-Determination Act of 1991, which requires any health-care institution receiving federal Medicare or Medicaid funding to inform patients of state laws concerning advance directives or living wills, through which patients may request to forgo specified forms of treatment in the event that they become incapacitated and unable to voice decisions directly.

The distinction between these two forms of assisted dying has become a critical one for legal and medical ethics. It marks the line between what is often called "passive voluntary euthanasia" and "active voluntary euthanasia," or, in starker terms, between "letting die" and "killing." It has also come to mark the line between what is understood as unnatural and natural death, between suicide and non-suicide. For instance, the first U.S. right-to-die law, the California Natural Death Act of 1976, which served as a model for subsequent statutes, specified that "the withholding or withdrawal of life-sustaining procedures from a qualified patient in accordance with the provisions of this chapter shall not, for any purpose, constitute a suicide."[3] Indeed, it is precisely to the extent that it is not considered a suicide that such a death is labeled "natural." To recognize a patient's right to forgo or discontinue medical treatment has thus been understood as a way of "letting nature take its course," even if this and similar terms may be merely, as a standard American legal textbook suggests, "sanitized locutions that have made it easier to understand and accept the distinction between passive and active euthanasia and implement the former while continuing to condemn the latter."[4] The discontinuation of life-prolonging medical treatment is therefore deemed consistent with the physician's ethical commitment to do no harm as formulated in the Hippocratic Oath, as well as with the state's "unqualified interest in the preservation of human life."[5] Assisted suicide, by contrast, has been normally understood as posing a challenge to conventional medical ethics and state interests, in that it requires the state or the state-authorized physician to help effect a death that may not have taken place otherwise, an unnatural death associated by legal and cultural history with criminal homicide and self-homicide.[6]

But the distinction between active and passive interventions, always tenuous, is becoming increasingly difficult to maintain.[7] For instance, the discontinuation of medical treatment has been generally recognized as a patient's right even if the consequence is death; in such a case, the physician has normally been understood not to have acted, but simply to have respected the autonomy of the patient and to have passively witnessed the patient's death ("passive voluntary euthanasia"). To some critics of assisted suicide, the distinction rests on intention. "In cases of refusing care, death need not be intended by the principal or assistant," wrote the then appellate judge Neil Gorsuch, "while in cases of euthanasia, death must be intended by the killer, and in cases of assisted suicide, one must intentionally assist the principal in the objective of ending his or her life."[8] But when a physician informs a patient who wishes to die that discontinuing one of her medications will result in death within hours or days, does the physician in this case play a merely passive role or does she instead actively issue a prescription for dying?[9] Does she simply fulfill a responsibility to refrain from unwanted treatment, or does she intend to help end a life?

The fragility of the distinction between action and inaction is further underscored by the doctrine of "double effect," according to which the use of narcotics in doses that foreseeably hasten death is nonetheless deemed consistent with "letting die," as long as the stated medical intention is to relieve pain. Notoriously difficult to classify, for instance, is the controversial practice of terminal sedation, in which a patient refuses intravenous fluids (exercising the right to refuse treatment), but then receives sedatives to alleviate pain that also render him unable to eat or drink, thus leading to death from dehydration or starvation while sedated. Doctors have thus reported that at times, and likely more often than is acknowledged, "the intentions and the prohibitions within the 'double effect' merged—that death was the only way to relieve their patients' suffering."[10] The legal and medical classification of active and passive modes of intervention can therefore come to appear more as a discursive convenience than an accurate description of medical practice, as observed by the physician Timothy Quill, a thoughtful and outspoken advocate of physician-assisted dying and party to the most recent U.S. Supreme Court case on the right to die. "By maintaining this distinction, the medical profession allegedly remains untainted by becoming an agent of death," Quill writes. "Yet, in the cloudy world of patient care, these distinctions become more illusory than real."[11]

What happens, then, when another is asked to become, or asks another to serve as, an "agent of death"? At the heart of this question, and of the fraught distinction between "letting die" and "killing," is the relationship between the one who dies and the surrogate. It thus becomes important to reflect on the accepted practice of "letting die" before turning to the debates that surround assisted suicide. In honoring a request to forgo or withdraw life-sustaining measures, does the surrogate merely respect a patient's autonomy through practicing restraint and withdrawing from the scene of a death, or does she make possible something that exceeds the autonomy of the patient and that could not happen otherwise?

The Invention of the Living Will

When Terri Schiavo died in 2005, after almost a decade of legal and political battles over whether or not to remove the feeding tube that had kept her technically alive for fifteen years, the media and others, from all sides of the controversy, derived a common lesson. "Wisdom of Writing a Living Will Is One Lesson Most All Agree We've Learned," read a typical headline—this one from the *Pittsburgh Post-Gazette*—from the day after Schiavo was officially pronounced dead.[12] Arthur Caplan, then director of the Center of Bioethics at the University of Pennsylvania, saw the Schiavo case as a watershed moment. "Post-Schiavo, it's become essential to have a living will."[13] Legal and health care organizations providing advice about living wills reported a massive increase in inquiries. In Wisconsin, legislators proposed making living wills mandatory for Medicaid recipients. From the front lines of the legal battle, George Felos, the attorney for Terri Schiavo's husband, Michael, delivered the same message: "If there's anything that would make somebody go out and get a living will, it should be this case. I mean, every American out there should get a written living will and specify what their medical treatment choices are, so at least something good will come of this case."[14] A similar message came from the White House. "I hear the numbers of people inquiring about living wills or writing living wills increased dramatically, and I think that is really good," Laura Bush was quoted as saying the day before Schiavo's official death. "The president and I have living wills."[15] The story of Terri Schiavo thus became a cautionary tale, exhorting its vast audience to decide—in legally binding and public form—under what conditions we would rather be dead than alive.

The nature and significance of the living will is illuminated by its legal history, which revolves around two earlier, prominent right-to-die cases, those of Karen Ann Quinlan, a New Jersey woman who suffered massive brain damage in 1975 at the age of twenty-one, and Nancy Cruzan, a Missouri woman who was the victim of a serious automobile accident in 1983, when she was twenty-six.[16] Both women were left in irreversible comas, or what has come to be called a persistent vegetative state, which the U.S. Supreme Court in *Cruzan v. Director, Missouri Department of Health* glosses as "a condition in which a person exhibits motor reflexes but evinces no indications of significant cognitive function."[17] Unable to breathe on her own, Quinlan was dependent on a mechanical ventilator as well as artificial hydration and feeding. Cruzan required hydration and a feeding tube. Like the Schiavo case, the stories of these two young women mobilized politicians and activists across the political spectrum. It was in the wake of *In re Quinlan* that previously stalled efforts to enact living will laws made headway in most states.[18] When the first of these laws, the California Natural Death Act, was introduced in 1976, the bill's sponsor, Barry Keene, made this explicit: "The image of Karen Ann Quinlan haunts our dreams."[19]

At issue in both cases was the role of the surrogate or guardian in authorizing measures that would lead to the death of someone no longer able to make decisions for herself and so deemed legally incompetent. In *Quinlan*, the New Jersey Supreme Court, over objections from doctors and other health care providers, appointed Karen's father as "guardian" and "surrogate," knowing that in this capacity he would request the removal of a mechanical respirator.[20] The court was clear that it could not "discern her supposed choice based on the testimony of her previous conversations with friends, where such testimony is without sufficient probative weight."[21] The court nonetheless found that Karen's right to privacy was not abrogated by her present incompetence, and that "the only practical way to prevent destruction of the right is to permit the guardian and family of Karen to render their best judgment, subject to the qualifications hereinafter stated, as to whether she would exercise it in these circumstances."[22]

Cruzan reached the U.S. Supreme Court a decade later and marked "the first case in which we have been squarely presented with the issue of whether the United States Constitution grants what is in common parlance referred to as a 'right to die,'" wrote Chief Justice Rehnquist in the majority opinion, thus lending the court's authority to this phrase.[23] But one of the striking aspects of *Cruzan*, as many have noted, is that the court did not directly rule on this right. Instead, it simply "assume[d] that the United States Constitution would grant a competent person a constitutionally protected right to refuse life-saving nutrition and hydration."[24] What many thought would be the central issue of the case was accepted as a given. The central dilemma of the case, then, was not whether or not there is a right to die (limited to the refusal of treatment and not extending to the right to assistance in dying), but rather how to define the relationship between the incompetent person and her surrogate. Rehnquist defines the issue succinctly: "an incompetent person is not able to make an informed and voluntary choice to exercise a hypothetical right to refuse treatment or any other right. Such a 'right' must be exercised for her, if at all, by some sort of surrogate." In effect, then, the court was deciding between two surrogates, the parents and the state, each promising a different course of action. Her parents wanted Missouri to accept their "substituted judgment" that their daughter would choose to refuse treatment, while Missouri wanted to require a higher standard of "clear and convincing evidence" of Cruzan's wishes. The Supreme Court, based on Missouri's "unqualified interest in the preservation of human life," found its higher standard to be constitutional. At the time of this decision, the parents were thus denied the ability as guardians to discontinue the artificial feeding and hydration that was keeping their daughter technically alive.

Quinlan and *Cruzan* thus took opposite approaches to the question of the surrogate. Whereas *Quinlan* allowed the parents to substitute their judgment in the absence of any clear evidence of Karen's wishes, *Cruzan*, without invalidating the earlier New Jersey decision, allowed Missouri to require such evidence. At stake in both cases, however, was an effort to circumscribe the judgment or the discretion of the surrogate in the service of what has come to be called the autonomy paradigm, according to which the power of decision ought to be located in the patient. The surrogate ought not to make a decision *for* the patient, but instead is said to serve as the representative of her will. In the absence of any clear evidence of what Quinlan or Cruzan wanted for themselves, the law is forced to reach a compromise. But rather than affirm the right of the surrogate to reach an independent decision, it tethers the surrogate's authority to the autonomy of the patient. This strategy, however, exposes an instability in the structure of legal surrogacy, for this autonomy could be exercised only from within a state of incompetence, from within Karen Quinlan's and Nancy Cruzan's muteness. It could only be "supposed," even where something qualifying as "clear and convincing evidence" could be produced. This point was demonstrated dramatically in the aftermath of the Supreme Court decision in *Cruzan*. Two months later, with the Supreme Court having affirmed the right to refuse treatment even as it simultaneously upheld the state's right to require evidence of autonomy, Cruzan's parents introduced new evidence in a Missouri court. Three of Nancy Cruzan's former coworkers testified that they recalled her saying she would not want to "live like a vegetable."[25] But whether or not this new evidence met the state's standard, which it had fought to uphold before the Supreme Court, was never established, since the attorney general, William Webster, this time did not oppose the Cruzans' suit, perhaps less for legal reasons than political ones, Peter Filene suggests. Webster was planning a run for governor of Missouri, and opinion polls were in favor of the Cruzans.[26]

The ways in which autonomous choice is exercised, the ways in which it is heard and received across the line from competence to incompetence, then, potentially undermines this autonomy and exposes it as a "myth"[27] or "fiction."[28] In this light, the Schiavo case is not, as has been suggested, "the most extraordinary end-of-life case, ever,"[29] but instead exemplifies the troublingly ordinary instability of the structure of surrogacy.

Autonomy as Ideal and Limitation

The living will as a legal instrument is born out of the autonomy paradigm, which requires a form of communication across a divide labeled by the law as the line between competence and incompetence. It is meant to supply the clear and convincing evidence that seemed to be missing in the Quinlan and Cruzan cases. Coming into force at the moment when the person is incapacitated, living wills are thus said to speak not just for but *as* the patient once he or she is deemed incompetent to declare his or her own wishes directly.

Although requirements for what constitutes a valid living will vary from state to state, with many even recognizing oral statements, their basic structure is a declaration of what measures should or should not be taken in the event of incompetence. A template provided by the New Jersey Department of Health is typical:

> I understand that as a competent adult I have the right to make decisions about my health care. There may come a time when I am unable, due to physical or mental incapacity, to make my own health care decisions. In these circumstances, those caring for me will need direction concerning my care and they will require information about my values and health care wishes. In order to provide the guidance and authority needed to make decisions on my behalf, I, _____, hereby declare and make known to my family, physician, and others, my instructions and wishes for my future health care.[30]

As this and related documents show, the living will seeks to express my autonomy precisely at the moment when I can no longer speak for myself and yet when I most critically am called upon to decide the matter of my life or death.[31] For proponents of the right to die, the living will is therefore an important instrument because it defends my will against the control of others. For when I am declared incompetent, I am for all intents and purposes dead to the law, excluded from its jurisdiction, socially dead, without the ability to exercise rights, as Rehnquist noted. I am subject to the power of the institutions or individuals designated to make decisions about my care. The living will thus embodies the possibility of self-determination. "In the wake of the *Schiavo* case, the execution of an advance directive has become a political act—an assertion of personal autonomy in the face of efforts to squelch the most basic of American rights."[32]

But this autonomy is subject to both contextual and structural limitations. By contextual limitations, I mean those that result from the fact that the living will is necessarily addressed to and interpreted at a time when the author is incapacitated, and as such is limited by the ability and willingness of its readers to respect its demands. For example, a series of studies has suggested that health care decision-making and treatment protocols have not always demonstrated awareness of the existence of a living will or of the wishes expressed in it. The living will thus risks being neglected.[33] Crucial medical decisions may also be required under hectic and confusing conditions that can contravene the best-laid plans. As Atul Gawande writes, "the arrow of events refuses to follow a steady course and that plays havoc with the surrogate's mind."[34] Finally, there may be conflicts between the wishes expressed in a living will and the decisions of a guardian. Thus, despite the fact that the living will was presented as the way to avoid another "Schiavo tragedy," that is not necessarily the case. Quoted in the *New York Times* in an article on the Schiavo case, William Colby, the Missouri lawyer who had represented the Cruzans, noted that living wills "are often useful, but they're not foolproof."[35] Schiavo's particular case reveals the ways that a broader political and legislative context can limit the efficacy of even the most explicit affidavit, since at the time of her initial heart failure, it was illegal in the state of Florida for a patient to request removal of a feeding tube. Due to this legal limitation, even if Schiavo had signed a living will prior to becoming incompetent, it would not have resolved her case.[36] Nor is there any guarantee that a living will's terms will be honored by those responsible for executing it. According to Terri Schiavo's guardian *ad litem*, Terri's parents "stated that even if Theresa had executed a formal living will, they would have fought to have it voided because they did not believe it was consistent with their beliefs."[37] As one legal scholar notes (though without reference to Melville's "Bartleby"), living wills risk becoming "dead letters."[38] Indeed, thus far there are no specific legal consequences for the failure to honor a living will. Although tort law may evolve, currently one cannot sue for "wrongful living" as one can for wrongful death.[39]

The living will is also subject to another set of contextual limitations relating to medical and legal discourse. It must make requests that are "clinically meaningful" as well as legally valid. The practices the living will can request must, for instance, affirm the distinction between "passive" and "active" interventions in dying, and can only (to date) request the former. The living will in this sense must affirm the image of natural death embodied in the idea of a "right to a natural death." Luis Kutner's observation in a 1969 article often credited with inventing the legal instrument of the living will still obtains: "Therefore, as of now, a doctor cannot be directed to act affirmatively to terminate a patient's life. He may, however, be directed and exculpated to act passively by inaction."[40] Scholars in health care policy have noted additional potential complications and misunderstandings that the health care context poses when someone unfamiliar with medical (as well as legal) discourse and practice is asked to certify a document containing technical language. To bridge the gap between lay and expert discourse, some have proposed living wills formatted as checklists. But such documents only further highlight the limitations imposed by the requirement of clinical and legal meaningfulness, for they can account only for generic scenarios and remain necessarily silent when it comes to more nuanced realities.[41]

These contextual limitations point to a more fundamental structural problem that arises in the living will. For as I write a living will, I speak for and as the incompetent person I will have become at the moment the living will is activated. This division between the competent self who signs the living will and the incompetent self who will be subject to its directives is not merely the result of a legal or medical determination about my competence. It is inscribed in the very form of the living will, which anticipates and divides the self who is able to sign from the self who will no longer be able to sign. To the extent that the identity of the one who signs is fundamentally invested in the power to sign—to the extent that the one who writes the living will is, essentially, one who can sign—this signatory is bound to the other who cannot sign in a relationship of radical heterogeneity. Otherwise put, the living will does not allow me to remain who I am at a future moment when I will have lost direct means of expression. Rather, it requires that I execute a judgment about a moment in time where I cannot place myself, about someone who will no longer be me.[42]

One possible practical consequence of this fissure at the heart of the living will derives from the fact that I can never predict exactly when I might cross the border or be understood to have crossed the border from competence to incompetence. I cannot wait until the last possible minute to write my living will, since I do not know when that last possible minute may be, and waiting risks missing the opportunity to write a living will at all. There is therefore a necessary gap of time between the moment I sign my living will and the threshold at which it is activated. But who can say that my ideas about how I wish to be treated in my incompetence-to-come will not have changed in the interval between the time of signing and the time that the living will comes into effect? This very real fear is confirmed by studies that show how personal ideas of what is considered worse than death can shift substantially over time. Summarizing eleven studies published in the 1990s, a Hastings Center Report concludes that "the bottom line is that, over periods as short as two years, almost one-third of preferences for life-sustaining medical treatment changed."[43] It may also happen, as with some Alzheimer's patients, that my will may shift even from within the state of so-called incompetence.[44] The existence of the living will, in such cases, could negate the very autonomy it seeks to preserve, since it memorializes a decision I may no longer affirm.

But even this critique does not take into account the full challenge to the image of autonomy the living will performs. For the living will does not simply fracture my life into moments of discrete autonomy, each of which battles for supremacy. Rather, it makes me the accomplice and repository of an image of a dead self, or a dead other, who mocks the image of autonomy and makes me responsible for its destruction. Rather than safeguard an image of the self against its dehumanization, the living will creates a new image of the self as dead. I become my own surrogate.

The Trust Structure of the Living Will

The image of the dead self produced by the living will may be more fully understood by examining the legal roots of this new form of testament. In the law review article by Luis Kutner referenced above, often credited as containing the first formulation of the idea of the living will, the living will is invented or imagined in an analogy with a legal trust. A prominent civil rights lawyer and cofounder of Amnesty International, Kutner sought through this innovation to expand the scope of personal autonomy by using established legal practices and norms in a creative, new way. Kutner's proposal for the living will proceeds from the observation that criminal law is ill-equipped to handle cases of voluntary euthanasia. Common law on homicide, he notes, does not concern itself with motive, only with premeditation. "Conceptually, if the elements of willful premeditation exist, the perpetrator of the act [that is, the surrogate] stands equally condemned regardless of the fact that he may have acted from an impulse of mercy."[45]

Despite the legal and conceptual identity of malicious and altruistic homicide, Kutner observes that judgment and sentencing of the two crimes have not, in practice, followed the same pattern. Perpetrators of "mercy killing" have often been left unprosecuted, found innocent despite factual evidence, or given light to no sentences. The law thus requires "adaptation" so as to recognize a right to assistance in dying. "How then can the individual patient retain the right of privacy over his body—the right to determine whether he should be permitted to die, to permit his body to be given to the undertaker?"[46] Kutner responds to this question through a creative adaptation of the law of legal trusts. I suggest here, however, that the attempt to expand individual rights through recourse to the form of the legal trust bears with it a set of corollary consequences that unsettle the very autonomy that the living will seeks to preserve. For as the living will empowers a surrogate to execute the autonomous decision of the one who creates that will, at the same time the trust form of the living will treats the body as property and thus subjects the autonomous will to a form of troubling dispossession.

Kutner formulates the analogy between the living will and a legal trust as follows: "The living will is analogous to a revocable or conditional trust with the patient's body as the *res*, the patient as the beneficiary and grantor, and the doctor and hospital as the trustees. The doctor is given authority to act as the trustee of the patient's body by virtue of the patient's consent to treatment."[47] This formulation suggests, on one level, the ways in which the living will adheres to a conventional structure of delegation. In English law, the institution of living trusts—that is, a trust in which the grantor is still living, as different from a testamentary trust created by the death of the grantor—originated with twelfth-century crusaders, who would convey their estates to friends to avoid various "feudal burdens" and "ancient restrictions," with the understanding that the trusted friend would manage the property to the benefit of the crusader's family in his absence, and restore it to him on his return.[48] But the return of the property under this system was only a moral and not a legal obligation; common law recognized the trustee as the full owner of the property. In the case where the trustee broke the landowner's trust and refused to return the property to the original landowner, common law would side with the trustee. In such cases, petition could be made to the King's Council, the Curia Regis, presided over by the lord chancellor and his office, the Chancery. It became standard practice for the lord chancellor to overturn any effort on the part of trustees to retain property. What at first were exceptions to common law enacted by the lord chancellor thus became regularized, giving birth to the law of trusts. Under chancery law, the property could be understood not as fully owned by the trustee, but as "managed property."[49] The interests of a third party, the beneficiary, could now have legal standing.[50] The living will thus divides the autonomous or willing self—the grantor/beneficiary—from the body, understood as the content or *res* of the trust. Under the model of trust law, the trust could now embody the will of the grantor to preserve and convey the property to the beneficiary, with the trustee as an inconsequential intermediary.

We might draw two implications from this analysis. The first concerns the notion of the body as *res*, as property. This idea of the body as property is fundamental to the idea that the state has an interest in preserving life. Although this is often referred to as the state's affirmation of the "sanctity of life," this sanctity is rooted less in the idea of divine mystery, omniscience, or beneficence than in the more mundane image of God as the owner of the body as property. It is in part this image that grounded the traditional legal prohibition of suicide. In Roman law, this prohibition was in force only in specific cases—the suicides of slaves, soldiers, and criminals seeking to escape prosecution. These limitations demonstrate that at stake in the prohibition of suicide was not concern for the well-being of the person but rather his value as property. The influence of this framework on European law is apparent in the first two official church pronouncements denying religious funeral rites to suicide, from the Council of Arles in 452 and the Council of Orléans in 533, which echoed Roman limitations on the ban on suicide, mentioning only slaves, servants, and accused criminals. Even when this code expanded to apply to all persons regardless of legal or social status, in the Council of Braga in 563, the law continued to draw on the political logic of the Roman ban, as in Thomas Aquinas's influential formulation: "Whoever takes his own life, sins against God, even as he who kills another's slave, sins against that slave's master."[51] This figure continued in Enlightenment thought, as in John Locke's claim that "though man in that state have an uncontroulable liberty to dispose of his person or possessions, yet he has not liberty to destroy himself . . . for men being all the workmanship of one omnipotent, and infinitely wise maker; all the servants of one sovereign master, sent into the world by his order, and about his business; they are his property, whose workmanship they are, made to last during his, not one another's pleasure."[52] Although it is often maintained that the law's recognition of the right to refuse medical treatment is a concession to personal autonomy, that in recognizing the living will the law allows the interests of the individual to outweigh the interest of the state in preserving life, the trust form of the living will thus suggests a different understanding of the relationship between the living will and the law. Rather than place a limit on state power, the living will affirms the underlying logic of property rights as the basis for the state's interest in the "sanctity of life."

The second implication follows from the first, namely that the grantor, to the extent that he cannot through the trust instruct any and all actions but must be limited to the legally and clinically meaningful, always already occupies the role of trustee. To follow Locke's logic, God would be the owner of the body, entrusted to man as trustee to manage God's property. When I write a living will, I do not, in this analysis, entrust what was mine to the trustee (the doctor, the hospital, the law, the state). Instead, I merely transfer the *res* from one trustee (myself) to another. The living will thus exposes the basis of autonomy as always already secondary or derivative, as always already a form of trusteeship or surrogacy in which the body is imagined as property. Whereas autonomy might seem to derive precisely from the ways in which a person is *not* property, the trust form of the living will poses a fundamental challenge to the image of the autonomous person that it was supposed to safeguard. Thus, on the one hand, the invention of the living will recasts autonomy as self-ownership, where self-ownership legitimates the delegation of a surrogate as a powerful and effective counterpoint to ceding decision-making to medical and legal authority. But at the same time, self-ownership proves to be a problematic paradigm, in that the right to self-ownership remains fundamentally dependent on the logic of property.

II. A Suicide That Is Not One's Own

"Here Lies the Water"

Whereas the living will, in attempting to adapt existing law so as to respond to the demand for the right to forgo medical treatment, figures the body as *res*, the request for assistance in suicide embodies both a more radical promise of autonomy as well as a more radical challenge to the law. Because it seeks to end life before the onset of incompetence, assisted suicide would seem to avoid the reification of the person and make possible a fully autonomous expression of the right to die. Yet the traditional criminalization of suicide also problematizes the attempt to adapt the law in such a way that assisted suicide could become legitimate. Whereas the living will confirms the legal status of the body as property in trust, suicide appears as the destruction of property. It seems to transgress the law and to claim sovereignty over the body for the self rather than God or the state. It seems to refuse to recognize the law as a legitimate guarantor of the body as trust, that is, as a legitimate surrogate. Whereas the living will accepts and affirms the derivative or

dependent nature of the self, suicide seems to sever itself from existing law
and to usurp the right to kill for itself.

But this distinction between a death authorized by law through the instrument of the living will and a death that breaks the law through suicide does
not entirely hold water. For there is a hidden complicity as well between the
law and suicide, although to perceive this complicity may require a perspective situated at the limits of the law, and on the threshold of life and death,
such as that of the gravediggers in *Hamlet*, whose plays on words and ideas
unearth the role of the law in producing the category of suicide:

> FIRST CLOWN: Here lies the water—good. Here stands the man—
> good. If the man go to this water and drown himself, it is, will he
> nill he, he goes; mark you that. But if the water come to him and
> drown him, he drowns not himself. Argal, he that is not guilty of
> his own death, shortens not his own life.
>
> SECOND CLOWN: But is this the law?
>
> FIRST CLOWN: Ay marry, is't—crowner's quest law.[53]

As they dig the grave for Ophelia, who is being given an official churchyard
burial despite her possible suicide, the first gravedigger effectively demol-
ishes any absolute distinction between suicide and non-suicide. For like the
shoreline, the line between activity and passivity, between drowning oneself
and being drowned, is perpetually shifting, thus unsettling any determination of guilt or innocence. Speaking truth to power, the second gravedigger
recognizes as much: "If this had not been a gentlewoman, she should have
been buried out o' Christian burial."[54] The same action or inaction, in other
words, can be construed in opposing ways. Suicide is defined not by something inherent to the act itself, but rather by its interpretation according to
the law, by the way the law draws a line in the sand.

The gravedigger's appeal to "crowner's quest law" foregrounds the logic
(or the lie) that constitutes suicide as a legal category, for the coroner or
crowner—*custos placitorum coronae*, "guardian of the pleas of the crown"—
was originally charged with guarding the property rights of the king. His later
charge—to determine the manner of death—marks a logical extension of this
interest in property rights, in that he becomes responsible for safeguarding
political sovereignty over the body of the subject considered as a form of
property. Suicide is thus understood as the destruction of the king's property
in a double sense: first, it deprives the sovereign of the services of his subject,
and second, it deprives the sovereign of the exclusive right to kill. This double
offense helps explain the traditional double punishment that a judgment of
suicide by the coroner would entail in much of pre-Enlightenment Europe:
first, forfeiture of property to the crown, thus depriving the suicide's heirs

of any inheritance, and second, excommunication or capital punishment, in which sovereign power over the body is reasserted. This second penalty could assume various forms: denial of burial rites, desecration of the corpse, as in English customs that prescribed burial at a crossroads with a stake through the body, dragging the naked corpse through the streets, even public hanging of the body. When the gravedigger suggests that the distinction between suicide and non-suicide may be arbitrary, he thus poses a subversive challenge to the very basis of sovereign power. In suicide, the law does not confront something inherently transgressive, but rather the law itself produces the crime precisely by casting the person as a form of property. Whereas the trust form of the living will adapted the law of property in an attempt to extend autonomy to the time of incompetence, criminal law concerning suicide imposes the logic of property on the body as a means of despotic control. It is as if the gravedigger is suggesting that there is no suicide without assistance from the law.

Indeed, the threat that the law may be implicated in suicide, that it risks undermining itself, was not lost on the U.S. Supreme Court as it grappled with the modern question of the right to die. In *Cruzan*, Justice Scalia thus seems to allude to *Hamlet* in his concurring opinion, which challenges the logic of the majority opinion even as it concurs with the outcome. Scalia insists that the issue in *Cruzan* is not merely the distinction between killing and letting die, but rather the legitimacy or illegitimacy of "suicide by refusing to take appropriate measures necessary to preserve one's life." He goes on to challenge the distinction maintained in the majority opinion:

> Suicide, it is said, consists of an affirmative act to end one's life; refusing treatment is not an affirmative act "causing" death, but merely a passive acceptance of the natural process of dying. I readily acknowledge that the distinction between action and inaction has some bearing upon the legislative judgment of what ought to be prevented as suicide—though even there it would seem to me unreasonable to draw the line precisely between action and inaction . . . . It would not make much sense to say that one may not kill oneself by walking into the sea, but may sit on the beach until submerged by the incoming tide.[55]

Scalia's position is conservative in that it does not acknowledge the potentially new and unsettling nature of the acts under consideration and insists on inscribing them into the traditional category of suicide. But his observation also plays to the gravedigger's more radical suggestion that in defining and criminalizing suicide, the law may not be a merely passive observer, but rather an active participant.

Indeed, the gravedigger's subsequent exchange with Hamlet suggests that implicated in the legally produced distinction between suicide and non-suicide is a more fundamental distinction, or a more fundamental confusion, between living and dying:

HAMLET: Whose grave's this, sirrah?

FIRST CLOWN: Mine, sir.
[Sings] O, a pit of clay for to be made
For such a guest is meet.

HAMLET: I think it be thine, indeed; for thou liest in't.

FIRST CLOWN: You lie out on't, sir, and therefore it is not
yours: for my part, I do not lie in't, and yet it is mine.

HAMLET: Thou dost lie in't, to be in't and say it is thine:
'tis for the dead, not for the quick; therefore thou liest.

FIRST CLOWN: 'Tis a quick lie, sir; 'twill away gain, from me to you.[56]

Whereas the gravedigger's critique of the power of the coroner called the law to account for deriving the distinction between a criminal and noncriminal death from property interests, Hamlet and the first gravedigger spar here over the question of who owns the site of death. Hamlet insists that the grave belongs to the dead, not the "quick," or living, and that the gravedigger is therefore lying when he claims it as his own. But the gravedigger's claim touches on a double truth: it belongs to him not only because he is the one digging it, but also, it would seem, because he too is mortal, that is to say, dying—a guest on this earth. The grave is as much his as it is Ophelia's, or, for that matter, Yorick's, who once occupied or still occupies the same grave. But this is also to say that death cannot be treated as property in the same way that the law treats the life of its subjects as property. One can only be a guest when it comes to death. Thus when the gravedigger says the grave is his, this is a "quick lie" not only in the punning sense that it is speedy and boomerangs back to Hamlet ("'twill away gain, from me to you"), turning Hamlet's words inside out and showing that it is Hamlet and not the gravedigger who lies. It also subverts the logic of life-as-property, for it suggests that living itself—quickness—may be a lie, or rather that the opposition between living and dying is a lie, that living *is* dying. The quick or living lie, in other words, is also the lie of living.

The gravedigger thus leads us to see that when the law draws the line between suicide and non-suicide, at stake is not simply the criminality of suicide. At issue is the very question of what counts as life before the law—of what or whom is granted legal protection and recognition, of what sorts of claims and demands the law can hear. Whereas the legal recognition of life remains inextricably linked to the property form, and thus revolves around the question of who "owns" life, the gravedigger excavates a site beyond legal jurisdiction. Occupying the indeterminate threshold where "here lies the water," the gravedigger gives the lie to the law.

From Wrong to Wrong

Echoing the gravedigger's quick lie, Scalia's disagreement with the majority opinion in *Cruzan* over what does and does not count as suicide exposes an equivocation or puzzlement in the way modern law confronts the question of suicide. For as suicide was gradually and unevenly decriminalized over the course of the last 250 years, from the discontinuation of anti-suicide laws in France after the Revolution to decriminalization in Great Britain in 1961, it remains within the orbit of criminal law only with respect to laws criminalizing assisted suicide. But this also created a unique and perplexing legal situation, in which it is criminal to be accessory to an act that is not itself criminal. Just as the effort to adapt existing trust law to create the legal instrument of the living will has as its consequence the legal inscription of the person as property, the attempt to apply existing criminal law to assisted death carries with it the burden of the conventional stigmatization of suicide.

The consequences of this legal dilemma are demonstrated in the majority opinion by Rehnquist in *Washington v. Glucksberg*, one of the two cases concerning physician-assisted suicide decided concurrently by the U.S. Supreme Court in 1997. Rehnquist begins the opinion by noting that it is accepted procedure of the court when confronting a due process claim to review the relevant legal history. But which history will this be? Notably, Rehnquist identifies this history as that of legal approaches to suicide. He thus sets out to demonstrate how the history of laws criminalizing suicide, despite their obsolescence, support the criminalization of laws against assisted suicide. As Rehnquist notes, early laws against assisted suicide derive from the criminality of suicide itself, as in the charge given to a Massachusetts jury in 1816: "Now if the murder of one's self is felony, the accessory is equally guilty as if he had aided and abetted in the murder."[57] But at the moment when he attempts to explain the continued criminalization of assisted suicide even after suicide itself is decriminalized, Rehnquist must depart from the law. Laws against assisted suicide remain legitimate, he maintains, because suicide "remained a grievous, though nonfelonious, wrong." The rationale for the criminalization of assisted suicide is now based not on any specifically legal logic, but instead on a moral evaluation. Rather than prosecute suicide as a felony, the law now finds itself concerned with the prevention of a "wrong."

The decriminalization of suicide thus seems to evacuate the legal claim to the body as property. Yet the continued criminalization of assisted suicide demonstrates that this decriminalization does not simply legitimate suicide. Instead, it recasts the felonious offense against the state's property interest in

the subject and against its exclusive claim over the right to kill into the modified discourse of the "nonfelonious wrong." Although the *Glucksberg* opinion
does not expound on the cultural logic of this modification, the ambiguity
of its language lays bare the central issue in recent legal considerations of
assisted suicide. For the "wrong" at issue is not only conceived of as a wrong
in the sense of an offense against the state or against the community, but
also a wrong in the sense of a mistake, an error. As noted earlier, as suicide
ceases to be a crime, it becomes the object of new frameworks of analysis.
Over the course of the nineteenth century, the study of suicide as a medical
problem, while not unprecedented, became systematic and predominant. By
1821, Etienne Esquirol, chief doctor of the asylum at Charenton and former
minister of the interior of France, could write in the influential *Dictionnaire
des sciences médicales* (*Dictionary of Medical Science*) that "the opinion that
views suicide as an illness or an acute delirium seems to have prevailed in our
times, even against the text of the laws and the anathemas of Christianity."[58]
Simultaneously, suicide became one of the privileged objects of the new disciplines of moral statistics and sociology. When Emile Durkheim published
his still influential 1897 work, *Suicide: Étude de sociologie* (*Suicide: A Study
in Sociology*), he could cite dozens of statistical studies from across Europe.[59]
Whereas discussions of suicide had previously focused on its legal, religious,
and moral legitimacy, these new disciplinary approaches sought to identify
the underlying causes of suicide, treating it as a symptom of physical, psychological, and environmental factors. As A. Alvarez puts it, " 'To be or not to be'
had given way to 'the reason why.' "[60] Those who attempt or commit suicide
are consequently treated with suspicion. They are driven by something other
than the desire to die, by social, psychological, or genetic forces, or else suicide results from a moral or imaginative failure, an inability to find a way
forward or a mistaken belief that suicide itself is a way forward. No longer
a crime, suicide becomes the sign of a fatal mistake. "In order to commit
suicide one cannot write a meaningful suicide note; conversely, if one could
write a meaningful suicide note, he would not 'have to' commit suicide,"
writes the psychologist Edwin Shneidman.[61]

    To the extent that they do not know their own motives, do not under-
stand the causes or consequences of their action, those who commit suicide,
once potential felons, now become victims of an error against which the law
must protect them. The assistant consequently appears as a potential felon
in that he abets this error and may even appear as its cause—as one who
exerts undue influence. For how can the law and the prospective assistant
know and guarantee that a request to exercise the right to die—in effect, a
suicide note written in advance—does not spring from something other than
the deliberate and fully autonomous desire to die, something for which there
may be or ought to be different recourse? Viewed in light of such suspicions,
the claim to the right to die misunderstands its own demand. It could be the
symptom of intolerable pain, which requires not death but improvements

in palliative care; or if not palliation, then an acceptance of the necessity of suffering. It could be a reaction to the emotional and financial burdens of illness, which require not death but better support mechanisms. It could be the consequence of a youth-obsessed culture in which old age is figured as privation, and as such calls for cultural reform. It could even result from a denial of death, from an impossible attempt to take control of what is absolutely other, absolutely unmasterable. It could appear, in sum, as the sign of some sort of constraint (institutional, cultural, expressive, moral) rather than as an expression of what has been called "the ultimate freedom."[62] It could be a cry for help rather than proof of a genuine will to die.

Pretty v. United Kingdom

If the demand for assistance in dying is always potentially wrong, in both senses of the word, how can the law come to hear and recognize this demand? The tensions that emerge as the law is asked to approve assistance in suicide, and as such to become itself an accessory, emerge with particular clarity in a case adjudicated by British and European courts in 2002, and that, in its central issues, closely mirrors the questions that have circulated in the United States and elsewhere. In 1999, at the age of forty, Diane Pretty was diagnosed with motor neuron disease (MND), also referred to as Lou Gehrig's disease or amyotrophic lateral sclerosis (ALS). Although some MND patients live long past the average life expectancy of two to five years—most famously the physicist Stephen Hawking—Diane Pretty would not exceed the average. Without any active assistance, she died of complications related to her illness in May 2002, two months after her final legal efforts to sue for the right to assisted suicide failed in the European Court of Human Rights.

Pretty's legal case began in the summer of 2001. By that time, she had become physically incapacitated. By the end of her life, there were several opportunities for her to refuse medical treatments or artificial feeding so as to hasten her death; but in each case, she did not want to undergo the pain that these courses of action would entail. Through her attorney, she therefore requested that the director of public prosecutions (DPP) issue an advance assurance that Pretty's husband would not be prosecuted if he were to assist her in dying. When the DPP refused, Pretty contested the DPP's decision in court, appealing to the English Divisional Court, the House of Lords, and finally the European Court of Human Rights (hereafter, the Court), claiming that the blanket ban on assisted suicide in Great Britain was incompatible with the European Convention on Human Rights (hereafter, the Convention).

One of the problems faced by Pretty's attorneys, Antje Pedain observes, was "to identify a Convention right into whose ambit of application the liberty to take one's own life might fall."[63] Although she claimed that her rights were engaged under several different articles of the Convention, the most controversial and decisive legal issues arose with respect to Article 8, which consists of two clauses.[64] The first posits that "everyone has the right to respect for his private and family life." The second clause qualifies the first, specifying that a European member state may legitimately interfere with this right "in the interests of national security, public safety or the economic well-being of the country, for the prevention of disorder or crime, for the protection of health or morals, or for the protection of the rights and freedoms of others."[65] The boundaries that define private life, in other words, are determined not by the claims of personal autonomy but rather by the negative determination on the part of the law that a given right does not undermine national interests. What qualifies as one's private life—a term in which the possessive adjective reinscribes the figure of self-ownership as something that derives from a politico-legal delineation of property interests—does so only to the extent that it does not interfere with the protective powers ascribed to the state. The right to private life thus exists only as the remainder of what is determined not to require protection.

The appeal for assistance in suicide thus takes place precisely on the threshold between private and public interests. An appeal that seems to derive from the right to private life may instead solicit the protection of the state. But underlying this distinction, as the gravediggers in *Hamlet* demonstrated, is also the very distinction between what counts as "life." Indeed, in determining whether Article 8(1) was engaged, the Court needed to decide if what Diane Pretty was requesting should be understood as an act that even pertained to her "life." The House of Lords decision, which preceded the appeal to the Court, unanimously found that Pretty's rights under 8(1) were not engaged. But their concurring opinions do not follow the same logic. Lord Steyn represents one position on this question, holding that "the guarantee under Article 8 prohibits interference with the way in which an individual leads his life and it does not relate to the manner in which he wishes to die."[66] From this perspective, dying would not be protected by the right to private life, but would instead constitute "a negation of the protection that the Convention was intended to provide."[67] The right to suicide would be self-contradictory, in that it would destroy the life it claimed to protect. The government would become accessory to the breach, not the upholding, of the right to private life; it would become accessory to murder. Consequently, rather than classify assisted suicide as an autonomous act, Lord Steyn's arguments place the appellant under the protection of the state. Lord Hope took an opposing view on this question. "The way she chooses to pass the closing moments of her life is part of the act of living, and she has a right to ask that this too must be respected."[68] Whereas Lord Steyn excludes dying from the scope of life, Lord Hope classifies dying as part of "life." To the extent that one can be said to possess one's death in the same way that one possesses one's life—or rather, that possessing one's death is a necessary corollary of the possession of life—Pretty's rights under 8(1) are engaged.[69]

Whether or not Pretty can be legally killed, then, depends in part on how the law draws the line between life and death. On the one hand, suicide is understood as an act of living that just happens to result in death. Following this logic, the Court draws connections with precedents concerning other forms of dangerous or life-threatening conduct, including consensual sado-masochistic activities and the refusal of medical treatment, where the Court had previously found Article 8(1) to be engaged.[70] On the other hand, suicide is understood as the destruction of the very possibility of "private life." Thus, pursuing the line of questioning opened by the gravedigger in *Hamlet*, one might ask whether the two sides of this debate, one that insists on the related-ness of suicide and living and the other that insists on their non-relatedness, are in the end truly opposed. For both maintain the distinction, challenged by the gravedigger, between living and dying, and simply come to different conclusions based on which side of the line they place Diane Pretty's request. The distinction required by law, then, does not describe an actual or objective condition, it is not constative, but rather elicits a performative utterance on the part of the appellant, in which the law thus serves as surrogate entrusted with protecting the "life" of the appellant.

The instability of this appeal is reflected in the difference between the position Diane Pretty adopts in and out of court. In her appeal to the Court, she echoes Lord Hope's position, submitting that "nothing could be more intimately connected to the manner in which a person conducted her life than the manner and timing of her death."[71] She claims the right to die on the basis required by the law, that it is part of life. But to a BBC interviewer, in a pro-gram aired the day after she died, she makes a claim that could not be made in court, again using her voice-activated keypad, as if echoing the gravedig-ger and troubling the very distinction on which her legal case depended: "I am dead."[72] This second statement, however, poses a practical problem for the law, which cannot hear a request to die from someone already dead. Thus in *Sanles v. Spain*, which raised nearly identical issues concerning the compatibility of the Convention and a ban on assisted suicide, the Court dis-missed the applicant's efforts to pursue the case of her brother-in-law, Ramón Sampedro (discussed in the introduction), after his death.[73] The Court can grant the right to die only if dying is delimited to an act of living.

The law thus confronts a limit when it confronts the other face of suicide. Indeed, "I am dead" does not subordinate itself to the law in a quest for rec-ognition and assistance, but instead wrests power from the law, legislates its own death for itself. It is an autonomous, poetical utterance. Faced with "I am dead," the law, like Hamlet, can only say, "thou liest."

The Death of the Surrogate

These questions arise, of course, only because the one who seeks the right to suicide cannot commit suicide on her own. "If I was able to kill myself,

I would," Diane Pretty told her interviewer.[74] Because Pretty cannot commit suicide on her own, the law is asked to assist or to authorize an act of assistance. But the law is therefore placed in an impossible position; for if, on the one hand, the right to assistance in suicide derives from the claim to self-ownership, on the other hand the very logic of ownership appears as an artifact of the legal inscription of the person as property. In the logic of the law, *self*-ownership is an illusion or a contradiction. To speak of the person as something that can be owned, even by oneself, is always already to be subject to the law and its property claims on its subjects.

In at least one argument advanced by the government, this meant that the one who wants to commit suicide, no matter what the reason, is by definition "vulnerable" and in need of protection or correction. The Court, in the Pretty case, did not accept the government's claim that Pretty was vulnerable to coercion. "The Court would note that although the Government argued that the applicant, as a person who is both contemplating suicide and severely disabled, must be regarded as vulnerable, this assertion is not supported by the evidence."[75] At the same time, as already noted, the necessity of appearing before the law and of claiming a right to die as an act of living has already placed Diane Pretty on the side of the law.

Indeed, in her suit she affirms the law even as she seeks assistance from it. Lord Bingham writes:

> On behalf of Mrs Pretty counsel . . . seeks to restrict his claim to the particular facts of her case: that of a mentally competent adult who knows her own mind, is free from any pressure and has made a fully-informed and voluntary decision. Whatever the need, he submits, to afford legal protection to the vulnerable, there is no justification for a blanket refusal to countenance an act of humanity in the case of someone who, like Mrs Pretty, is not vulnerable at all.[76]

In order to ask the law to assist her in dying, she must speak as one of the living, on behalf of the living, in a double sense. She represents others like herself who seek a new rule of law, who ask the law to afford legal protection not only to the vulnerable but also to the competent. But in so doing, she also speaks indirectly on behalf of the vulnerable, of those who may not really wish to die even if they may be led to request it. The bioethicist John Keown is thus correct when he suggests that her lawsuit concerns not only her private life but the lives of others. "What she's not entitled to do it seems to me is to undermine the protection which the law gives to all members of our community, including many other sufferers of motor neurone disease and other terminal illnesses, and that's precisely what she would have achieved if the European Court had granted a right to assisted suicide."[77] But what Keown does not take into account is the critical fact that in pursuing her case within the realm of the law, she affirms rather than undermines the interests of the law in the protection of life. In asking the law to recognize her as not vulnerable and to assist her in her competence to take her life, she affirms the law's right to distinguish between competence and incompetence, vulnerable and non-vulnerable.

The question then arises of what makes Diane Pretty non-vulnerable. It is not merely her competence, for as long as dying is classified as an act of living, the decision to die is vulnerable to error, since it necessarily excludes from view the fact that dying is also the end of the act of living, and is radically incompatible with life. The fact that dying puts an end to living cannot be overlooked. Instead, what grounds her claim is, in effect, the paradoxical claim to be already dead. It is her illness and the designation of this illness as terminal. It is the claim that she has no life left to preserve, that death is imminent in such a way that it will not make a difference if she dies now or later, or that, indeed, dying now can help her avoid "the suffering and indignity that she will endure if the disease runs its course."[78]

It is in this light that we might understand the nature of those laws that have been passed, in several U.S. states as well as several European countries, permitting the practice of assisted suicide, all of which require evidence both that the decision is voluntary and that the one making the request is incurably or terminally ill. In the Netherlands, which was the first European country to legalize physician-assisted dying in 2002, and where the legal specifications are least precise, a physician is exempt from prosecution as long as he "holds the conviction that the request by the patient was voluntary and well-considered" and as long as both physician and patient "hold the conviction that there was no other reasonable solution for the situation he was in."[79] In Belgium and Luxembourg, whose laws are nearly identical, the request must be "voluntary, well-considered, and repeated, and is not the result of any external pressure" and the patient must be "in a medically futile condition of constant and unbearable physical or mental suffering that cannot be alleviated."[80] All U.S. state laws legalizing physician-assisted death require repeated oral requests to the physician as well as a formal written petition. In addition, the diagnosis, which marks a moment at which medicine fulfills a legal rather than therapeutic function, must specify that the patient has less than six months to live.[81] In this double requirement, autonomy is recognized only in conjunction with a claim that the one who makes this claim lies outside or beyond life. It is as if six months can be instantly rounded down to zero with no remainder. The recognition of an autonomy outside the law, of a power to declare one's own death, comes at the expense of being already dead to the law. If the law prohibits assisted suicide, it is because it fears undermining the interest in the preservation of life—that is, in defining the line between life and death—that constitutes the law in the first place. If it permits assisted suicide, it does so only by disclaiming responsibility. The one who dies must declare that "I accept full moral responsibility for my actions."[82] She must let the law off the hook, declare herself outside the law, already dead.

The one who seeks the right to suicide is then caught in a double bind. To the extent that she claims to be alive, she becomes subject to the state's interest in the preservation of life. She becomes, in the very demand to be treated as an exception, a representative of the vulnerable, affirming their vulnerability by contrast with her supposed competence. Seeking recognition from the law, she becomes something more or other than herself, losing control of her proper name, which becomes symbolic of a conflict within the law itself: *Pretty v. United Kingdom*.[83] Yet to the extent that she declares her own death, she places herself outside the law, outside the realm in which a claim for recognition might be answered. She exposes the fact that at the heart of the problem is that a surrogate is needed to produce an event that in the end destroys the relation with the surrogate, and consequently destroys the surrogate as such.

III. The Death of Bartleby

Before the Law

The surrogate, then, cannot be insulated from risk—the risk of enabling a mistake and thus becoming accessory to murder, or else the risk of destroying the very relation that authorizes this action. The surrogate cannot reliably depend on the legal vehicles of autonomy—the living will, the "fully informed" request for assistance in suicide—because they are always liable to error. They risk hiding a vulnerable life that is not ready or does not want to die, or they risk converting the singular wish to die into an exception that, as such, reinforces the very vulnerability it seems to disclaim. Even if it is established that the one who wishes to die is "free from any pressure," the very fact that she appears before the law implies a motive beyond or other than her own death. She does not simply want assistance in dying. "Diane and Brian decided that if the law was against them they should try to change it."[84]

But to change the law so that it could recognize a right to die cannot simply mean creating new rules. Rather, it entails changing what it means to appear before the law, changing the way the law faces the tension that traverses the demand to die, as both a part of life and the termination of life. This possibility, this question, is engaged most radically in a literary text that stages a haunting encounter between a lawyer and a troubling, hardly intelligible appeal, an appeal that does not accept the distinction between living and dying, suicide and non-suicide, action and inaction—that is, the enigmatic appeal of Melville's Bartleby the Scrivener. For just as Bartleby cannot be said to commit suicide, neither can he be said not to commit suicide. "*Bartleby does not commit suicide*, at least not in any conventional sense," writes Timothy J. Deines. "If readers can agree on nothing else about this text, surely they must recognize this fact."[85] But must we? Or rather, might it be that Bartleby commits suicide in an unconventional way? In what follows, I suggest that Melville's tale enacts the legal questions circulating around the right to die. How can the law hear a demand that is incompatible with the very form of the law? How could one serve as the surrogate of such a demand?

The Narrator as Surrogate

First published in *Putnam's Monthly* in 1853, "Bartleby, the Scrivener: A Story of Wall Street" is narrated by a New York lawyer—relevantly, for this reading, a lawyer specializing in equity law, and who at the time of his encounter with Bartleby had recently been appointed to the post of master of chancery. He hires Bartleby as the direct consequence of this new appointment. "Now my original business—that of a conveyancer and title hunter, and drawer-up of recondite documents of all sorts—was considerably increased by receiving the master's office. There was now great work for scriveners."[86] But Bartleby famously does not turn out to be the efficient copyist his employer had sought. The lawyer instead finds himself baffled as his employee begins first to "prefer not to" perform his assigned work and then to "prefer not to" leave the law offices, even when the lawyer himself, desperate to free himself from his mysterious charge, moves out. Although Bartleby was meant to copy out the legal documents prepared by the attorney, in narrating Bartleby's tale the lawyer comes instead to copy out Bartleby's story, from his time in the law office, to his death in prison after being arrested as a vagrant, to the rumor that the enigmatic scrivener had once worked in the Dead Letter Office in Washington.

The lawyer's specialization in the law of trusts thus extends to his relation to Bartleby. For the story of Bartleby, too, will be a sort of recondite document in which he assumes the role of Bartleby's trustee:

> But I waive the biographies of all other scriveners for a few passages in the life of Bartleby, who was a scrivener the strangest I ever saw or heard of. While of other law-copyists I might write the complete life, of Bartleby nothing of that sort can be done. I believe that no materials exist for a full and satisfactory biography of this man. It is an irreparable loss to literature. Bartleby was one of those beings of whom nothing is ascertainable, except from the original sources, and in his case those are very small. (13)

Although the lawyer cannot repair the "irreparable loss to literature," the document he prepares on the life of Bartleby, the document entitled "Bartleby, the Scrivener," is a form of conveyance in which he serves as trustee and Bartleby as *res*.[87] This conversion of Bartleby into the *res* of a trust is confirmed by the conflation, in the term "life," of lived experience with the record of that experience.

Yet the responsibility the lawyer assumes in becoming Bartleby's trustee, he also frankly acknowledges, is undermined by the strangeness of the one whose "life" he holds in trust. Normally, he would rely only on "original sources," but these hardly exist. What can be known of Bartleby he knows through two sources: his status as an eyewitness, and hearsay. Absent adequate sources, it might seem that prior knowledge or expectations concerning others like Bartleby could supply a means of grasping his life. Yet conventional narrative expectations also prove insufficient: "I have known very many of them [scriveners] professionally and privately, and if I pleased, could relate divers histories, at which good-natured gentlemen might smile, and sentimental souls might weep" (13). The attorney may be alluding here to popular fictions such as James Maitland's *The Lawyer's Story*, which was serialized in the *Sunday Dispatch* between February and May 1853. Like Melville's tale, Maitland's story is narrated by a lawyer who takes on an extra copyist "who interested me considerably, in consequence of his modest, quiet, gentlemanly demeanor and his intense application to his duties." *The Lawyer's Story*, however, turns quickly into a mystery in which the lawyer uncovers his former copyist's biography, helping him discover his parentage and recover a large inheritance.[88] Maitland's mystery is thus resolved when his scrivener's previously enigmatic identity is attached to property ownership, when he becomes the beneficiary of a trust and in turn becomes capable of entrusting and conveying his self, in the form of property, to another. What Maitland's lawyer discovers, in other words, are the sorts of materials that Melville's lawyer might want so as to flesh out Bartleby's biography. Indeed, the notion that "materials" are needed to tell someone's story grounds the person in matter, in "the corporeal, as opposed to the spiritual or mental," as the *Oxford English Dictionary* has it. What the lawyer would require to tell a "full and satisfactory biography," in other words, is that identity behave like matter, like property. Indeed, the lawyer seems to treat his employees as a body of property, "my corps of copyists" (19). Bartleby, by contrast, presents the narrator with a "chief character" (13) whose life suffers from (or flaunts) a lack of materials.

Presenting himself as "an eminently *safe* man" (14), one who is inherently limited in outlook and bound to conventional legal and moral frameworks, the lawyer cannot but fail to respond adequately to the demands placed on him by the "unaccountable" Bartleby (27, 37). In this common reading, Bartleby dies because he has been abandoned by the attorney, who now tells Bartleby's story so as to justify, successfully or not, this abandonment. Bartleby's death becomes proof of the attorney's failure and burdens him with a guilt only indirectly acknowledged in the tale. According to this reading, the tale exposes a discrepancy between the demands placed on the attorney by Bartleby and the attorney's recognition of those demands.

Yet, as has also frequently been noted, it is not at all clear what, if anything, Bartleby wants or needs, and therefore what the attorney could or might do in order to act responsibly toward this strange and unsettling figure. For as one exchange between the lawyer and Bartleby makes clear, however much Bartleby resists elaborating on the significance of his preferring not to, one thing he does insist upon is the distinction between preferring and willing:

> "You *will* not?"
> "I *prefer* not." (25)

Whereas the lawyer is trained to execute others' wills, Bartleby prefers not to will, prefers not to formulate his appeal in terms of the structure of autonomous willing. Rather than a living will, Bartleby issues what we might call a *living preference*. It is in this vein that I propose Bartleby as a figure for the right to die. I suggest that Bartleby's formula, "I would prefer not to," encodes the paradoxical demand for the right to die, and that what seem to be the attorney's failed efforts to respond to this demand may instead represent the only possible form of response, even if that response assumes the irreducible risk of violence and misrecognition.

"Murder for Sweet Charity's Sake"

The suggestion that Bartleby may be appealing for assistance in dying is amplified by the lawyer's image of Bartleby as someone who is terminally ill. The lawyer reaches this conclusion in the context of a meditation on the limits of pity or sympathy for another. "So true it is, and so terrible too, that up to a certain point the thought or sight of misery enlists our best affections; but, in certain special cases, beyond that point it does not. They err who would assert that invariably this is owing to the inherent selfishness of the human heart. It rather proceeds from a certain hopelessness of remedying excessive and organic ill" (29). Elsewhere in the text, the lawyer is acutely aware of the ways that philanthropy may serve self-interest, seeing in Bartleby the opportunity, as he put it earlier, to "cheaply purchase a delicious self-approval" (23). But in this account, the failure to sympathize results not from selfishness, but rather from a certain emotional pragmatism. At the point where any remedy becomes hopeless, the lawyer suggests it is no longer useful or necessary to feel pity and the pain that accompanies it: "To a sensitive being, pity is not seldom pain. And when at last it is perceived that such pity cannot lead to effectual succor, common sense bids the soul be rid of it" (29). The notion that Bartleby's case is hopeless and incurable thus creates a crisis for the philanthropic ethos. To remain sensitive to one such as Bartleby would expose the self to unbearable pain, such that Bartleby's terminal condition comes to pose a threat to the self.

Rosemarie Garland-Thomson provocatively suggests that this "collapse of sympathetic benevolence" grounds "the cultural logic of euthanasia," in which euthanasia carries the connotation not of the neutral-to-positive "good death" it signifies etymologically, but rather of nineteenth-century eugenic theories aimed at propagating "good genes."[89] Bartleby, Garland-Thomson suggests, is "a figure for disability, one whose bodily appearance or function will not conform to cultural expectations and standards."[90] Labeled as "flawed," he is "in need of regularization, and ultimately—if not curable—expendable." The narrator's affective process exemplifies this logic. The failure to cure Bartleby results in a collapse of sympathy, such that when the lawyer deems Bartley incurable, "the only solution is to 'rid' himself of the scrivener."[91] In this view, then, the lawyer's diagnosis of Bartleby as "the victim of an innate and incurable disorder" is in fact a murderous outward projection of his own moral failure and is symptomatic of a larger cultural logic. "We collectively 'prefer' not to accept disability as a fundamental part of human experience. Melville's 'Bartleby' lays bare the logic of that preference," Garland-Thomson concludes.[92] Bartleby's preferring-not-to thus comes to appear as a projection of the narrator's, proceeding from the collapse of sympathy. Bartleby appears to him as "intransigently disabled," such that Bartleby's preferring-not-to (rather than a being-unable-to) itself provides a pretext for the collapse of sympathy and for the lawyer's ultimate eliminationism.[93] Indeed, as indicated in her conclusion, Garland-Thomson shifts the locus of Bartleby's formula from Bartleby himself to the narrator and to his readers.

Because Melville's text is a first-person narrative, and because even the words attributed in the text to Bartleby are reported by the narrator, this reading cannot be dismissed. Indeed, in narrating the story of this encounter with Bartleby, the lawyer takes the necessary risk that his testimony will be self-incriminating, that he will ultimately appear as Bartleby's murderer. I would suggest, however, that "Bartleby" does not settle the matter, and that another possibility emerges alongside this eliminationist reading, for the lawyer is overtly aware of the ways he resembles a potential murderer, even as he tries to imagine a different way of making sense of what murder might entail. This awareness emerges in a later passage not discussed by Garland-Thomson in which the lawyer identifies with John Colt, whose violent murder of Samuel Adams, a printer, when the latter visited his office to collect a debt, was the subject of sensational news coverage in 1841–42.[94] Imagining committing a murder in his own office, Melville's lawyer sees himself in Colt. But whereas Colt was driven to murder out of "irritable desperation," the lawyer claims that his imagined murder of Bartleby would derive from a different motive: "Men have committed murder for jealousy's sake, and anger's sake, and hatred's sake, and selfishness' sake, and spiritual pride's sake," he writes, "but no man that ever I heard of, ever committed a diabolical murder for sweet charity's sake" (36).

According to the line of interpretation suggested by Garland-Thomson, the notion of "murder for sweet charity's sake" would be an ideological ruse in which more venal motives are presented as altruistic. The claim to act out of charity would simply mask the desire to eliminate difference. This reading would have the authority of recent history, in which "mercy killing" served as a euphemism for eliminationism in the Nazi *Aktion Gnadentod*, or "Mercy Death Program" (commonly referred to as the T4 program; see chapter 3). Yet the lawyer's self-awareness, his insistence on the difference between this form of murder and others, suggests the additional possibility that what is at stake here is not a disingenuous or deluded appeal to charity, not false consciousness, but rather an attempt to imagine and to formulate a different relationship to the killing of another—to tell the story of a deed committed by "no man that ever I heard of"—an unheard-of, unprecedented kind of death. Situating himself both as potential criminal and as judge, he is asking the question asked by the U.S. Supreme Court and by the European Court of Human Rights: what would it mean to participate in the death of another, to commit an act that for all intents and purposes looks like murder, but that is undertaken in response to the other's appeal?

An Unheard-of Appeal

It is worth recalling that this allusion to a never-heard-of form of murder takes place in the midst of a narrative that itself tells the story of an unheard-of sort of scrivener—"the strangest I ever saw or heard of" (13), who requires "unheard-of exemptions" (26), and who sends his employer into a state of "unheard-of perplexity" (35). What Bartleby requires of the lawyer, it would seem, are modes of interpretation and response that are persistently without precedent. The repetition of the "unheard" might alert us as well to the particular mode of resistance that Bartleby's strangeness poses for the lawyer. What Bartleby solicits is something that falls outside the range of hearing, or we might say, of *a* hearing. It is something that cannot be brought before the bar of the law and be heard according to the law's system of rules and precedents.

Indeed, this troubling advent of the unheard, of a silence that does not simply mark an absence of sound but rather a disturbing kind of appeal, characterized Bartleby from the start. "I should have been quite delighted with his application, had he been cheerfully industrious. But he wrote on silently, palely, mechanically," observes the lawyer after first hiring his new scrivener (19–20). Whereas the force of a contract, of a signature, derives from its ability to represent the presence or voice of the signatory, the scrivener's work is devoid of "cheer," from Latin *cara*, or "face." Bartleby's activity is faceless and voiceless, and as such treats writing as nothing but an automatic gesture. Rather than the transfer of presence and significance from one format to another, from voice to text and from text to copy, writing appears as an act that bypasses meaning and treats letters as mere marks.

Bartleby's unheard-of nature also sheds light on his preference not to examine his copies. "It is, of course, an indispensable part of a scrivener's business to verify the accuracy of his copy, word by word," the lawyer explains. "Where there are two or more scriveners in an office, they assist each other in this examination, one reading from the copy, the other holding the original" (20). Thus when Bartleby responds to the lawyer's request that he assist him in checking a legal document, using what will become his repeated formula for the first time—"Bartleby in a singularly mild, firm voice, replied, 'I would prefer not to'" (20)—what he prefers not to do, it would seem, is to imbue the document with voice, whether to read the document aloud or to become its hearer. In the protocol for checking accuracy, the voice becomes the medium through which two documents can be compared to each other, any differences can be eliminated, and their sameness can be affirmed. Indeed, it is the very possibility of the identity of the documents that makes meaningfulness possible, for it is only on the basis of this identity that writing can appear as the mere transcription of a meaning that lies outside it and determines it. After all, how could a contract be valid if every copy displayed variations?

Bartleby's preferring not to copy thus reorients the relationships that define the law office, disrupting their reliance on the presence of voice as the medium of communication and transmission and instituting another mode of relation hinging on the unheard and the unheard-of, on the problem of attending to what, due to its very unexpectedness, does not or cannot be properly heard, registered, and repeated. This new mode of relation manifests itself, for one, when the lawyer and his employees find themselves unwittingly echoing Bartleby's language:

> Somehow, of late I had got into the way of involuntarily using this word "prefer" upon all sorts of not exactly suitable occasions. And I trembled to think that my contact with the scrivener had already and seriously affected me in a mental way. And what further and deeper aberration might it not yet produce? This apprehension had not been without efficacy in determining me to summary means.
>
> As Nippers, looking very sour and sulky, was departing, Turkey blandly and deferentially approached.
>
> "With submission, sir," said he, "yesterday I was thinking about Bartleby here, and I think that if he would but prefer to take a quart of good ale every day, it would do much towards mending him, and enabling him to assist in examining his papers."
>
> "So you have got the word too," said I, slightly excited.
>
> "With submission, what word, sir," asked Turkey, respectfully crowding himself into the contracted space behind the screen, and by so doing, making me jostle the scrivener. "What word, sir?" (31)

This brief exchange between the lawyer and Turkey parodies the practice of examining copy, with the lawyer seeking from Turkey verification that they have in fact heard the same word. Their normal business of examining legal documents such as contracts is disrupted as they enter the "contracted" space of Bartleby's language. But Bartleby's word, like Bartleby himself, defies examination. Even as this word defies the lawyer's will and makes its way "involuntarily" into his speech, even as it insinuates itself as well into Turkey's speech, at the same time it remains uncommunicated and unheard: "What word, sir?"

Bartleby's "singular" voice, in other words, seems to evade the pathways of normative legal and social communication, in which meaning is always subject to comparison and verification. It introduces something unheard and unheard-of into the law office and inspires the lawyer to confront, however hesitantly and insufficiently, the possibility of the unprecedented, of something that seems inherently contradictory—a charitable murder.

The Master of Chancery

Yet Bartleby, like Diane Pretty, remains committed to the law. Indeed, Bartleby's haunting of the law office, the fact that he declines to leave the office despite the lawyer's pleas and despite, eventually, the lawyer's own evacuation of the premises, suggests that at stake for Bartleby is a question of how, if at all, his preferring not to might be recognized by the law and by the lawyer as its representative. Indeed, even as the lawyer attempts to coax Bartleby to leave the law office, he unwittingly seems to acknowledge this commitment. "How would a bar-tender's business suit you?" he asks (41). Although the lawyer may seem to be proposing a different profession, within the language of the law a bar-tender might be another name for a barrister, a tender of the bar, that is, of the law.[95]

The attempt by a master of chancery to make sense of the strange figure of Bartleby suggests further connections to chancery or equity law. Chancery law, Naomi Reed notes, "dealt not with questions of law but of equity, of '[j]ustice administered according to fairness as contrasted with the strictly formulated rules of common law.' . . . As a Master of Chancery, then, the lawyer must have some special skill in understanding the uniqueness of a situation."[96] But this special skill, Reed suggests, is vitiated by the fact, conveyed by the lawyer, that between the time of the events narrated and the time of the narration, the Courts of Chancery in New York State had been closed. Despite his training in equity law, the lawyer, telling his story now in this post-Chancery era, therefore understands Bartleby "through the logic of law rather than the logic of equity."[97] Thus, in Reed's reading of the final line of the story ("Ah Bartleby! Ah humanity!"), the lawyer in the end fails to grasp Bartleby's uniqueness and views him instead as an instance of a general rule, as a synecdoche of humanity. The logic of abstraction, of equivalences—and, with reference to intersections of law and economy, the logic of the money form and of the commodity—prevails over the logic of uniqueness and strangeness, over the logic of Bartleby. Thus Bartleby remains, in the lawyer's resonant phrase, "the unaccountable Bartleby," in that he cannot be accounted for in the system of exchange or equivalence that rules both the logic of law and the logic of the market. Bartleby, in turn, in disrupting the operation of the law office also more radically "disrupt[s] the apparently smooth running of a logic of abstract equivalence"—that is, the law of capitalism.[98]

Reed's analysis of "Bartleby" is exemplary of the strain of interpretation mentioned earlier and also represented by Garland-Thomson, according to which the story narrates a moral failure on the attorney's part, such that Bartleby becomes a figure of difference—a dispossessed or silenced other, or in a stronger form, a figure of resistance, representing something like an alternative logic or illogic that contests the logic of the law altogether. Gilles Deleuze, in a paradigmatic reading of Bartleby as the "pure outside [*exclu*]," identifies this as a "new logic, a *logic of preference*," although Deleuze declines to relate Bartleby's death to this new logic.[99] Reed, by contrast, suggests that Bartleby's death marks the ultimate form of "withdrawal from circulation" in the commodity state. Her reading thus allies itself with a dense critical nexus that associates Bartleby with civil disobedience, seeing him as, for instance, an originary figure to "occupy Wall Street."[100] In this view, his death becomes a condemnation of the world, even the result of a hunger strike. Bartleby dies for the sake of difference.[101]

Yet Reed's identification of Bartleby with a logic or economy of difference—with the logic of equity over the logic of law—glosses over the ways in which both chancery and common law are forms of law. Indeed, when the New York Court of Chancery was abolished in 1847 (that is, in the lawyer's story, between the death of Bartleby and the publication of his narrative in 1853), this was not done so as to suppress the particular power of equity law to appreciate uniqueness. Instead, it was because, according to one turn-of-the-century legal historian, "the equitable jurisdiction of the court, at first administered somewhat liberally, according to the original idea of the court of chancery, had become crystallized in a body of law and rules apparently as inflexible as the common law."[102]

This sheds additional light on the significance of chancery law in Melville's text, for it reminds us that chancery law derives from sovereign power, since chancery courts emerged historically as courts of appeal wherein litigants could bypass or appeal common law court decisions, addressing their suits directly to "the king's conscience" or, by extension, to his chancellors, who served as the king's surrogates and were assigned the power to sign and seal the king's documents. Especially in its early manifestations in English law, Chancery court would thus have the ability to overrule the common law court and as such attest to the king's prerogative to make law—that is, to the king's position outside the law. A master of chancery, what the lawyer called "the master's office," thus names a form of power that, if it can recognize uniqueness outside and against a system of abstract equivalence, does so on the basis of its own exceptionality and of the force of law which attaches to that exceptionality.

Metaphors of Sovereignty

Whereas the force of chancery law is derived from the sovereign exception, which in its essential form grants the sovereign the right to kill with impunity, the lawyer occupies his "master's office" only uneasily. Indeed, even as he imagines the unheard-of notion of a murder that would not be motivated by criminal intentions but instead by charity, he continues to frame this act as murder and to condemn himself in advance. He remains a trustee, whose power as such derives entirely from another and who remains the other's subject. His specific law practice revolves, we recall, around "rich men's bonds and mortgages and title-deeds" (14).

Nevertheless, the law office does appear repeatedly as the space of sovereign law-making, and more specifically, of that exceptional privilege of the sovereign, the right to kill. I want to highlight two such moments. First, upon the lawyer's second attempt to enlist Bartleby in the task of examining copies, when Bartleby again states, "I would prefer not to," the lawyer describes himself as "for a few moments . . . turned into a pillar of salt" (21), alluding to the punishment of Lot's wife when she breaks the divine injunction not to look back upon leaving Sodom. The second occurs when the lawyer, thinking he has successfully evicted Bartleby, returns to work the next morning:

> I was fumbling under the door mat for the key, which Bartleby was to have left there for me, when accidentally my knee knocked against a panel, producing a summoning sound, and in response a voice came to me from within—"Not yet; I am occupied."
> It was Bartleby.
> I was thunderstruck. For an instant I stood like the man who, pipe in mouth, was killed one cloudless afternoon long ago in Virginia, by summer lightning; at his own warm open window he was killed, and remained leaning out there upon the dreamy afternoon, till some one touched him, when he fell. (34–35)

In his "I would prefer not to," it may be the case that Bartleby "gives up the authority to speak" and performs an "abdication," as Maurice Blanchot suggests.[103] In both of these instances, however, it is Bartleby—and not, as one might expect, the lawyer—who is associated with sovereignty, with a divine or natural right to kill—that is, with a form of killing that is not murder.

But beyond this power to kill ascribed to Bartleby, something else, it would seem, takes place in these moments: the "motionless" (19), "stationary" (41), "unmoving" (42) Bartleby imposes his own immobility on the lawyer, who becomes, in effect, a monument to Bartleby's power—a pillar of salt, a pet-rified man. This paradoxical transmission of immobility—paradoxical in that immobility itself seems to move, to be transferred, from one figure to another—disrupts the model of a sovereignty based on the right to kill. For what Bartleby's power performs here is not simply a killing that is not mur-der, but more unsettlingly a killing that is not simply a killing. The pillar of salt and the petrified man figure forms of death that at the same time survive death, that undermine the finality of death by producing, in and through the event of death, a sort of proxy for the one who dies. Indeed, what links the pillar of salt and the petrified man is that both occupy the position of witness: just as Lot's wife is transformed into a pillar of salt precisely at the moment when she turns back to witness the destruction of Sodom, and just as the pillar itself therefore becomes the witness of her very act of witnessing, so the man struck by lightning is frozen gazing out the window, witnessing the scene of his own destruction.[104] As Bartleby comes to occupy the place of the law, the lawyer thus finds himself, and the law, transformed. The power of the law consisted previously in its inscription of the person into a system of property ownership, and on that basis both prohibited suicide and arrogated to itself the right to kill. Autonomy, accordingly, meant to assume the place of the legislator: to claim self-ownership as well as the right to kill oneself or to be killed without that act constituting a crime. But Bartleby's power here seems to create something that escapes its own grasp, a figure of witnessing that sees and memorializes its own destruction.

This transformation of the space of the law under the influence of Bar-tleby's power anticipates the surprising images of sovereignty with which Bartleby is associated in the hour of his death. First is the image of pharaonic power the lawyer finds in the prison yard:

> The yard was entirely quiet. It was not accessible to the common prisoners. The surrounding walls, of amazing thickness, kept off all sounds behind them. The Egyptian character of the masonry weighed upon me with its gloom. But a soft imprisoned turf grew under foot. The heart of the eternal pyramids, it seemed, wherein, by some strange magic, through the clefts, grass-seed, dropped by birds, had sprung. (44)

In this metaphoric transformation of the prison into an enchanted mauso-leum, the walls that seemed to imprison Bartleby become forms of protection, creating a space without sounds, where nothing can be heard and where the lawyer appears not as Bartleby's persecutor but as an attendant to his eternal reign. As with the pillar of salt and the petrified man, Bartleby is associated with a power, "some strange magic," whereby death survives itself.

This strange sovereignty finally animates the moment when the lawyer pronounces Bartleby dead through an allusion to the book of Job. Bartleby, he says, quoting the King James Bible and preserving its orthography, is asleep "with kings and counsellors" (45). In the book of Job, this passage occurs as Job curses the day he was born. "Why died I not from the womb? . . . For now should I have lain still and been quiet, I should have slept: then had I been at rest, with kings and counsellors of the earth."[105] Job, of course, despite voicing a wish to have died, renounces any claim to exercise the right to die himself. Submitting to a law outside himself, he is God's servant or slave (`ebed). When the lawyer suggests that Bartleby sleeps with kings and counsellors, he thus suggests that Bartleby dies the death that Job did not and could not die. Whereas Job accepts his position as God's property and his lack of autonomy, Bartleby's curse ("I would prefer not to") fulfills itself in his death. Lying on his side with his knees drawn up, he appears in the fetal position as if indeed he "died from the womb."

But the lawyer is not simply a neutral witness to Bartleby's death. For he cannot but be aware that he himself is a "counsellor," and that his evocation of Job pronounces his own death along with that of the scrivener; he, too, is asleep with Bartleby. The attorney, in this light, does not simply abandon Bartleby and leave him to die in prison. Instead, he assists Bartleby's death, even if he grasps his own role only belatedly. He petrifies Bartleby just as Bartleby petrified him, acquiring the right to kill Bartleby only by Bartleby's own prerogative. What Bartleby said to the lawyer when he first visited him in prison—"I know you . . . and I want nothing to say to you" (43)—may, then, not be a condemnation so much as the recognition of a pact fulfilled, a recognition that the lawyer has finally if unwittingly fulfilled a promise that leaves nothing more to be said—or rather, that was transmitted in an unheard-of manner in the first place.

The Surrogate of Dead Letters

If it is perhaps the case, then, that the lawyer does not simply abandon Bartleby to a ruthless world; if he does not, as is so often maintained, act negligently or maliciously towards the vulnerable figure who seems to place himself at his mercy; if instead he himself becomes subject to Bartleby's strange appeal, his curse, such that his action or inaction ultimately recognizes and makes possible a right to die that relinquishes and disrupts both the myth of autonomy and its opposite, the position of victim; if he finds himself confronted with an appeal that prefers not to assume the conventional form of a living will and that as such calls to account the inadequacy of any effort to ensure that the relationship between the one who seeks the right to die and the law is "safe"; if it is the case, finally, that the lawyer comes to perceive and submit himself to a power that transforms him and teaches him how to become Bartleby's accomplice in the unheard-of act of a murder for sweet charity's sake; if the lawyer becomes not Bartleby's persecutor but his surrogate and witness, it must also be underscored that this surrogacy is based entirely on a series of metaphorical operations. In the encounter with Bartleby, the lawyer becomes like Lot's wife or the Virginia pipe-smoker just as Bartleby becomes like an Egyptian pharaoh or a Job who defies his God. In the attempt to hear the unheard, the lawyer is not simply historian or biographer, but more accurately a poet whose story depends fundamentally on his ability to speak through metaphor, to find words and figures that would somehow transmit what Bartleby, and what his effect on others, was like. Thus the ethical question concerning the lawyer's responsibility to Bartleby is necessarily bound up with a rhetorical question concerning the nature and validity of metaphor. If the lawyer becomes Bartleby's surrogate by discovering a hidden likeness between the "unaccountable" Bartleby and the images he uses to represent Bartleby, by the same token metaphor risks projecting or inventing a likeness where there is none.

Indeed, this question of the ethics of comparison haunts the lawyer's famously ambiguous conclusion—"Ah Bartleby! Ah humanity!" In one reading, as noted, Bartleby becomes the representative or symbol of a general or generic humanity. The lawyer's sermonic eloquence underscores this possibility, for his language associates him with figures such as Judas and Pontius Pilate as well as with a failed or "prudent" version of the Good Samaritan.[106] Correspondingly, Bartleby—as the bearer of "good tidings"—appears as a Christ figure betrayed by the lawyer, or, in a more generous reading, one whose death exerts a redemptive force and allows the lawyer to perceive his own failings, however belatedly.[107] The lawyer would then become Bartleby's surrogate to the extent that they both appear as representations of humanity in general, to the extent that they share what he earlier calls "the bond of common humanity." Bartleby would thus be absorbed in the end by the same logic that absorbed and compromised Diane Pretty's appeal. His singularity vanishes behind images that transform him into a representative figure. The one who preferred not to participate in verifying the accuracy of copies, and who eventually "gives up copying" altogether, comes to appear in these images as himself a copy.

But another perspective on the significance of comparison is opened in the coda to the tale, in which the lawyer at last reveals the contents of the "vague report" (13) that he had mentioned in the opening paragraph of his narrative. Although he has deferred this rumor until the end of his narrative, its shadow nonetheless hangs over the entire tale. Bartleby, the rumor has it, was formerly employed in the Dead Letter Office in Washington:

> When I think over this rumor, hardly can I express the emotions which seize me. Dead letters! does it not sound like dead men? Conceive a man by nature and misfortune prone to a pallid hopelessness, can any business seem more fitted to heighten it than that of continually handling these dead letters, and assorting them for the flames? For by the cart-load they are annually burned. Sometimes

from out the folded paper the pale clerk takes a ring:—the finger it was meant for, perhaps, moulders in the grave; a bank-note sent in swiftest charity:—he whom it would relieve, nor eats nor hungers any more; pardon for those who died despairing; hope for those who died unhoping; good tidings for those who died stifled by unrelieved calamities. On errands of life, these letters speed to death. (45)

Whereas the comparisons the lawyer proposed earlier in the tale are motivated by his attempts to grasp Bartleby's apparent singularity, the comparison that surfaces here arises impulsively and compulsively, due to "emotions" that defy expression. Comparisons to the Colt-Adams murder, the Virginia pipe-smoker, Lot's wife, and Job are all derived from frames of reference that belong to the lawyer's everyday world. But the relation he draws between dead letters and dead men, by contrast, appears entirely unmotivated. Indeed, whereas the lawyer claims that the comparison is due to similarity in sound— "Dead letters! does it not sound like dead men?"—"dead letters" does not in any conventional way sound like "dead men." "Dead" does not "sound like" "dead," but simply repeats it, while "letters" and "men" share no apparent phonetic similarity. In a tale that stakes ethical relationships on the validity of metaphorical comparison, in which inaccurate metaphors risk taking the surrogate down the path of murder, the claim to hear a similarity where there does not seem to be one thus entails a radical risk. In associating dead letters and dead men, the lawyer thus gives a hearing to the unheard.

Rather than a mistake, it may be, I suggest, that in the end it is precisely by hearing the unheard comparison of dead letters and dead men that the lawyer finally hears the full significance of Bartleby's appeal. For in this comparison, Bartleby becomes not merely a singular person who burdens the lawyer with the responsibility of a vexed and unstable surrogacy, not simply a *res* in the lawyer's trust, but rather comes to appear as himself a surrogate. Indeed, the lawyer's understanding of Bartleby's relation to the dead letters he is said to have handled in his former employment is surprising. Since the lawyer is an "elderly man" (13), and the tale he tells is of a scrivener—that is, a kind of writer—who dies, it might seem natural for him to associate dead letters with their writers. In fact, in a well-known letter to Nathaniel Hawthorne, Melville, too, makes this connection. "My dear Sir, a presentiment is on me,—I shall at last be worn out and perish. . . . What I feel most moved to write, that is banned,—it will not pay."[108] Banned writing, a writing that would not reach a readership, would effectively be dead letters. The difficulty or impossibility of reaching a readership is here associated with the death of the writer, perhaps metaphorically in that his life or identity as a writer is stifled, or perhaps even literally, with the lack of pay leading to starvation, as with the dead letters imagined by the lawyer containing banknotes for the starving. Surprisingly, however, this is *not* the association the lawyer makes. Rather than stand for the death of their writers' words, dead letters here come to stand for their addressees. The undelivered banknote leads to the starvation of the addressee; the undelivered pardon causes the intended recipient to die of desperation. Indeed, it is as if what makes dead letters dead is not simply that they are undeliverable, but that their undeliverability is itself a cause of death.

Rather than treat dead letters as mere refuse, Bartleby, in the lawyer's account, becomes their reader. As such, he becomes the surrogate of letters on the threshold of death, at the moment they are about to be burned by the cart-load. Bartleby thus interrupts their deaths. As the clerk receives the ring, the banknote, and the pardon, dead letters become living letters or living wills, with Bartleby as their trustee. He becomes their memorial and stands in the place of an addressee where none exists. He thus makes the address of the letters possible; he gives a hearing to what would otherwise remain unheard. But at the same time he does not try to save these letters from death. He does not try to track down their intended recipients or determine their original intention. Instead, as he consigns these letters to the flames, he becomes the bearer of these letters in their very death. Bartleby thus comes to embody the appeal for the right to die, whether through a living will or petition for assistance in suicide, in a form that does not require this appeal to formulate itself in terms of autonomy and to make itself recognizable to the law or to set aside its self-contradictory nature, its radical ignorance with respect to what it demands. As the surrogate of dead letters, Bartleby thus confronts the law with the challenge, and also the opportunity, of hearing the unheard, of recognizing in the dead letter of the appeal for the right to die an essential unreadability. To respond to an appeal that does not and cannot know its own will, and that as such escapes any effort to contain it within the normative framework of law, means to assume the risk that this response may always possibly be a mistake, a murder. Yet at the same time, as Kafka so troublingly declared to his physician, not to respond would equally be murder. To occupy the place of the surrogate is to assume this irreducible risk, even if—or perhaps, even because—one prefers not to.

Chapter 2

✦

The Modernist Art of Death

Balzac, Baudelaire, Benjamin

> Among the numerous enumerations of the *Rights of Man*
> that nineteenth-century wisdom rehearses so frequently and
> complacently, two rights of considerable importance have
> been neglected, which are the right to contradict oneself, and
> the right to *take one's leave.*
>
> —Charles Baudelaire

In the previous chapter, we saw how the necessary mediation of a surrogate
puts in question the attempt to conceive of the right to die as an expression
of personal autonomy. Here, I turn to another argument for the right to die,
which understands it not as evidence of autonomy but rather as an act of self-
definition or self-authorship: in brief, an aesthetic act. To appeal for the right
to die, in this light, is to practice an art of dying. Katha Pollitt alluded to this
idea when, discussing Carolyn Heilbrun's death in an article quoted in the
introduction, she wrote of "the right to shape the arc of your life."[1] We might
recall as well Justice Stevens's contention that the right to die recognizes "the
individual's interest in choosing a final chapter that accords with her life
story."[2] The physician Atul Gawande similarly asserts that "all we ask is to
be allowed to remain the writers of our own story," and that consequently
people "want to end their stories on their own terms."[3] In this image of life
as narrative, death presents the opportunity to complete a story that remains
formless, that in fact is not yet a story, until the moment of completion, at
which point it acquires form and meaning. "A man who dies at the age of
thirty-five," Walter Benjamin observes, "will always be remembered as a man
who died at the age of thirty-five."[4]

The normative form of this argument is perhaps most effectively developed
in the thought of the legal philosopher Ronald Dworkin. Dworkin's argument proceeds from an analysis of the ways that distinct and even opposed
legal principles tend to become confused with each other in the adjudication
of the difficult and often unprecedented situations that arise in right-to-die

cases. In particular, he observes that in the majority opinion in the Supreme Court case of *Cruzan v. Director, Missouri Department of Health*, what claim to be arguments based on respect for autonomy are motivated instead at crucial moments by the consideration of interests other than autonomy: by paternalistic concerns for the best interests of someone considered vulnerable as well as by moral convictions attributed to the state concerning the inherent sanctity of life. Dworkin's critique of *Cruzan* turns on a key insight. Chief Justice Rehnquist's opinion for the majority supports Missouri's right to require clear evidence of a desire to forgo life-prolonging medical treatment on the grounds that such a requirement prevents the irrevocable harm that would ensue from allowing someone to die who had not clearly articulated that choice. The Missouri rule was therefore interpreted as protecting patient autonomy. Yet, Dworkin observes, Rehnquist's reasoning does not allow for a logically valid but opposite outcome, in that it "assumes that no serious harm is done in keeping alive someone who would have wanted to die." In fact, Dworkin adds, it may well be the case that "forcing people to live who genuinely want to die causes serious damage to them."[5] What is ostensibly an argument based on autonomy turns out to derive instead from a set of moral assumptions on the part of the law concerning what constitutes "irrevocable harm."

Dworkin's response to this unmarked confusion of arguments seeks a way through or around the conflict and confusion between respect for autonomy, on the one hand, and concern for the best interests of the patient or the interests of the state, on the other. Because claims for the right to die based on autonomy can never be sufficiently grounded, as discussed in chapter 1, Dworkin recognizes the necessity of developing a way of judging another's interests. At the same time, he insists that to assume as a default position that the patient's or the collective's best interests are served by keeping someone alive (or nominally alive) leads to potential injustice. Consequently, he proposes that a person's interests, and therefore what the "sanctity of life" might mean to that person, should be determined on a case-by-case basis:

> We cannot understand what death means to people—why some would rather be dead than existing permanently sedated or incompetent, why others would want to "fight on" even in terrible pain or even when they are unconscious and cannot savor the fight; why so few people think that whether they live or die once they fall permanently unconscious does not matter to them at all—we cannot understand any of this, or much else that people feel about death, unless we turn away from death for a while and look back to life. In almost every case, someone who is permanently unconscious or incompetent was not born into that condition: the tragedy lies at the end of a life that someone has led in earnest. When we ask what is best for him, we are not judging only his future and ignoring his past.

We worry about the effect of his life's last stage on the character of his life as a whole, as we might worry about the effect of a play's last scene or a poem's last stanza on the entire creative work.[6]

Whereas the argument from autonomy was primarily concerned with whether or not someone was qualified to issue a demand to die, and as such was concerned with death as a moment of decision isolated at a particular moment in time, the argument from self-authorship situates the appeal for the right to die within a narrative context and imagines it as a formal ending, the conclusion to a plot. Indeed, elsewhere Dworkin employs similar figures and explicitly links death to narrative, writing that "death is special, a peculiarly significant event in the narrative of our lives, like the final scene in a play, with everything about it intensified, under a special spotlight."[7]

At both of these moments, the image of life as a work of art appears, on first reading, as a mere analogy: our concern for the best death is similar to our concern for a proper ending to a work of literature. Yet Dworkin's language, playfully but consequentially, also conflates life and art. Read according to the simple analogy between life and art, dying is "life's last stage" in the sense that it is the last step in a process, similar in its finality to the last act of a play. But as this "stage" appears surrounded by references to tragedy, character, and plays, the temporal, processual meaning of "stage" slips into its theatrical meaning. "Life's last stage" comes to name the final proscenium on which we appear, our farewell performance. Similarly, when Dworkin speaks of the "character" of a life, he means primarily its major traits or distinctive qualities. But in context, this term, too, takes on its sense of dramatis persona. This double meaning resounds when Dworkin later asserts that "none of us wants to end our lives out of character."[8] On the one hand, this means that we want our deaths to be consistent with an inner sense of self, with our moral character. But on the other hand, it suggests a thoroughly, inescapably performative or theatrical dimension to death, in which death, "under a special spotlight," places us in a heroic role. Finally, life is not simply *like* a narrative, with death correspondingly *like* the end of a narrative; instead, as in Justice Stevens's related image, Dworkin speaks of the "narrative of our lives." Life *is* a narrative, with the end of the narrative spelling death. In developing a way of determining another's interests apart from judgments of autonomy and conventional moral judgment, Dworkin thus replaces legal questions concerning competence and rationality with questions more closely associated with literary criticism. Legal judgment cedes to aesthetic judgment.

In some ways, this notion of death as the conclusion to a well-wrought story draws on the long tradition of the art of dying, the *ars moriendi*, most systematically charted in the many guidebooks that circulated in medieval and early modern Europe. But whereas this tradition, to which I return shortly, judges a death to be good and proper to the extent that it emulates an existing model, most prominently the death of Christ, Dworkin rejects the validity of any standard or generic notion of a good death. "Whether it is in someone's best interests that his life end in one way rather than another depends on so much else that is special about him—about the shape and character of his life and his own sense of his integrity and critical interests—that no uniform collective decision can possibly hope to serve everyone even decently."[9] What allows a given death to appear as a good or fitting ending is therefore not the way it conforms to existing conventions, but instead the extent to which it seems good or proper with respect to the unique and singular life it concludes.[10] In this view, a death would be one's own not because one possesses that death in the form of property that one therefore has the right to destroy, but instead because it belongs to one's life story, which seems to dictate or require an ending that would be out of place in any other story but one's own.

But this claim to the specialness or singularity of every death is tempered by the demands of aesthetic judgment. For to the extent that death participates in producing a life as a creative work, to the extent that death places me on stage and allows me to turn my life and death into an artistic performance, I become not simply an actor but also a spectator and critic, along with others who are called upon to judge my performance. Where Dworkin found fault with Rehnquist for confusing the protection of autonomy with moral judgment, in Dworkin's argument we see that the value of a given death is similarly judged by criteria that cannot be derived exclusively from a singular life or death narrative, though in this case these criteria are aesthetic rather than moral. In Dworkin's argument, this aesthetic criterion is coherence or integrity. "People think it important," he writes, "not just that their life contain a variety of the right experiences, achievements, and connections, but that it have a structure that reflects a coherent choice among these—for some, that it display a steady, self-defining commitment to a vision or character or achievement that the life as a whole, seen as an integral creative narrative, illustrates and expresses."[11] Again the argument from self-authorship distinguishes itself from the argument from autonomy: whereas the latter sought to determine the extent to which a decision was free and voluntary, what matters in Dworkin's argument is the extent to which an appeal for the right to die (or to reject the right to die) produces a coherent and integral narrative. At issue, in other words, is formal rather than conceptual unity, with a significant ethical consequence: if the creative narrative of a given life requires a certain kind of death in order to achieve its overall integrity, it would also be the case that an unsuitable death would interrupt the achievement of this integrity. If the last stanza, last act, or last chapter is discordant, the entire work is ruined.

The criterion of formal unity therefore poses a problem when it comes to evaluating any given death. For the one whose death is at stake, if she is imagining and planning a death that will do justice to her life narrative, if she is attempting to write and direct the final scene in her play, this evaluation requires her to assume the impossible position of spectator to her own demise. As autobiography becomes autothanatography, the writing of one's death, the subject is confronted with "its radical loss of self-identity," as Ellen Burt observes.[12] The attempt to turn death into a decisive and culminating experience is bound to fail before the impossibility of experiencing death. Autothanatography thus requires the sacrifice of an image of the coherent and integral subject; it is an art of ruin. This structural impediment to the coherence of autothanatography in turn poses a problem for the lawmaker, judge, physician, or surrogate charged with assisting the other's death. For if the subject cannot produce a coherent autothanatography, then any determination by the surrogate of whether or not a given death is consistent with "life as a whole" remains suspect. It may always be the case that the principle of coherence one claims to see achieved in a given death may result from the necessarily retrospective ordering of a life narrative. The ending, rather than acquire its meaning from what precedes it, may instead create or impose meaning with respect to what precedes it.[13] As aesthetic criteria, in other words, coherence and integrity risk leading to the oversight or even suppression of the singularity of a life and death.

In this light, the question arises of what sort of self-authored death could produce its own aesthetic criteria, its own standard of judgment, rather than submitting itself to the criterion of integrity. To address this question, I propose to explore a literary corpus that stages the aesthetics of death along different lines from those proposed by Dworkin. Whereas Dworkin's emphasis on narrative coherence recalls a classic, Aristotelian model of literary form, I suggest in this chapter that in order to grasp the problematic if also productive relationship between the right to die and aesthetic judgment, one might look instead to the theory and experience of literary modernism. My focus is on a constellation of texts that revolve around a striking if enigmatic claim made by Charles Baudelaire—namely, that modernism in art is linked from its very origin to the advent of a new form of death, which he calls "modern suicide." This form of death, as we shall see, does not conform to conventional models of suicide. Instead it announces a new and unfamiliar terrain in which the modern subject imagines what it might mean to become the author of one's own death. First among the texts where this terrain is most profoundly explored is Honoré de Balzac's 1831 novel *La Peau de chagrin* (usually translated as *The Magic Skin* or *The Wild Ass's Skin*), whose protagonist Baudelaire identifies as one of his "modern suicides." But I will also have occasion to consider texts by Walter Benjamin, Karl Marx, and others who observe in the nineteenth century the advent of new questions and figures of dying that anticipate and haunt contemporary debates about the right to die.

I pursue this inquiry in three parts followed by a brief epilogue. The first part situates the notion of modern suicide with respect to the history and theory of modernity in the mid-nineteenth century. The second part charts the ways that *La Peau de chagrin* reflects these contexts, while the third part and epilogue turn to the novel's creative vision of a modernist art of death.

I. Death and Modernity

"Who Shall Say?"

My focus on the incipient modernism of the early to mid-nineteenth century is motivated by the sense that this moment marks a certain threshold or passage into the time of modern death, that it is here that we witness the first indications of the radical transformation of death that Malte would later find firmly entrenched in the Paris of the early twentieth century. Although the question of euthanasia would not emerge as an overt social concern until later in the nineteenth century, this period marks the emergence of the denaturalization of death and its consequent imbrication with forces of technology and commerce, as embodied in Malte's image of the hospital as a factory producing death in the image of ready-to-wear garments.

This denaturalization of death is signaled, for one, by its medicalization over the course of the nineteenth century. As Jonathan Strauss observes, perhaps even more than mental illness, images and theories of death proved instrumental in the rise of the medical profession in Paris and "exercised an underappreciated force in the self-definition of nineteenth-century French society."[14] In turn, this development in "the capital of the nineteenth-century" both reflected and influenced social and cultural change throughout western Europe and the Americas. On an institutional level, the medicalization of death is indicated in such changes as the discontinuation after the Revolution of a decree requiring physicians to offer confession to the dying, thus shifting the authority over death from the church to medical experts.[15] Hospitals, once administered by the church, also became gradually secularized, with the nuns who formed an important contingent of their staff gradually expelled.[16] And death itself came to be viewed as a medical condition. For instance, in Xavier Bichat's influential and frequently reprinted 1799 treatise *Recherches physiologiques sur la vie et la mort* (*Physiological Studies on Life and Death*), death itself appears as the fundamental object of medicine, in that it is viewed as a positive force to which life is but a reaction. "Life," Bichat declares, "is the set of functions that resist death."[17] Although competing medical theories outpaced Bichat's so-called vitalism by the mid-nineteenth century, his treatment of death as primarily a medical problem, and thus as subject to medical control, established a lasting paradigm for modern medicine—the paradigm against which the right-to-die movement emerges in its effort to wrest control over the end of life away from medical authority and to place it in the hands of the individual.

Concurrent and intertwined with the medicalization of death are premonitions of a degraded, unheroic notion of death, of death that seems to be losing its very finality and certainty, its deadliness. The anxiety projected in Edgar Allan Poe's tales may be exemplary of this strain of the nineteenth-century imagination. In "The Premature Burial," for instance, it takes the form of a fear of being suspended in a deathlike state and consequently of being mistaken for dead and buried alive. Not only the subject of literary fiction, this fear informed medical theory as well as sometimes fervent public reactions, such as a niche but not insignificant market for caskets equipped with alarm bells and breathing tubes.[18] Poe's narrator testifies, if exaggeratedly, to a broader dissolution of a traditional conception of death. "The boundaries which divide Life from Death are at best shadowy and vague," he declares. "Who shall say where the one ends, and where the other begins?"[19] This blurring of the line between life and death could also result in an opposite but complementary anxiety, dramatized in Poe's "The Facts in the Case of M. Valdemar." Valdemar allows himself to become the experimental subject of the narrator, a mesmerist. On the verge of death, he enters a hypnotic trance in which he remains for seven months. When the mesmerist then attempts to end the trance, Valdemar cries out to be allowed to die at last: "For God's sake!—quick!—quick!—put me to sleep—or, quick!—waken me!—quick!—*I say to you that I am dead!*"[20] The fear of being mistaken for dead while still alive finds its corollary in the fear of not fully dying or not being permitted to die. In both cases, death fails to arrive at the proper time, as if to witness a decline in the authority associated with fate or nature.[21]

Baudelaire's notion of modern suicide, I suggest, represents a germinal attempt to grapple with the question of how to die in the wake of the degradation of death. For the French poet, as we will see, the modernity of a given death relates first of all to an aesthetic question, the question of its *beauty*. Baudelaire thus joins Dworkin in relating death to the work of art and in attempting to judge its significance according to aesthetic criteria. But where Dworkin proposes integrity as the central aesthetic criterion, Baudelaire proposes what he calls *modernity* (*modernité*). Although this notion and its relationship to death (and to suicide) requires further thought, it raises the question that motivates this chapter: how can one become the author or artist of one's own death not simply with respect to one's own experiences, one's own character, but rather with respect to the very historical event of the degradation of death, with respect to an era that seems to contradict the very possibility of a death of one's own?

Modern Suicide and Modern Art

Baudelaire's claim concerning modern death arises in the context of a discussion of aesthetics, in what Walter Benjamin identifies as "the classic passage devoted to the theory of the modern," from the French poet's seminal essay in art criticism, "On the Heroism of Modern Life," which concludes the volume of critical essays published as the *Salon of 1846*. Baudelaire's essay situates itself on the threshold of two epochs. "It is true that the grand tradition is lost, and that the new tradition is not yet made," he asserts. The central question of the essay concerns what sort of modern art can replace the vanishing "grand tradition," which the poet associates with classical antiquity as well as with contemporary artistic practices that "interest themselves incessantly in representing the past." Whereas the grand tradition subscribes to a Platonic ideal of beauty as "absolute and eternal," modern art begins with the rejection of this claim. "Absolute and eternal beauty does not exist," the poet proclaims, "or rather it is only an abstraction skimmed from the general surface of different beauties. The element of particularity of each form of beauty comes from the passions, and just as we have our particular passions, so we have our beauty."[22] Baudelaire thus situates himself as the witness to an epochal divide, an event of discontinuity that invalidates former modes of representation—and along with those modes of representation, modes of knowing and feeling—and that requires the invention of new aesthetic practices and criteria adequate to the "particular passions" of modernity. At issue, in other words, is not simply an aesthetic theory, but rather a theory of modernity that links history and art in a new way. If classical art effectively overlooked the significance of history in an attempt to give expression to what it perceived as timeless ("absolute and eternal"), then modern art, the poet suggests, cannot be separated from its own historicity, from what the poet will later call (however paradoxically) its "representation of the present."[23]

In identifying various manifestations of "the heroism of modern life," the poet will turn later in the essay to what have become the more often cited emblematic figures of modernity—the dandy, the criminal, the prostitute. But before these figures appear on the scene, the first manifestation of the particularity of modernity he discusses are what he calls "modern suicides." It would thus appear that death, along with art, has undergone or is undergoing an epochal change, that modernity coincides with and is attested to by this new way of dying. Baudelaire writes:

> Except for Heracles on Mount Oeta, Cato of Utica, and Cleopatra, whose suicides are not *modern* suicides, what other suicides do you see in the old masters? In all the lives of antiquity . . . you will not find the suicide of Jean-Jacques, or even the strange and marvelous suicide of Raphaël de Valentin.[24]

Benjamin, in a passage I turn to later, was fascinated by the link Baudelaire suggests here between modernity and suicide. But he finds the poet's particular examples "meager": Jean-Jacques Rousseau and Raphaël de Valentin, the protagonist of Balzac's 1831 novel, *La Peau de chagrin*.[25] Indeed, these examples are as surprising as they are provocative. In light of Baudelaire's embrace in his early years of an idealist Romanticism, one might have expected as counterpoints to his classical examples such Romantic heroes as Werther or

Chatterton. The Rousseau example is admittedly inscrutable. The claim that Rousseau killed himself does echo contemporary accounts of the philosopher's life. Madame de Stael, writing just one year after Rousseau's death in 1778, was firm in her conviction that he had poisoned himself, while Olivier de Corancez reports having learned, shortly after Rousseau's death, that his friend had shot himself in the head with a pistol.[26] In *La Vie et les ouvrages de J.-J. Rousseau*, first published in 1823, V. de Musset-Pathay, the first editor of Rousseau's collected works, concludes, based on what he claims was extensive independent research into the question, that both de Stael and Corancez were correct: the philosopher had in fact committed suicide twice over, first poisoning himself and then, "so as to cut short the slowness of the effects [of the poison] and the duration of his sufferings, he ended them with a pistol shot."[27] But the allusion to Rousseau nonetheless remains opaque, since Baudelaire gives absolutely no indication as to why he views this death as specifically *modern*.

The example of Raphaël de Valentin, however, is allowed slightly more context. For one, it is explicitly qualified as being "strange and marvelous." In addition, Balzac's novel seems to be at issue in an explanatory footnote that the poet appends to this passage aimed at justifying his examples of classical suicide. The note reads in its entirety:

> The first [Heracles] kills himself because the burning of his robe becomes intolerable; the second [Cato] because he can no longer aid the cause of liberty; and that voluptuous queen [Cleopatra] because she has lost her throne and her lover; but none of them destroy themselves in order to change their skin in view of metempsychosis.[28]

For his classical examples, Baudelaire shows that each commits suicide in response to the imminent loss of something fundamental to his or her self-image—for Heracles his invincibility; for Cato his freedom; for Cleopatra her erotic power. Classical suicide, in this light, displays what Dworkin called "commitment to a vision . . . that the life as a whole, seen as an integral creative narrative, illustrates and expresses." Each of these suicides dies "in character." They stage deaths that come to appear inevitable, deaths with which they come to be identified as closely as with any other aspect of their stories. Consequently, these figures can become standard subjects of traditional painting, in that no matter how a given artist or rendering depicts their deaths, they remain recognizable.[29] Their suicides as represented in art allow them to remain themselves—that is, to appear always as valid replications of their self-image, just as the art that takes these figures as its subject matter is grounded in and legitimized by an economy of imitation—what Baudelaire earlier called "the grand tradition." Whether depicted by Giampietrino in 1525, by Guido Reni, Guercino, or Cagnacci a century later, or by Jean François de Troy in eighteenth-century France, Cleopatra remains Cleopatra.

Understood in this way, classical suicides appear as autonomous acts that issue from rational decisions designed to preserve an image of the sovereign self—its integrity and coherence.

In declaring the end of the grand tradition, Baudelaire thus also declares the end of the possibility of this sort of heroic, idealized death. It is against such classical idealization that the poet seems to allude to *La Peau de chagrin*, which centers on a pact the protagonist forms with a magical skin—identified at one point in the novel as the pelt of an *onagre*, a wild ass—that is said to represent Raphaël's life span: as it grants his wishes, it shrinks in size and correspondingly shortens his life. Raphaël de Valentin undergoes, in other words, "a change of skin." Instead of an act of self-confirmation or consolidation, this death appears to be open-ended and to expose the self to radical transformation: it takes place, the poet claims, "in view of metempsychosis"—that is, in view of a transmigration of the soul whose destination is undetermined and which radically calls into question Raphaël's ownership over his own body. Rather than preserve an existing self-image from its imminent death, it courts a rupture of the self, an alienation of the self from the bodily skin, and is oriented towards alterity.[30] Whereas classical suicide draws its beauty from the tradition it preserves through imitation, modern suicide breaks with tradition and announces something new. Its beauty derives not from the way it expresses an absolute and timeless value, but instead precisely from the way it embodies "our particular passions," which would seem to be nothing more nor less than a passion for the particular itself, for the modern, for the strange and new. As such, its aesthetic value is intrinsically dependent on its encounter with, openness to, and passion for the externalities of modern life. Anticipating the later definition of the artist in "The Painter of Modern Life," the modern suicide is "an I insatiable for the not-I."[31] Raphaël's "modern suicide," in this light, seems to announce the emergence of a form of dying that is specifically and decisively modern—a modernist form of death.

Although Baudelaire does not expand further on his understanding of *La Peau de chagrin*, Balzac's novel powerfully develops this relationship between modern art and modern death. It does this, I will suggest, specifically by situating the question of modern death in relation to two principal externalities that condition the emergence of a modernist art of death. First, there is the externality of "tradition," which confronts Raphaël with a set of conventional aesthetic models in relation to which he must stage his death and which threaten him with a sense of inescapable belatedness. Second, and entwined with tradition, are the social and cultural conditions associated with the degradation of death—most powerfully and ineluctably, the sense that the commodification of everyday life transforms even death into an exchangeable product. To speak of modern suicide as exemplary of the "heroism of modern life," in other words, means to grasp the ways in which this heroism does not simply revolt against the conditions of modernity, but rather comes to bear witness to conditions inimical to the newness and singularity that would be required for a truly modern suicide. Raphaël's death, viewed through the lens of Baudelaire's theory of modern art, thus gives more specific form to the question of modern death. It asks: How can one die a death that is truly of one's own when death has become an object of desire, whether that desire is tied to a hunger for aesthetic spectacle or for economic gain? How can one create an art of death in a world in which everything—even death—seems to have a price?

These questions are at issue from the opening pages of Balzac's novel. To recall the structure of the novel: the first section, "The Talisman," describes the entrance of a still unnamed young man into a casino, his interrupted intention to drown himself in the Seine, and his discovery of a magic skin, the *peau de chagrin* of the novel's title. The second section, which takes place at a lavish banquet, revolves around Raphaël's retelling of his own story, at the center of which are two unrequited loves: Raphaël's for the unobtainable duchess Foedora, and the impoverished Pauline's tender love for Raphaël. The third section, "The Agony," charts the consequences of Raphaël's pact with the skin for his mode of living, and of dying. This last section is followed by a brief epilogue that expounds on the images of Pauline and Foedora after the death of Raphaël.

What follows does not aim to be a comprehensive treatment of Balzac's novel, such as Samuel Weber's essential monograph.[32] Instead, in pursuing the image of modern death, I concentrate on the two phases that constitute the movement towards Raphaël's "strange and marvelous" death: in the second part of the chapter, the critique of the insufficiency of extant modes of conceptualizing and responding to suicide, located mainly in the first section of the novel; and in the third part, the radical reconceptualization of what it means to live and die that takes place when Raphaël's pact with the *peau de chagrin* comes into effect.

II. Suicide Interrupted

The Art of Death

The question of modern suicide arises in *La Peau de chagrin* first with respect to the aesthetic conventions imposed by literary tradition. From the opening pages, that is, the predicament faced by the protagonist—and, in parallel, by the novel itself—concerns the question of how to stage death or occupy death's stage in a way that does not merely replicate existing conventions or conform to existing expectations—how, in other words, to enact a "strange and marvelous" death. Balzac's novel, like Baudelaire's theory of art, thus links the possibility of literary modernity to the advent of modern death.

A brief examination of the genre of the *ars moriendi* highlights the ways in which the desire for an unconventional death may be allied with a specifically modernist literary mode. As noted earlier, the tradition of the art of dying is fundamentally imitative. From its origins in the early fifteenth-century *Tractatus artis benes moriendi* to the "artistic climax of the tradition" in Jeremy Taylor's 1651 *Holy Dying*, the genre fundamentally takes the form of a conduct book instructing readers in the "crafte of dyinge," as the English translation of the Latin *Tractatus* put it.[33] The good death conforms to a prescribed pattern: "therefore such things as Christ did dying on the cross, the same should every Christian man do at his last end, after his cunning and power."[34] Just as Christ prayed, cried out, wept, commended his soul to God, and "gave up wilfully his spirit," so should Moriens (as the dying Everyman is often referred to) undertake these five steps.[35] Imitation is thus linked to, and understood as evidence of, submission to divine authority, with Moriens enjoined to recognize death as natural and necessary: "And sith, as it is aforesaid, we may not, in no wise, neither flee nor escape, neither change the inevitable necessity and passage of death, therefore we ought to take our death when God will, wilfully and gladly, without any grutching [complaining] or contradiction."[36]

This injunction to emulate a conventional model echoes through more recent analogues to traditional *ars moriendi*, among which we might include Dworkin's argument for the right to die. As observed above, although Dworkin frames his analysis of the right to die as description, it contains a prescriptive dimension: coherence and integrity do not simply name what we may already aim for, but instead provide and instruct us in the formula for a good death. Despite the desire to posit integrity as something generated entirely by the individual person, its necessary evaluation by others means that in order for integrity to be recognized as such, it must conform to a certain set of expectations as to what constitutes integrity; it must, that is, emulate available models of integrity.

We might also look to more obvious recent versions of the *ars moriendi*. The stage theory of death proposed by Elizabeth Kübler-Ross in her enormously influential 1969 book, *On Death and Dying*, and in later writings serves as one such model, as the anthropologist James Green observes. Kübler-Ross, Green notes, was equivocal concerning the application of her model. To the extent that the stages of dying are merely descriptive, they cannot be said to constitute a recipe for dying well, and indeed Kübler-Ross would often say that these stages could and do occur in any order and often overlap. Her writings nonetheless contain a normative dimension, with the stage of "acceptance" positioned as a final stage that is achieved after working through the other four stages of denial, anger, bargaining, and depression.[37] Those who adopt the stage model of dying as a "script" are therefore recognizing a possibility inherent in Kübler-Ross's work, even as they perpetuate the tradition of the *ars moriendi*, with the five steps in the imitation of Christ replaced by the five stages of grief. Green also cites Mitch Albom's best-selling memoir, *Tuesdays with Morrie*. Structured as a series of lessons, the book depicts the author's encounters with a retired sociology professor, Morrie Schwartz, as a "contemporary teaching about dying."[38] Such "modern versions of the ars moriendi" function as "script lines."[39]

To Green's examples we might add several more controversial instances tied specifically to the right-to-die movement. In the book that Hemlock Society founder Derek Humphry first circulated to members of his organization before later trade publication, *Let Me Die Before I Wake*, he offers detailed accounts of how others have ended their lives along with cautionary tales of failed attempts, and concludes with a description of the method he would use to end his own life, thus providing models to be copied to achieve a good death. "The only way to be reasonably certain of a good death," he writes, "is to plan it, and plan, if at all possible, when one is still in good health."[40] The French *Suicide: Mode d'emploi* (*Suicide: A User's Manual*), published in 1982 but banned in France since 1991, backed up its advocacy for "a certain and easy death" with a detailed list of medications and dosages deemed effective as well as recommendations for staging a successful suicide.[41] Finally, we might recall the recuperation of a classical, idealized image of suicide in the name of the Hemlock Society, the first major U.S. right-to-die organization, which evoked the model of Socrates's death as "a noble and self-chosen one" worthy of emulation.[42] Whether or not they advocate the right to die, such works, like their medieval and early modern predecessors, model dying as an emulative process in which a good death is achieved by positing death as inevitable and coming to accept this inevitability.

"A New Genre of Death"

What would it mean, then, to break with the tradition of the *ars moriendi* and to create an art of dying that departs from previous models—to create, that is, an anti-mimetic art of dying? The opening scenes of *La Peau de chagrin* introduce us to an anonymous young man, eventually identified as Raphaël de Valentin, who is plotting his own death. His predicament becomes apparent in the opening pages of the text. When he enters the casino where he will gamble away his last gold coin, he immediately exhibits "the gloomy impassivity of suicide" (61; 25), and as he places his bet the casino becomes a theater where "each of the spectators wanted to see, in the fate of that gold coin, the drama and the closing scene of a noble life (63; 27).[43] He is cast here in the role of Romantic hero, echoing familiar icons such as Werther, whose story famously inspired several emulators (though fewer than is often supposed); Chatterton, the English poet whose suicide came to be seen as his most poetic act, and who became a celebrated icon of late eighteenth- and early nineteenth-century English and French culture; and René, the suicidal hero of Chateaubriand's wildly popular 1802 novel. By mid-century, the critic Sainte-Beuve would look back at this image of Romantic suicide with disdain. "The obsession and challenge of all the Renés and Chattertons of our time has been to be a great poet or to die," he writes.[44] But the habitués of Balzac's casino do not need Sainte-Beuve to anatomize contemporary stereotypes. When Raphaël predictably loses his bet, one of them announces knowingly: "A scorched soul who's going to throw himself into the river" (63; 28).

As if it were not already apparent in the casino, the narrator, too, sees the young man's death as both generic and overdetermined:

> How many young talents, shut up in a garret, wither and perish for lack of a friend, for lack of a woman to console them, alone in the midst of a million fellow beings, while a bored crowd, glutted with gold, looks on. Seen from this angle, suicide assumes gigantic propor-tions. Between a voluntary death and the fecund hope that summoned a man to Paris in his youth, God alone knows what a chaos there lies of abandoned projects and poems, of stifled cries of despair, of fruit-less efforts and aborted masterpieces! Every suicide is a poem sublime in its melancholy. Where in the ocean of literature will you find a book that can vie with the genius of a news-item such as this:
>
> > *Yesterday, at four o'clock, a woman threw herself into the Seine from the Pont-des-Arts.* (64–65; 29)

Although some have read this passage as a genuine affirmation of the sublim-ity of suicide,[45] whatever genius or sublimity might be associated with the young man enters this passage only in the form of cliché, with the news item ironically displayed as a failed alternative to the novel we are reading—a novel that, like its protagonist, seeks a way out of or beyond the predeter-mined, anonymous, reductive script embodied in the news item, and a way towards an original story.[46]

Like the gamblers and the narrator, the young man, too, recognizes the imitative dimension of his story: "He made his way towards the Pont Royal imagining the last thoughts of his predecessors" (67; 29–30). Imitation can of course function, on one level, as a mode of legitimation. In Goethe's *The Sorrows of Young Werther*, for instance, the hero activates, or tries to activate, this positive form of imitation, staging his death as a eucharistic rite, with a goblet of wine and a sacred text (in his case, the Romantic favorite, *Emilia Galotti*) laid open on his desk.[47] As in traditional manuals of *ars moriendi*, the "good death," in this view, is fundamentally imitative, modeled after the Pas-sion of Christ. It should be noted that Goethe's novel may not entirely endorse this emulative mode: the cold tone of the editor's final report of Werther's death seems to insist on the failure of the protagonist's efforts to inscribe him-self into a tradition of heroic self-sacrifice. And yet, as has often been noted, the editor's implied criticism of Werther in the final section of the novel may itself evoke a counter-movement of sympathy in the reader, thus indirectly validating Werther's self-image and his achievement of a beautiful death.[48]

The as-yet-unnamed protagonist of Balzac's novel, however, is no Werther. For one, the novel does not give the reader the opportunity to develop sympathy for the young man; he appears from the very first scene already in the cliché image of the Romantic suicide. Moreover, where Werther's letters implicate readers in his first-person perspective, the opening scenes of Balzac's novel view the protagonist resolutely from the outside. He is an anonymous type. If he were to commit suicide at this point, rather than evoke the sympathy of the reader, he would do nothing but justify Sainte-Beuve's sarcasm. Indeed, in light of a comment such as Sainte-Beuve's, Balzac's invocation of the convention of the Romantic martyr becomes heavily ironic.

However, from the moment the young man "surprises himself carefully brushing off the dust" from his sleeve, it is clear that he will not commit a conventional suicide—not because he now rediscovers a will to live, but because this self-surprise sets him apart from his predecessors and shows him to himself in a light to which no conventional form of suicide would be adequate: "A death in plain daylight seemed ignoble to him, and so he resolved to die by night, in order to deliver an indecipherable corpse to the society that misapprehended the greatness of his life" (68; 30–31). The language of Raphaël's thoughts remains indebted, on one level, to the myth of Romantic suicide. He wants his death to signify "greatness." Yet it also acknowledges the paradox of this desire, the threat that his inscription into a Romantic mythology would undermine that very greatness by making his death too readily legible, too much of an imitation. Whereas Emerson would write that "imitation is suicide," for Raphaël suicide is imitation.

Raphaël is aware, then, that the way he dies will be subject to judgment and will shape the way his life is understood by others. But this awareness is burdened with the sense that tradition and its existing stock of images of suicide are not available to him as a positive resource; it is, as Baudelaire proclaimed, lost. Consequently, he must produce an *indecipherable* corpse so as to remain outside and opposed to the standardized interpretations that others are bound to draw from his action. He wants the meaning of his death to reside not in any particular message it might communicate, not in any particular truth it might reveal, but rather in its enigmatic nature—in its resistance to meaning. "Do not look for the principle of my death in the vulgar reasons which lead to the majority of suicides," he later declares (81; 48).

Raphaël claims the right to die, then, precisely as a way to evade the fate of the commonplace, precisely as a means of self-authorship. *La Peau de chagrin* thus proposes what is at once a new argument against and a new justification for suicide. When the as-yet-unnamed young man decides against drowning himself, he does so not out of a rediscovered will to live, nor out of fear of pain or punishment. Nor is he constrained by moral considerations; the question of whether his action would be right or wrong does not cross his mind. Instead, he does not commit suicide at this moment because to do so would be to conform to a preexisting image of suicide. His death would be perceived as nothing but an imitation. Indeed, when Raphaël later narrates the events leading up to his interrupted suicide attempt, he includes an exchange with his friend Rastignac, in which the latter, in a passage that anticipates Dorothy Parker's incisive poem "Resumé," details the shortcomings of common methods of suicide one by one:

> "I prefer death to this life. So I am earnestly looking for the best way
> to end the struggle. . . . What do you think of opium?"
> "Oh no! Extremely painful," Rastignac replied.
> "Asphyxiation?"
> "Too vulgar!"
> "The Seine?"
> "The drag-nets and the Morgue are very filthy."
> "A pistol-shot?"
> "Suppose you miss? You're disfigured for life." (191; 172)

In contrast to these conventional ways of killing oneself, Rastignac, for his part, proposes debauchery: "The best solution I've found is to wear oneself to death by living for pleasure." But this, too, is utterly conventional. Were Raphaël to follow Rastignac's suggestion, he would be nothing but a copy of his friend. Instead, Rastignac issues a challenge that henceforth defines Raphaël's quest: "If you want to create a new genre of death by fighting that kind of duel with life, I will be your second" (192; 173).

Whereas the traditional *ars moriendi* prescribes the willful acceptance of divine authority over death "without any grutching or contradiction," this "new genre of death" requires that Moriens actively refuse life, that he battle against life, as Rastignac put it. The new death, it would appear, does not come in its own time, does not simply require waiting and acceptance. Moriens must instead take death into his own hands and claim the right to take his own leave, however contradictory that may be, as Baudelaire suggested. The new genre of death is therefore a form of suicide. And yet it must also be a *new* form of suicide, where this newness can emerge only in opposition to the interpretive categories and conventions that give suicide its meaning. Suicide becomes justified now not on the basis of its rationality or necessity, not as proof of autonomy or as an act of self-sacrifice, but rather to the extent that it represents a new, original act—to the extent, one might even say, that it is no longer simply recognizable as suicide. To attest to new conditions under which death takes place, one must die in a new way.

Under the Sign of Suicide

But the exchange between Rastignac and Raphaël, which takes place chronologically before Raphaël's encounter with the *peau de chagrin*, hardly makes it clear that a new genre of death is achievable. Rastignac appears in the novel as the more experienced and worldly of the two friends, and in issuing his challenge to Raphaël, he may be speaking less inspirationally than skeptically, gesturing toward the limitations of individual efforts to create a new genre of death, to display anything like heroism in the modern world.[49] When he suggests that Raphaël will have to duel with life, "life" encompasses not just its biological sense, but also social life, the conditions of modernity that, in Rastignac's metaphor of the duel, are set in deadly opposition to the individual—in deadly opposition, paradoxically, to the individual's death, to his authorship of his own death. It remains unclear, in other words, whether Raphaël's "modern suicide" can attain the form of resistant indecipherability it seeks, or whether instead it is bound to appear as a mere symptom of the modern degradation of death. In claiming the right to die, does Raphaël assert and attest to a freedom to create his own death, or does he carry out the secret dictates of the modern necropolis?

This question acquires increased specificity and urgency in light of Walter Benjamin's commentary on the notion of modern suicide in Baudelaire, to which I now turn before returning to *La Peau de chagrin*. We might first recall that the notion that modernity transforms and is shaped by a shift in the meaning of death—what he calls a change in "the face of death"—is a key theme in Benjamin's thought. His essay "The Storyteller" memorably encapsulates this concern. In this essay, the nineteenth century is said to mark the acceleration and culmination of a process wherein "bourgeois society—by means of medical and social, private and public institutions— . . . enable[d] people to avoid the sight of the dying." In what amounts to a condensed version of the story Philippe Ariès would unfold forty years later in *The Hour of Our Death*, Benjamin observes that whereas death was once a "public process in the life of the individual, and a most exemplary one," now the dying are "stowed away in sanatoria or hospitals." This sequestration of death, Benjamin even suggests, may not be merely a "secondary effect" of bourgeois society but rather "its subconscious main purpose."[50]

Benjamin links this sequestration of death to literary modernity—to the "decline of storytelling" and to the "rise of the novel in modern times." "It turns out," he writes, "that this change [in the face of death] is identical with the one that has diminished the communicability of experience to the same extent as the art of storytelling has declined." This connection between the degradation of death and the decline of storytelling hinges on Benjamin's image of the dying man:

> Today people live in rooms that have never been touched by death . . . and when their end approaches they are stowed away in sanatoria or hospitals by their heirs. It is, however, characteristic that not only a man's knowledge or wisdom but above all his real life—and this is the stuff that stories are made of—first assumes transmissible form at the moment of his death. Just as a sequence of images is set in motion

inside a man as his life comes to an end—unfolding the views of himself under which he has encountered himself without being aware of
it—suddenly in his expression and looks [*seinen Mienen und Blicken*]
the unforgettable emerges and imparts to everything that concerned
him that authority which even the poorest wretch in dying possesses
for the living around him. This authority is at the very source of the
story.[51]

The traditional scene of death, taking place in the home with the dying man
surrounded by family and community, appears in this image also as the
quintessential scene of storytelling—indeed, the very moment when storytelling becomes possible. With a complication to which I will return at the
end of this chapter, death appears here, to recall Dworkin's argument, as an
intensified moment at which a whole life comes into focus in the form of an
"integral creative narrative." Yet for Benjamin, modernity precisely spells the
decline of this possibility for storytelling. As death is removed to the invisible confines of the hospital, the scene of transmission is lost to view and the
authority of death is degraded.

This analysis of the relationship between modern death and literary
authority illuminates Benjamin's somewhat oblique but extraordinarily sug-
gestive commentary on the problem of modern suicide in Baudelaire, from
the section devoted to "Modernity" in his long essay, "The Paris of the Second Empire in Baudelaire." Resonating with "The Storyteller," Benjamin
suggests here that Baudelaire's writing brings into view an essential relationship between modernity and death. But whereas modern death in "The
Storyteller" gives evidence of the demise of communicability, modern suicide
presents a more complicated problem of transmission. Benjamin writes:

> The resistance that modernity offers to the natural productive élan of
> an individual is out of all proportion to his strength. It is understand-
> able if a person grows exhausted and takes refuge in death. Modernity
> must stand under the sign of suicide [*im Zeichen des Selbstmords
> stehen*], whose seal is placed beneath a heroic will [*der das Siegel
> unter ein heroisches Wollen setzt*] that concedes nothing to a mental-
> ity inimical to it. This suicide is not a resignation but a heroic passion.
> It is the achievement of modernity in the realm of the passions. In this
> form, as the *passion particulière de la vie moderne*, suicide appears in
> the classical passage devoted to the theory of modernity.[52]

Even as Benjamin declines to discuss suicide in terms of "modern beauty," he
seems to translate Baudelaire's concern for suicide as an aesthetic act through
his semiotic metaphor, with suicide appearing as a "sign" and producing a
"seal." In this dense passage, suicide appears in the first instance as a reaction
to modernity, which drives the individual to suicide with murderous force.

As in "The Storyteller," modernity at this moment deprives the individual of a proper death, of achieving authority through death, and instead requires radical submission on the part of the individual, who "grows exhausted" and "takes refuge in death." Antithetically, however, suicide does not represent an unequivocal victory for modernity. Instead, the decision to take refuge in death is figured as a paradoxical but powerful form of semiosis. On the one hand, as in "The Storyteller," the communication of experience undergoes a crisis. The will is radically heterogeneous with respect to a world to which it makes no concessions, in which it has no place and no voice. But on the other hand, the sign and the seal of suicide appear as figures that grant authority to that which remains radically excluded from the modern world. In the figure of suicide as the seal affixed beneath a heroic will, as if the will were a document signed at the bottom by suicide, suicide appears as a form of authorization, as a signature that bears no meaning in itself but instead functions performatively to certify the authenticity, the communicability, of that which it seals. Modern suicide thus paradoxically bears witness to its own sequestration.[53] Whereas bourgeois modernity seeks to hide the dying from sight, suicide produces a mark or trace that indicates, without being able to make known or visible, an event that insistently transmits the event of its own erasure.[54]

It is this figure of suicide as a sealed communication that seems to inspire Benjamin's rejection of Baudelaire's examples of modern suicide, which, as noted earlier, he finds "meager," and his recourse instead to instances of suicide he finds in the historical archive, to "raw material [that] has deposited itself in those very strata that have turned out to be the foundation of modernity."[55] Although Benjamin does not expand on the significance of Baudelaire's reference to *La Peau de chagrin*—perhaps surprisingly, given the role that the novel plays in his own history of reading and book collecting[56]— the problem he illuminates with respect to the meaning of suicide at this moment of emergent modernity is nonetheless relevant to my inquiry in that it provides a concrete social and historical context for the dilemma faced by Raphaël de Valentin. For, like Balzac's novel, Benjamin's text attends to the insufficiency of traditional models of heroism, and of heroic suicide. At the same time, it provides a powerful alternative reconceptualization of modern heroism, and consequently of modern suicide, in terms of what Benjamin described earlier in the essay on Baudelaire as an "ironic" or "threadbare" heroism that is specific to modernity.

This notion of ironic heroism is developed most strikingly in Benjamin's discussion of Marx's *The Eighteenth Brumaire of Louis Bonaparte*. According to Marx, Benjamin notes, the conditions for heroic action and for the heroic image are historically determined. Whereas under Napoleon I the army provided an opportunity for "the flower of farm youth" to become heroes, under Napoleon III the army "consists largely of *remplaçants* . . . just as the second Napoleon is himself a *remplaçant*, a substitute for Napoleon."[57] Two related points emerge from this observation: first, that the democratization of heroism which occurs in modernity, according to which the heroic prestige and self-image that were formerly the exclusive domain of an elite become accessible across social classes, simultaneously threatens to vitiate the prestige of the heroic altogether; and second, that heroism is associated with singularity or irreplaceability, whereas modernity, in trafficking in "replacements" and not singular individuals, suffers a crisis of heroism.[58] Modern heroism is ironic because the forces that make it possible also work to limit or subvert it.

As Benjamin turns to the historical archive in search of his own evidence of modern suicide, the specific instances of heroic suicide he identifies bear out this notion of ironic heroism:

> Around that time the idea of suicide became available to the working masses. "People are scrambling for copies of a lithograph depicting an English worker who is taking his life because he despairs of earning a livelihood. One worker even goes to Eugène Sue's apartment and hangs himself there. In his hand is a slip of paper with this note: 'I thought dying would be easier for me if I die under the roof of a man who stands up for us and loves us.'" In 1841 Adolphe Boyer, a printer, published a small book entitled *De l'état des ouvriers et de son amélioration par l'organisation du travail* [*On the Condition of Laborers and Its Improvement through the Organization of Work*]. It was a moderate presentation that sought to recruit the old corporations of itinerant journeymen which stuck to guild practices for the workers' associations. His work was unsuccessful. The author took his own life and in an open letter invited his companions in misfortune to follow suit. Someone like Baudelaire could very well have viewed suicide as the only heroic act that remained for the *multitudes maladives* [ailing multitudes] of the cities in reactionary times.[59]

Like the farmers who sought heroic opportunities in Napoleon's army, the workers Benjamin cites wage war against oppressive labor conditions. As with the farmer-soldiers, the heroism of workers' suicide is double. First, it performs a democratizing function. When Benjamin emphasizes a new availability of the idea of suicide to the working class, suicide here stands not simply for the neutral act of self-killing, but rather becomes a form of self-sacrifice and powerful protest that, like military honor, had formerly been conceived of as an exclusive property of elites. A long tradition in the image of suicide is herein invoked, which divides self-destruction into illegitimate forms associated with weakness, despair, and sin, and legitimate forms associated with courage, self-sacrifice, and martyrdom. To commit suicide as a heroic act, to claim suicide as a form of heroism, is itself a way in which the working class assumes a new form of power.[60] Second, it acquires heroic stature by asserting the singularity of the individual, by contesting the regime of replaceability. Suicide appears as the most radical form of labor strike.

Yet this restriction of heroic possibility to suicide, rather than resuscitate the image of heroism, testifies to its degradation. Indeed, it is not mere coincidence that Benjamin's specific examples of suicide are associated with integral elements of "the age of mechanical reproducibility"—a lithograph, a printer, and Eugène Sue, whose name is synonymous for Benjamin with the rise of the mass-marketed novel. What these individual deaths attest to may be less the ability of the individual person to have a meaningful impact on the modern world than the discrepancy between their actions and their absorption into commodified images of the alienated *multitudes maladives*. What is heroic about Benjamin's modern suicides is, however ironically, that they attest not to the specialness or uniqueness of the lives they conclude, but rather to their replaceability. The only possible act of modern heroism destroys its actor.

A Marketplace of Death

Despite his dismissal of Baudelaire's examples of modern suicide, Benjamin's ironic reading of modern heroism resonates throughout *La Peau de chagrin*. Balzac's novel develops this irony in its protagonist's attempt to produce his own corpse in a form that both testifies to and distinguishes itself from "modern life." If Raphaël is a figure of the modern artist—of the modern suicide as modern artist—this is because his death makes visible the very degradation of death, its sequestration or invisibility. For in attempting to establish the newness of his death, he does not struggle in high Romantic mode with poetic forefathers. Instead, the threat to originality emerges from a cultural marketplace in which literary images of suicide circulate in the form of mass-produced cultural products. The gamblers who first recognize in him the stereotypical traits of the Romantic suicide are not like Coleridge drawing poetic inspiration from the life and death of Chatterton. The drama they think to witness takes place instead in the quintessential space of modern consumption, the casino, while the narrator correspondingly imagines the instant assimilation of the "sublime poem" of suicide into a *fait divers* printed in a daily paper. The protagonist, for his part, thinks immediately of suicides notable mainly for the widespread publicity they received: those of the English Lord Castlereagh and the ultraroyalist academician Louis-Simon Auger, royal censor under Louis XVIII, who drowned himself in the Seine in 1829.[61]

Beyond his concern with situating his death in relation to those he designates his "predecessors," Raphaël must also confront the meaning of his death with respect to the curious economy that surrounded drownings in nineteenth-century Paris. We are first alerted to the existence of this economy by Raphaël's reaction to a sign he notices as he approaches the bridge from which he initially intends to jump—"First-Aid for the Drowning" (65; 30). This notice leads the young man's thoughts not to any appreciation of civic responsibility, but instead to a calculation of the value of his corpse to those who might fish it out of the Seine: "Dead, he was worth fifty francs" (66; 30).

The system of rewards with which he is shown here to be instantly familiar was part of a coordinated urban policy modeled on Holland and Denmark and established in Paris in 1806.[62] The *New Paris Guide* published by the English-language bookseller Galignani throughout the nineteenth century, from at least its 1830 edition on, explains this system and specifies proudly (or reassuringly) that "forty-nine sets of apparatus for succour are deposited upon the banks of the Seine."[63] When a drowning person was rescued alive, rescuers, those who notified the Corps de Garde des Ports et Quais, and officers and soldiers who participated in the rescue could all expect specific monetary rewards prescribed by law, with half the specified amounts awarded in the case that the person could not be revived.

This system of rewards, however, also invited macabre abuses. An essay published in the same year as *La Peau de chagrin* explains its troubling consequences. Collected in a fifteen-volume anthology that set as its goal to "provide an overview of modern Paris,"[64] this essay characterizes the river that runs through the heart of the city as the site of a set of complex commercial, legal, bureaucratic, and political calculations revolving around the production of suicides:

> A reward for humane actions had formerly granted . . . forty francs for every man rescued from drowning, and twenty for every one drowned. But it was very soon found necessary to reverse this system of encouragement, with the view of putting an end to the industry of certain persons associated together for the purpose of half drowning, and rescuing one another. . . . Scarcely was this more rational rate established before it was found that many swimming philanthropists took it into their heads to give the victim, once he had sunk beneath the waters, the leisure to become worth double the reward—that is to say, time to drown . . . . The former order of things has consequently been restored; twenty francs are paid for a dead man, and forty for one who still has life in him. Only now, to prevent falling again into the snare of the former abuse—that of the mutual drownings—a man saved a second time entitles his preserver to no reward.[65]

The administrative protocols that developed around deaths-by-drowning in post-Revolutionary Paris, memorably explored in Richard Cobb's *Death in Paris* and adapted to the screen in Peter Greenaway's haunting short film, *Death in the Seine*, provide the dense background for Raphaël's understanding of what his suicide would amount to were he to drown himself in the Seine.[66] But the significance of civic concern for suicides in post-Revolutionary Paris as chronicled by Cobb seems to have undergone a radical change in meaning by the time of the July Monarchy, when the novel is set. Cobb finds it "consoling to discover that an urban society as allegedly brutal as that of eighteenth-century Paris should never have become habituated to suicide."[67]

But the young man in the novel, it would seem, matters only for what he is worth to others. While the novel does not specify the precise terms of the reward system in place at the moment Raphaël contemplates suicide, it seems to take place, in Raphaël's mind if not actually, during that curious interval when the bodies retrieved from the Seine were worth more dead than alive. The first-aid system appears here not as a resource for public health but as a mechanism for turning death to profit.

Indeed, the civic pride on display in Galignani's guide assumes more sinister form in Balzac's vision of a city ready to consume the anonymous young man not only economically but also narratively. For not only will the body itself produce profit, but so will the newspaper stories generated by it: "He could read the articles, deploring the incident, written by journalists in the interval between enjoying themselves at dinner and watching a ballet-dancer's smile; he could hear the chink of silver being paid to the boatmen by the prefect of police for the recovery of his body" (66; 30). Just as he was keenly aware of his belatedness with respect to the heroic associations of Romantic suicide, so Raphaël is attuned to the logic of commodification. If he dies, he will not die as himself, but rather as a commodity, interchangeable with anyone else, and will himself become an object of exchange between equally interchangeable persons: the casino employees and habitués, the rescuer and the public official, the morgue attendant and the journalist, all of whom view his death through the lens of profit. This lends a new meaning to Raphaël's desire to produce an "indecipherable corpse," *un cadavre indechiffrable*: it must be indecipherable not only in the sense of resisting decoding, but also in the sense of resisting conversion into *chiffres*, into numbers. Or in other words, he seeks to become, like Bartleby, an unaccountable body.

III. The Indecipherable Corpse

Modern death, as analyzed by Benjamin and as evidenced in the market-place of death along the Seine, thus has a double effect. On the one hand, it alienates Raphaël from his own death and delivers it to him in the form of value that is no longer simply his own, but that derives from the social. As he comes to be aware of the ways that what seems to be an expression of civic morality—the first-aid or health care system of nineteenth-century Paris—in fact degrades death and treats the person or corpse as a commodity, his death is represented to him in quantifiable and standardized form—as a death that is exchangeable for any other death just as it is exchangeable for money. Raphaël's experience thus might be seen to anticipate questions that arise today when efforts to legitimize the right to die are said to be motivated by underlying economic considerations, for instance, the desire to reduce the cost of medical care or to make viable organs available for transplantation. We might recall as well the charge frequently leveled against Jack Kevorkian, whose highly publicized assisted suicides were often said to exploit those he helped to die in order to feed his own desire for fame. On the other hand, however, the language of *La Peau de chagrin* strikingly suggests that it is precisely this system of monetizing death that provides Raphaël with the form in which to produce his own mode of death—namely, indecipherability. If Raphaël's modern suicide is to be "strange and marvelous," this is because it will both attest to and evade the strange new conditions of modern death. The magic skin, as we will see, enacts the tension between, on the one hand, the alienation of death by systems of quantification and commodification, and, on the other hand, the possibility of transforming this very sense of alienation into a new mode of transmission.

A Modern Faust

The significance of Raphaël's encounter with the *peau de chagrin* is illuminated by the novel's underexplored but explicit allusion to the Faust tradition, which situates Balzac's novel with respect both to literary tradition and to the problem of the commodification of death.[68] As a latter-day Faust, Raphaël engages in a testing of the limits of the human, most radically through an effort to transgress mortal boundaries. But where Raphaël's Faustian precursors grapple with these questions, tragically and comically, on a mythico-cosmological plane, Balzac's thoroughly modern Faust confronts a mechanistic world in which death no longer appears as a power controlled by divine or transcendent authority.

The novel echoes the Faust story from its opening pages, where, as Raphaël enters the casino, the narrator sees the hat check policy as "concluding an infernal pact with you by exacting a sort of pledge" (57; 59). It confirms the allusion through a series of explicit references to the Faust myth in general and to Goethe's *Faust* in particular.[69] These superficial allusions point toward deeper affinities between the two works relating to their common preoccupation with the era of commodification.

Indeed, commodification in an earlier form is already a central concern of the Faust tradition before Goethe. In Marlowe's *Doctor Faustus*, this concern revolves around the heretical notion that the soul can be bought and sold. As Richard Halpern points out, the commodification of the soul figures a critical dimension of the political economy of capitalism. "In order to become a commodity, soul must not only supply a use value to the purchaser but it must be alienable by the seller. It must, that is, be a form of property."[70] The alienability of the soul provides, on the one hand, a sense of self-ownership (if I can sell my soul, it must belong to me), and on the other hand, the conditions of possibility for the alienation of labor. The fixed ten-year term of Faustus's contract with Mephistopheles in Marlowe's play can therefore appear as a labor contract in which an expendable quantity of soul is signed over by Faustus in exchange for other goods and services.

In Goethe's *Faust*, as György Lukács observes, the exchange takes place not for goods but for capital itself.[71] What Faust (who, like Raphaël, is aware of the Faust tradition) demands in exchange for his soul in Goethe's version is not the fulfillment of his desires during a fixed quantity of time, but rather to remain *unsatisfied* in his desires. The power that Mephisto provides to Faust is analogous to the power of capital in that it allows Faust to continue producing both wealth (wealth of experience as well as material wealth) and, centrally, to continue producing new desires that remain to be fulfilled—that is, to produce himself as a desiring subject. By entering into his pact with Mephisto, Faust "will become a symbolic capitalist, but his capital, which he will throw incessantly into circulation and seek endlessly to expand, will be himself," Marshall Berman writes.[72] Faust's pact, then, takes the form of a wager: he bets he will never be fully satisfied and that he will consequently avoid the full execution of the contract. He remains, in theory, able to extend his life interminably as long as he refuses or fails to be satisfied. Consonant with the projects of the ultrawealthy "immortalists" and "healthspanners" discussed in the introduction, capital holds out the promise of transcending human limitations, particularly of transcending mortality. For this reason, Faust's pact with Mephisto can be figured, however ironically, as a rebirth, anticipated by the scene where he is recalled from the brink of suicide by the Easter celebration.[73]

In Marlowe's and Goethe's versions of the Faust story, the labor contract and the speculative economy of capital thus seem to provide the opportunity for unprecedented modes of experience, even if in the end they close in on their respective subjects to reassert human limitations and the ultimate authority of death. Without mentioning the *Faust* intertext, Weber hints at the ways that *La Peau de chagrin* might be seen to replicate a Faustian economy: "The skin offers its property as a magical 'means of production' and of possession in exchange for the vital substance of the producer."[74] In this reading, *La Peau de chagrin*, following in the path of Goethe's *Faust*, posits an abiding tension between the desiring subject and his death. What Raphaël, like his Faustian precursors, ultimately wants, according to this logic, is to live; the pact he enters into allows him to live anew, to be rescued from the deathlike state of his previous existence, but at the price of death. *La Peau de chagrin*, however, deviates significantly from this Faustian pattern. Where Marlowe's Faustus is a contracted laborer and Goethe's a capitalist speculator, Raphaël appears in his turn as a consumer. But this role also signals a decisive break from key parameters in the Faustian paradigm.

The Death-Commodity

This rupture begins to be felt when Raphaël discovers the magic skin—the vehicle for this strange and marvelous death—in the quintessential space of commodification, a store. Described in lavish detail, the antiquities shop

where Raphaël finds the *peau de chagrin* presents a vast jumble of miscella-
nea. "The beginnings of creation and the events of yesterday were paired off
with grotesque good humor. A roasting-jack was posed on a monstrance, a
Republican sabre on a medieval arquebus. . . . All the countries in the world
seemed to have brought here the debris of their sciences and arts" (71–72;
35). Stripped of their specific histories and geographies, the objects amassed
in the shop become mere "debris," related to each other solely on the basis
of exchange-value. The potential buyer's desires and fantasies, projected onto
objects like glossy advertisements, manufacture value. "Espying a medieval
dagger with a hilt as cunningly wrought as a piece of lace, with rust patched
on it like bloodstains," we read in one such moment, "he thought with a
shudder of mighty trysts interrupted by the cold blade of a husband's sword"
(71; 36). The consumer's gaze unanchors things from use-value and sets them
adrift in the liquid space of commodification: "The ocean of furnishings,
inventions, fashions, works of art and relics made up an endless poem. Forms,
colors, thoughts came to life again; but nothing complete presented itself to
his soul" (71–72; 37). The shop becomes a world of phantoms lacking solid-
ity, a world of simulacra, a version perhaps of the Daguerrian diorama whose
alluring illusion Balzac would propose as an image of modern life in *Le Père
Goriot*, published four years after *Le Peau de chagrin*.[75] Here, meaning is
reduced to price. "A little writing-desk that had cost a hundred thousand
francs and had been bought back for a five-franc piece stood next to a secret
lock whose price would formerly have sufficed for a king's ransom. . . . An
ebony table, a gem of artistic creation, carved from designs by Jean Goujon,
which had cost years of toil, had perhaps been picked up for the price of a
load of firewood. . . . Precious caskets and furniture wrought by the hands
of magicians were jumbled together indifferently" (73; 39). This indifference
extends even to Raphaël himself. Just as he was instantly recognizable as
a predetermined "type" upon entering the casino, just as his intended self-
drowning threatened to assimilate him to the marketplace mechanisms that
turn death to profit, in the antiquities shop he seems to merge with the world
of the commodity: "Pursued by the strangest of forms, by fabulous creations
poised on the confines between life and death, he walked along as in the
enchantment of a dream. Indeed, in some doubt as to his own existence, he
felt himself at one with these curious objects: neither altogether living nor
altogether dead" (73; 39).

The oneiric, phantasmagoric quality of this world suspended between
life and death strikingly anticipates Marx's theory of the commodity. It has
been observed that Marx's writings show little direct interest in death.[76] But
death does occur as a crucial figure in his account of commodification. "The
existence of things *quâ* commodities," Marx writes, "and the value-relation
between the products of labour which stamps them as commodities, have
absolutely no connection with their physical properties and with the material
relations arising therefrom. There it is a definite social relation between men

that assumes, in their eyes, the phantasmagoric form of a relation between things."[77] As products of labor enter the marketplace, as they acquire value no longer simply according to the actual labor invested in their production or according to their use, but rather according to their exchangeability for other products, not only are these products themselves transformed into commodities, but also the commodity form functions as a mode of representation that transforms the way people see themselves and others.

As relations between people come to appear as relations between things, moreover, this transforms the very image of life. The production of use-value through labor is the very condition of possibility for life, Marx contends: "So far therefore as labour is a creator of use value, is useful labour, it is a necessary condition, independent of all forms of society, for the existence of the human race; it is an eternal nature-imposed necessity, without which there can be no material exchanges between man and Nature, and therefore no life."[78] But the commodity form, which breaks definitively from use-value (the exchange value of commodities has "absolutely no connection with their physical properties"), also interrupts the possibility of life, as life is reduced to quantifiable time and lived experience is translated into wages and buying power. This is also to say that in a world mediated by the commodity form, where everything and everybody are replaceable, the very meaning of death also erodes. Death no longer means the loss of an irreplaceably singular human experience, human story, or human person. Instead, commodified man is immersed in the phantasmagoric realm of the *peau de chagrin*, where existence comes into question and one is "neither altogether living nor altogether dead."

This entanglement of the question of life and death with the absorption into the world of the commodity is actualized in the *peau de chagrin* itself, which is located in the deepest recesses of the shop and seems to articulate the shop's overall logic. The skin is the quintessential commodity, the object that fixates Raphaël's desire and that absolutizes the commodity form. It is not quite sufficient, then, to say that Raphaël exchanges his life in return for the fulfillment of his wishes. This is because, on the one hand, the *peau de chagrin* does not, in Faustian mode, grant desires that cost him his life, but rather it embodies and fulfills a death wish. He does not exchange life for death, but rather one death for another. Indeed, because it will prove impossible to cease desiring, the moment the young man enters into the pact with the talisman is effectively the moment of his death, with his ultimate physical demise as merely the belated realization of this moment. In this sense, the *peau de chagrin* simply replaces the Seine as the instrument of Raphaël's death. The merchant, in fact, characterizes the pact with the skin in these terms. "After all," he declares, "you are bent on dying. Well, your suicide is merely postponed" (88; 55). The novel, in this light, becomes, as Victor Brombert suggests, "the story of a slow suicide."[79] On the other hand, however, even as the *peau de chagrin* fulfills Raphaël's death wish, it also crucially *prevents* Raphaël from dying, as becomes clear in a scene where Raphaël proves utterly invulnerable in a duel (274–76; 264–65). One wish that the *peau de chagrin* cannot fulfill, then, is the wish to die; suicide in its traditional form becomes impossible.

Indeed, it may not even be appropriate to speak of Raphaël's new relation to death in terms of desire or wishes. For to the extent that the *peau de chagrin* responds to his early resolution to produce an indecipherable corpse, it also renders indecipherable the very quality of resolution itself, the agential basis of suicide. From this point on, it is no longer clear if he dies because he wants or decides to die or not, since the *peau de chagrin* means that every desire, no matter what it is for, even the limit case of the desire not to die, is also, at the same time, the desire to die. If Raphaël claims the right to die a death of his own, in other words, this demand only takes place with regard to a framework in which choice itself is radically curtailed. The *peau de chagrin*, in other words, does not present Raphaël with a choice between radically different ways of living or of dying, but rather presents itself as something that always already underwrites Raphaël's identity and possibilities.

Nowhere is this clearer than in Balzac's revision of the classic Faustian compact scene. The signing of the pact constitutes a momentous decision for his precursors, in which they themselves are made to write up the contract and then sign away their souls with their own blood after extensive deliberation and bargaining. But Raphaël's relationship to the contract he enters into is entirely different. First, rather than write up the contract himself, Raphaël encounters the contract in already written form, as its reader rather than its author. For the *peau de chagrin* is also, of course, a parchment, with the terms of its contract written upon it in "characters incrusted in the cellular tissue of this marvelous skin, as if they were produced by the animal to which the skin had once belonged" (83; 49). As Raphaël reads the terms of the contract, moreover, they already seem to become infused in a way into his being, when we consider how this text is presented in the novel: first, in Arabic calligraphy, then in French, after which, and only after which, an explanation for this act of translation is given, when the merchant then attributes the translation (which he says is from Sanskrit, despite the Arabic characters) to Raphaël himself (84; 50–51). The translation of the "Sanskrit" text thus seems to take place automatically within Raphaël, such that he is committed to the contract in and through the act of reading.

A second indication of this evacuation of agency, this suspension of the capacity for decision, is confirmed when the pact is said to be in effect. For Raphaël does not even quite decide to commit himself to the pact, but rather seems to enter into it without quite knowing what he is doing. He simply declares, as if conducting an impetuous experiment, "Let's see! [*Voyons!*]" (liberally but not implausibly translated by Hunt as "Let's put it to the test!", 87; 54), and then sets the experiment in motion by wishing for an extravagant banquet. What takes place, at this moment, does not, then, take the form of a deliberate commitment to the terms of the talisman, but rather exposes choice and agency as mere illusion. Indeed, by the time Raphaël puts the talisman to the test, he is already in its grip. Thus when the antiquarian declares, "You have signed the pact, and there is no more to say," he does so despite the fact that Raphaël has not signed anything but has only read what now turns out to have been an alienated form of his own signature in the form of the text of the skin.

Finally, the terms of the compact themselves undermine the hierarchical power structure at issue in the Faust tradition. This shift is indicated almost invisibly, since it eludes most readers, in the mistranslation of the terms of the compact from Arabic to French. The Arabic text that appears "reproduced" in the novel has as its central line, as translated by Alois Richard Nykl: "And by each of thy wishes I shall diminish thy days."[80] In this version, which more closely adheres to the Faust tradition, the skin voices agency and control over the life and death of its subject; notably, it does *not* say that it, too, will shrink along with the days of its possessor. By contrast, in the French version, the skin declares that "*à chaque vouloir je décroîtrai comme tes jours,*" that "with each wish I will diminish like your days." Rather than assert itself as the cause of its possessor's death, then, the French version links the skin's size and its possessor's life only according to a relation of similarity, *comme.* The *peau de chagrin* and Raphaël's life thus become likenesses of each other, each reflecting the other's approach to death but without either one clearly causing the diminution of the other.

The consequences of this evacuation of external authority are several. For one, we might note that the fulfillment of desire plays, in the end, a rather minor role in Balzac's novel. Raphaël neither summons Helen from the realm of the dead nor participates in a Walpurgisnacht. Second, unlike Dorian Gray's portrait, which Balzac's novel anticipates, the *peau de chagrin* does not encode any moral judgment concerning its subject's desires: it remains strictly neutral with respect to Raphaël's wishes, and appears to contract equally whether his wishes are altruistic or decadent, petty or grand. Third, and equally telling, while the *peau de chagrin* itself is said to resist understanding and is perceived by Raphaël as magical, each time one of his desires is realized, it is accompanied by a plausible explanation. When he first wishes for "a royal banquet, a carouse worthy of this century," for instance, nothing materializes out of thin air; instead, upon leaving the antiquities shop, he encounters friends who invite him along to a dinner sponsored by a wealthy patron. Similarly, his wish for wealth is answered by news that he has inherited the fortune of a distant uncle in the colonies. It thus remains a deliberately and powerfully open question as to whether the skin exerts fatal power over its owner or whether instead its action is a figment of his imagination—that is, whether the skin causes Raphaël's demise or he causes its.[81] Thus in place of the moral cosmology of the Faust tradition is now the strictly mechanical, impersonal, and symptomatic relation established between Raphaël and the talisman. One can no longer say whether the magic skin is a projection of Raphaël's desires or if he by contrast becomes a projection of its powers and properties. What takes place between Raphaël and the skin, then, is not an "exchange," as Weber puts it, at least not to the extent that an exchange must leave its participants distinct from each other and in an ongoing relation to each other. Raphaël is not alienated from himself though his pact with the skin. Rather he becomes, without reserve, someone or something else.

Raphaël on Life Support

In place, then, of the model of a self-authored death that derives its meaning from its adequacy to a coherent and integral life story, Raphaël finds his own relationship to death radically transformed, or exposed to him in a radically new way, by the death-commodity, the *peau de chagrin* to which he is bound through an act, a pact, of reading. The significance of this bond is encapsulated in the word used throughout the novel to describe the action of the skin: it "contracts" (*se contracter*), a term that resonates not only with physical meaning, describing the diminishing circumference of the skin, but also with legal and medical significance. It is contracted to Raphaël and he to it, in the legal sense, just as he contracts the skin as a sort of disease, in the medical sense. This "*force contractile*" (227) of the skin—its contractile but also, implicitly, its contractual and contractible force—translates the question of transmissibility and communicability that Benjamin located as the central concern of modern suicide. If it subjects Raphaël to conditions that invalidate the dream of Romantic heroism, if it turns every desire into the confirmation of a phantasmagoric existence suspended between life and death, if it therefore deprives him of the right to die on his own terms, at the same time this contractile force makes possible, I argue, the transmission of this very experience of subjection—that is, of a modernist art of death.

This possibility emerges as Raphaël comes to reckon with the contractile force of the skin not simply as something external to him that controls his life from without, but rather as a force that dissolves the distinction between interior and exterior, his skin and the *peau de chagrin*. Rather than fall victim to the political economy of the *peau de chagrin*, in other words, he displaces and internalizes that very economy. Thus the forces that seem to suppress his effort to claim authorship over his own life and death, the resistance that modernity poses to his "natural élan," come to appear, in the final part of the novel, as aspects of his own person and body. More specifically, the phantasmagoric and supernatural quality of the *peau de chagrin* is translated into a form of terminal illness. Indeed, as soon as he realizes that the pact is in force, he experiences this realization as the revelation of a disease. "Now he believed in the *peau de chagrin*. He listened to himself breathe, he already felt ill, and he asked himself: 'Am I not consumptive? Did not my mother die of tuberculosis?'" (209; 192). This figure of illness, which extends throughout the last part of the novel, signals not only the advent of radically new conditions of dying, but also a new conceptualization of the self. For this illness is not simply a given. Rather, it allows Raphaël to become, for himself and for others, an enigma that both requires and resists deciphering.[82]

Raphaël will therefore take a number of steps to design his life in such a way as to accommodate its new conditions. These conditions reflect the conditions of modern death diagnosed by Benjamin—its sequestration and degradation. Yet, strikingly, in Balzac's novel we see Raphaël not simply resigning himself to these conditions. In the same way that Raphaël becomes a system of exchanges so as to ironically appropriate the commodity form, the final section of the novel shows him creatively inventing the conditions of modern death, and in so doing transforming how modern death might take place.

The nature of this transformation emerges first of all as the novel explores the consequences of the fact that the *peau de chagrin*, just as it deprives Raphaël of the ability to decide to die, also cannot fulfill the wish to live on indefinitely.[83] Raphaël's creative solution to this situation is to seek to eliminate desire altogether. To accomplish this, he employs three different strategies, each of which represents a different facet of modern death.

In the first, he sequesters himself, assuming responsibility for the sequestration of death rather than having it imposed on him. Ensconced in his guarded mansion, he arranges his daily life so that a servant anticipates his desires. Everything he might possibly want is planned in advance, allowing him to avoid ever having to express a desire, and visitors are barred from entering his rooms. But if this strategy seems to slow or halt the shrinking of the *peau de chagrin*, it does so only by forcing Raphaël into a deathlike state, into what we might anachronistically but not inappropriately call a persistent vegetative state. "He often tells me," reports Raphaël's malapropism-prone servant, "that he wants to live like a piece of *vergetation* [*comme une végétation*], he wants to *vergetate*" (215; 199). The desire to live (perhaps encoded in the phallic *verge* of *végétation*), in forcing the elimination of desire, thus commits Raphaël to a machine-like or corpse-like existence.[84] We see this when a former professor, despite Raphaël's household regulations, manages to gain entry to his student's mansion:

> Almost joyous to become a sort of automaton, he abdicated life in order to live . . . . In the lap of luxury, he led the life of a steam engine. As the old professor gazed on this young corpse, he shuddered; everything seemed artificial in this weak and meager body. (217; 201)

As Raphaël becomes a vegetable, an automaton, a steam engine, a corpse, and a form of artificial life, the magic skin thus delivers him to a state of suspension between life and death, to a phantasmagoric existence.

Whereas this first strategy leads him to perform the role of a being suspended between the human and the inhuman, between life and death, his second strategy shapes his very vision of the world and of himself. "To set himself apart from all temptation, he carried an eyepiece of which the cleverly designed microscopic lens destroyed the harmony of the most beautiful features by giving them a hideous appearance" (225–26; 240). Again turning himself into a sort of machine—a microscope or camera lens—he subjects the world and himself to a gaze that destroys any ideal image that he would have wished to preserve through heroic suicide and replaces it with a new, unrecognizable image. But this lens, we might also note, does not simply replace the image of the external world with an illusion. Instead, it remains a lens that, through its microscopic action, simply reveals an unsightly dimension in what appears beautiful on the surface; if the world appears in a new and unrecognizable form, it is not because this new way of seeing departs from reality but rather because it reveals it from a new perspective. In becoming a means of changing the way in which the world appears, in becoming a medium of representation, Raphaël becomes, in fact, like the skin itself, which also appears as a scientific instrument that produces a strange but nonetheless revealing image of life when Raphaël mounts it on a canvas and traces a line around it so as to measure its diminution over time. In contrast to the painterly subjectivity of Dorian Gray's portrait, the magic skin, one could say, displays the supposed neutrality and mechanicity of photography, whose invention is contemporaneous with Balzac's novel. Indeed, Balzac understood photography as a sort of *peau de chagrin*: he believed that it worked by peeling away the spectral layers that he thought constituted physical bodies.[85] Each photograph would reduce the life span of its subject, thus literally representing the death of the subject.[86] The microscopic lens Raphaël wears as well as the *peau de chagrin* itself are versions of this deadly form of representation. They become medical instruments through which Raphaël's death is externalized and returned to him as representation.

Raphaël's third and final adaptation sets his story definitively in the context of the rise of the medical profession in nineteenth-century Paris. If his compact with the *peau de chagrin* forces or allows him to see life through its mechanical, quantifying perspective, it also appears as itself a prosthesis or graft. It is not simply a representation of his bodily life but is part of him. As such, the skin becomes itself subject to medical intervention. We see this when Raphaël, as if in search of a new experimental treatment, turns to scientific experts to act directly on the skin, as if by arresting its deterioration or by trying to enlarge it, the talisman and its host will be healed of the disease in which they are interlocked. But not surprisingly, when the ironically named Master Spieghalter (for if the talisman is a sort of mirror that reflects Raphaël's life span, Master Mirror-Halter decisively fails to halt its action) attempts to use a hydraulic press to compress and stretch the skin, the machine bursts its castings and breaks apart, like the apparatus in Kafka's "In the Penal Colony." The solvents and voltaic battery to which the chemist Baron Japhet subjects the skin are equally ineffective. The failure of efforts to act upon the skin directly lead, then, to the suspicion that the skin, rather than causing Raphaël's perceived illness, may be its visible symptom. He therefore turns to medicine: "'In order to die,' he said, forming a conclusion to the thought he had begun in a dream, 'it must be that my organism, this structure of flesh and bone animated by my will and which makes of me an individual *man*, gives evidence of some detectable lesion. The symptoms of impaired vitality must be known to the medical profession: a physician should be able to tell me if I am in a state of health or sickness'" (253–54; 241). But the "oracles of modern medicine" (256; 244) he consults are as incapable as the chemist and engineer of grasping the novel complex of symptoms that Raphaël and the *peau de chagrin* together present.

This disjunction between medical understanding and the novelty of Raphaël's condition comes to a climax in a scene that uncannily anticipates the medical practices that often surround the end of life today. In a final attempt to avoid expressing any desire, Raphaël requests that his physician (Horace Bianchon, making his first appearance in *La Comedie humaine*) drug him into "a state of continual somnolescence" (288; 279), from which he emerges only briefly each day to eat and immediately return to sleep. But unbeknownst to Raphaël, the doctor instructs Raphaël's servant to "keep him distracted" (288; 279), and so the servant arranges a surprise banquet in place of his employer's usual spartan meal, exposing Raphaël to temptations that seem to herald his imminent demise. The physician thus turns out to be a version of the antiquarian, who observed that Raphaël had merely been "distracted from dying"—and who, like the antiquarian and anticipating the economic calculations that may motivate efforts to prolong life in today's medical-industrial complex, profits from the deferral of Raphaël's death.

But in assuming that he knows what is in his patient's best interests and prescribing a course of action that conforms to his therapeutic assumptions, he in fact further, if unwittingly, submits Raphaël to the fatal dynamics of the *peau de chagrin*. For what the physician does not and indeed cannot see is that Raphaël's encounter with the magic skin produces a condition that does not conform to medical categories, as Raphaël and the talisman become interchangeable, each the cause and symptom of the other. Indeed, is it the *peau de chagrin* that, like a disease, kills Raphaël? Or vice versa, is it Raphaël who destroys the *peau de chagrin*? Or else, is it the *peau de chagrin* that keeps Raphaël alive, and he it? Although Raphaël turned to medicine hoping to learn if he was healthy or sick, what the *peau de chagrin* comes to mean is that it is no longer possible to say what characterizes "illness" and what "health," what distinguishes natural physiological processes (nature taking its course) from "artificial life."

The assistance that Raphaël requests from the physician thus attests to something new and strange that exposes the limits of medical knowledge and defies its foundational categories. Medicine and science, it would seem, cannot grasp the novel significance of Raphaël's "modern suicide." At the same time, however, Raphaël's indecipherability, we might note, remains bound up with the modernity of medical science. For it is precisely medicine's failure that allows Raphaël's case to appear utterly intractable, to assume the form of an indecipherable enigma.

Pauline

If Raphaël appears to Baudelaire as a "hero of modern life," precisely in that he undergoes a "modern suicide," if he appears as the artist of his own death, this may be, then, because even as he succumbs to the degradation of death—to its commodification, medicalization, and deauthorization—he does not simply vanish into the space of invisibility to which modernity consigns death. His death is not simply a resignation. Instead, it seems to make the invisibility of modern death visible and transmissible, much like Malte as he speculates on the frosted-glass windows of the ambulances speeding across the Place du Parvis Notre Dame.

For Benjamin, we might recall, this undertaking appeared, in one light, as an impossibility. The authority of the storyteller, Benjamin argued, required that death be a public event, that for experience to "assume transmissible form," the dying man's face must be witnessed, for it is in his expression and looks that "the views of himself under which he has encountered himself without being aware of it" can first be imparted. Modern death, in its removal from the realm of witnessability, also, then, silences the storyteller. In Benjamin's essay, we might also recall, the novel—the literary genre inhabited by Raphaël—is the form assumed by this silence. Whereas stories, even when written down, remain linked to oral traditions, Benjamin observes, the novel displays "an essential dependence on the book." Whereas the storyteller delivers his tales to listeners, Benjamin writes that "the birthplace of the novel is the individual in his isolation, the individual who can no longer speak of his concerns in exemplary fashion, who himself lacks counsel and can give none."[87]

Yet at the moment of death—the key moment which produces the authority that is at the very source of the story—the image of the storyteller suffers a crisis. On the one hand, it is only at the moment of death that experience becomes transmissible, for before that moment, Moriens does not even recollect, does not even have to view, the critical moments that comprise his story. And yet the moment that experience becomes transmissible in the form of a story, the moment it becomes possible to communicate the "integral creative narrative" of a life, is also the moment of silencing. For Moriens's story is transmitted only through an image, through his "expression and looks," which give themselves to be read in silence, as it were, by the witnesses to his death. If modern death at first appeared to spell the end of the oral tradition by sequestering the dying and thus to signal the advent of the decline of communicable experience, if the novel appeared as the prime symptom and proof of this decline, isolating readers in their solitude much as the dying are isolated in asylums and hospitals, the link that Benjamin identifies between the moment of death and the transmissibility of experience also suggests the possibility of a story that speaks through silence and that turns the very conditions of modernity into the conditions of communicability.[88] Thus from within the lament about the decline of storytelling and communicability, another counter-story emerges, one that suggests another channel of transmission that takes place through the silent reading of the novel. Thus, if, on the one hand, the age of the novel ruptures the traditional connection between the publicly witnessed death and the communication of experience, on the other, it creates the possibility of another sort of meaning, one that is linked to the very silence of textuality, to what can be read in the silent face of the dying man.

Indeed, it is just such a communication that emerges in Raphaël's final episode, as his lover Pauline, from whom he has previously hidden himself as part of his strategy of avoiding objects of desire, appears at his bedside, and he attempts to tell her, and convince her, of the power of the *peau de chagrin*. Placing what is left of it in her hand, "as tiny and fragile as the leaf of a periwinkle," he bids her farewell: "If you look at me again, I will die" (291; 282). What follows is a version of the archetypal scene of death described by Benjamin, but with a critical difference:

> She took the talisman and went to fetch the lamp. Under the flickering glimmer playing both on Raphaël and the talisman, she examined minutely both her lover's face and the last particle of the magic skin. Seeing Pauline so beautiful, moved by love and terror, he was no longer able to control his thoughts: the memory of the tender scenes and delirious joys of passion sprang up in triumph in his long-drugged soul, starting into flame like the embers of a fire banked down but not extinguished.
>
> "Pauline, come to me! . . . Pauline . . ."
>
> A terrible cry burst from the girl's throat and her eyes dilated; her eyebrows, violently contorted by the effect of untold anguish, were drawn apart with horror at what she could read in Raphaël's eyes: an onset of frenzied desire, in which she had once gloried. But, as this desire grew, she could feel the skin contracting, tickling her palm as it lay in her hand. (291–92; 282; ellipses in original)

As in Benjamin's image, the moment of death is anticipated by the sequence of unbidden thoughts and dormant but unforgettable scenes that flash before Raphaël's eyes. Crucially, however, what elicits this panoramic vision here is an act of reading, as Pauline "attentively examines" his face and as she "reads" his eyes. But as Pauline reads Raphaël's face and eyes, she also reads the *peau de chagrin* and is touched by its contraction. Her act of reading, then, is not simply a witnessing of the other's death, but also, it would seem, its cause. "If *you* look at *me* again, I will die," Raphaël says—not "if I look at you." This odd twist, in which what kills is the other's gaze, turns Pauline into the assistant, the surrogate, of Raphaël's death, the means by which his strange and marvelous modern suicide will be accomplished. In order to die, Raphaël must submit himself to her reading of him, but in so doing he also submits himself to a death that is no longer simply his own.

This transmission, then, is not without consequences: at the moment when Pauline, feeling the talisman twitch in her hand, is convinced of its power, she also submits to it, entering unwittingly, like Raphaël, into its pact. For she, too, now imagines that the fulfillment of her desire—her desire to extend Raphaël's life—requires her death; barricading herself in a neighboring room, she attempts to take her own life, crying out, "If I die, he will live" (292; 283). If this gesture might at first seem to represent a form of romantic self-sacrifice that would redeem Raphaël and save him from his fate, if Pauline might appear as Gretchen to Raphaël's Faust, ready to plead for his redemption, it would appear instead that Pauline, too, has become subject to, has contracted, the alienation of death. She becomes, as it were, a double of Raphaël, attempting to change places with him, to become his *remplaçant*. No real heroism is possible here, no beautiful, Romantic death. Instead, her attempt to kill herself becomes a grotesque parody of the death of Cleopatra: breaking down the door, Raphaël finds her "half-naked, writhing on a sofa," having tried "vainly to pierce her own heart" and now attempting to strangle herself with her shawl (292; 283).

Pauline, too, thus becomes bound to the law of the *peau de chagrin*, such that she can only accomplish her desire for Raphaël to live by courting her own death. But as for Raphaël, the *peau de chagrin* does not simply allow her to die. Instead, in the final tableau of the novel, the two lovers are locked together in a phantasmagoric figure suspended between life and death:

> The dying man sought for words to express the desire that was consuming his strength; but only the choking sound of the death-rattle broke from his lungs; each breath he took, fetched from farther within, seemed to come from his very entrails. At last, no longer able to form even sounds, he bit Pauline's breast. Jonathan appeared, terrified by the shouts he had heard, and tried to tear from the girl the corpse over which she crouched in a corner.
>
> "What do you want?" she demanded. "He is mine. I have killed him. Did I not foretell it?" (292; 283)

Everything, it would seem, hinges on this last desire, which is perhaps the quintessential desire. For if every desire Raphaël previously expressed was also always necessarily the desire to die, in this final wish, life and death become indistinguishable; the wish to live is the wish to die, and vice versa.

But if this wish is condemned to silence, it is not simply because the forces of modernity have overwhelmed him and deprived Raphaël of the authority to create his own death. It is because it is only at the final moment, at the moment when speech fails, that the experience of the *peau de chagrin*, the story of modern death, becomes transmissible. As Raphaël's teeth sink into Pauline's skin, the image of Cleopatra's heroic, classical suicide is again parodically evoked; he becomes the asp that bites her breast. But this again disrupts the Romantic image of self-sacrifice, for the moment of his death would also, in this light, appear to poison Pauline, to communicate to her a deadly experience. Indeed, if at this moment the narrative seems to forget the actual *peau de chagrin*, if the moment when it ought to have contracted into nothingness and vanished is missing from the novel, this may be because the skin does not quite vanish but is rather displaced as Raphaël is conjoined no longer with the *peau de chagrin* but with another skin, with the *peau* of P(e)au-line, who will herself pronounce what appears to be the verdict of the *peau de chagrin*, "He is mine, I killed him." This bite is thus simultaneously an act of dying and an act of transmission. As Raphaël's servant enters the room and "tried to tear away from the girl the corpse over which she crouched in a corner," Pauline's living body and Raphaël's corpse remain locked together, blurring the boundaries between life and death. It is this indistinction, in the end, that delivers to the reader an indecipherable corpse.

Epilogue: A Novel Ending

The *force contractile* of Raphaël's death, then, does not come to an end, does not simply die, but is instead relayed through Pauline's act of reading, which itself repeats Raphaël's reading of the *peau de chagrin* and contracts her to its terms. Rather than provide a coherent ending to his life, Raphaël's death exhibits a radical incoherence—the incoherence of his final wish and choking voice, of his body, and finally of the novel itself, which does not simply end at this moment but instead spills over into a short, oblique "Epilogue," a textual supplement that resists resolution.[89] At issue in this epilogue, in fact, is precisely the act of reading, for the epilogue is structured as a dialogue between the narrator (presumably) and an imaginary or representative reader, who sets the epilogue in motion by voicing a desire for resolution, coherence, and closure: "And what became of Pauline?" (292; 284). But the desire for completion is repeatedly frustrated. For in each of the three responses this question receives, Pauline appears in ethereal, irresolute forms: as a mirage glimpsed in a flame, as a "queen of illusions" or an angel, and as a phantom glimpsed in the mist by tourists on a Loire River cruise. At one such moment, in fact, addressed to the reader, her figure is said to have "tickled your hand" (*"votre main chatouillée"*) exactly in the way that the *peau de chagrin* previously tickled the hand of Pauline (293; 285). As the book we are reading approaches its last words and shrinks to nothingness, as its last pages tickle our hand, it does not, however, simply come to an end.

Benjamin, to recall, lamented the removal of death from the space of modern life: "Today people live in rooms that have never been touched by death." And yet the final pages of *La Peau de chagrin* suggest that modernity, and the modern storytelling that takes place through Balzac's novel, may not simply be *untouched* by death either. As the *peau de chagrin* is transmitted through the tickled hand from Raphaël to Pauline to the reader, we might wonder to what extent we are subject, perhaps without fully realizing it, to its *force contractile*. If this means that, as for Raphaël, self-authorship is a mere fantasy mired in an anachronistic image of heroism and a misrecognition of the modern degradation of death, it may also suggest a different relationship between death and art. Rather than produce and confirm the integrity of a life, as Dworkin suggested was needed in order to judge another's right to die, *La Peau de chagrin* stages modern death as a vexed moment that calls upon its reader to receive, and in turn to make transmissible, a persistent sense of incompleteness, a persistent sense of the senselessness of endings.[90] It suggests, along with Baudelaire in the epigraph to this chapter, that the right to take one's leave evades coherence and intelligibility and instead allies itself to the poetic, literary right to self-contradiction. If life, then, is a novel in which one chooses a last chapter to accord with one's life story, then the last chapter that accords with the modern history of death is one that recognizes in the demand for the right to die an ongoing enigma, something that remains unresolved. What Baudelaire calls the beauty of modern suicide resides in this enigma, in the beauty of a desire to die that itself undoes death.

Chapter 3

Death with Dignity after Auschwitz

Do you always have to be there just because you were there once?

—Jean Améry

In October 2014 Dr. Wim Distelmans, president of the Belgian Federal Commission for the Control and Evaluation of Euthanasia, led a group of approximately seventy doctors, psychologists, and nurses on a study tour of Auschwitz, organized under the rubric "Death with Dignity" (*Waardig Levenseinde*). A controversial and outspoken advocate of legalized physician-assisted death, Distelmans had been appointed to the commission shortly after the Belgian voluntary euthanasia law was passed in 2002.[1] In many ways, Distelmans's plan was surprising, since advocates of the right to die, including Distelmans himself, have generally sought to distance the legalization of physician-assisted death from any association with Nazi Germany and its so-called "euthanasia" program.[2] Indeed, several Jewish groups as well as the administration of the Auschwitz Memorial protested the premise of the study tour. Shimon Samuels of the Paris office of the Simon Wiesenthal Center called it a "travesty" and declared that "the connection he's making is perverse."[3] The British *Daily Mail*, referring to Distelmans as "Dr. Death," quoted unidentified "Jewish and anti-euthanasia campaigners" as calling the trip "offensive and shocking."[4] Following the trip, Distelmans received an email from the deputy director of the Auschwitz Memorial to similar effect: "We feel that the attempt to link the history of Auschwitz with the current debate about euthanasia is inappropriate."[5] Others attributed more sinister implications to the tour. Tom Mortier, a Belgian chemist who became politically active after Distelmans granted his mother's euthanasia request, wrote together with British anti-euthanasia activist Kevin Fitzpatrick: "It is gratifying for us to see Dr. Distelmans connect the dots between euthanasia in Brussels and the atrocities of Auschwitz. It confirms for us the dark future of Belgium's legal euthanasia."[6]

For Distelmans, by contrast, Auschwitz appeared as a "logical" site to "clarify confusions." "Among all the issues surrounding the end of life, one is constantly confronted with existential pain, questions of meaning, self-reflection, dependence and self-determination, finitude, and especially (in)dignity," read a prospectus for the trip. "It therefore seemed logical to us to plan the next study tour to the place that preeminently symbolizes a death without dignity [*een mensonwaardig levenseinde*]: Oświęcim, better known as Auschwitz, the extermination camp of the Nazis in Poland. This place seems to be a thought-provoking location to reflect in a seminar on these issues and to clarify confusions."[7] In contrast to claims that there is no connection between Auschwitz and death with dignity, and to claims that legalizing physician-assisted death announces an imminent repetition of Auschwitz, Distelmans proposes a different way of understanding the historical relationship between the Shoah and the present. Death with dignity, he suggested to a reporter from *Der Spiegel*, represents "the opposite of what occurred in Auschwitz."[8] In undertaking the trip, then, "he wanted his colleagues to understand his definition of freedom—and he hoped they would admit that there can only be freedom if people can liberate themselves from the power of others."[9]

The battle lines dividing Distelmans from his critics are drawn here according to the familiar if contested strategy of testing contemporary ethics, law, and social policy against the touchstone of Nazism and the Holocaust. To the extent that it is said to resemble Nazi policies or to perpetuate aspects of Nazi ideology, the legalization of the right to die represents a form of state criminality, nothing but "medical killing." By contrast, the right to die is said to achieve moral, social, and political legitimacy precisely by distinguishing itself from Nazi atrocities. At the fulcrum of this dispute is the meaning and validity of the notion of death with dignity. While one side asserts that human dignity is necessarily violated when medico-legal authority is enlisted to end life, the other argues that human dignity requires the recognition of a right to die with medico-legal assistance.

Yet beneath these positions, and unresolved by either, is the more essential and difficult question of what it means to bring these two terms together, the question of the relationship between dignity and death. If Distelmans has good reason for locating Auschwitz at the crucial point of contact for these terms—as I too argue in this chapter—it is also the case that the history and legacy of the Holocaust does not simply clarify confusion by supporting one side or the other in the bifurcated politics of the right to die. Both Distelmans and his critics oversimplify the significance of Auschwitz for the present. Far from stabilizing the meaning of death with dignity, and far from bearing no relation at all to current debates, Auschwitz and its aftermath expose death with dignity as a vexed concept that, in both direct and indirect ways, bears powerful witness to the unsettling and unsettled question of what it means to die, and to live, "after Auschwitz."

The first part of this chapter offers an abbreviated genealogy of the concept of death with dignity, focusing on the ways that it emerged in Europe and North America as a salient political concept in the shadow of the Holocaust. Although mobilized as an alternative to the tainted vocabulary of euthanasia, the concept of death with dignity remains haunted by the murderous notion of "life unworthy of life," which provided the ideological framework for the

Nazi "euthanasia" killing centers as well as for the death camps. Whereas the Nazi state deployed a biopolitical (or thanatopolitical) logic in the extermination of those categorized as unworthy of life, in the postwar period it is ironically Auschwitz and the conditions of existence it has come to represent that occupy the position of the "unworthy of life" against which the image of death with dignity is defined.

Thus even as Holocaust death proves decisive in producing the image of death with dignity, at the same time it raises persistent questions concerning the very possibility of such a death, the very possibility of dignity—not because death in or after Auschwitz is necessarily undignified, as Distelmans suggested, but rather because Holocaust death imperils the structure of recognition and witnessing upon which the image of dignity relies. It makes death with dignity illegible, unwitnessable, unrecognizable. I develop this argument in the second and third parts of the chapter, focusing on a constellation of texts and questions related, first, to Jean Améry's testimony concerning suicide and voluntary death both in and after Auschwitz, and finally, to Améry's own death.

I. Death with Dignity as a Post-Auschwitz Concept

From Euthanasia to Death with Dignity

If the notion of death with dignity, as Distelmans rightly notes, is surrounded by confusion, this is first of all because it enters the discourse of the right to die less due to any positive significance than out of an attempt to replace other terms. First, it enters public discourse as a replacement for the vocabulary of suicide (as in "physician-assisted suicide") and the stigma it carries. Second, it replaces the older term "euthanasia," which might be said under Nazism to have passed through what the poet Paul Celan names "the thousand darknesses of deathbringing speech."[10] The history of the movement from euthanasia to death with dignity exposes the continual haunting of the contemporary notion of the right to die by a disavowed past.

This history began with extensive prewar efforts to legalize a right to die under the name of euthanasia. Prior to the late nineteenth century, euthanasia—etymologically, a "good or easy death"—appeared in contexts in which it was "exclusively a matter of divine providence or good fortune, and beyond human control."[11] But the late nineteenth century witnessed a reinvention of the term, which now came to signify primarily medical euthanasia, or "the use of anesthetics to guarantee a swift and painless death," with the first proposal for medical euthanasia dating to 1870.[12] What once described the quality of a death came to name instead the action taken by medical authority to produce death.[13] This redefinition of euthanasia as a medical procedure marks its point of intersection with the age of postnatural death, since it subjects the question of what constitutes a good death to human judgment and, more precisely, to social regulation.

From the earliest proposals for legalized medical euthanasia, the controversial implications of the social regulation of death have been apparent. An 1885 editorial in the *Journal of the American Medical Association*, for instance, declares that "the idea itself is ghastly, and the principle would put into the hands of unscrupulous parties a certain and easy method of being rid of an objectionable relative."[14] A member of the Medico-Legal Society in London registered the further concern in 1906 that "some of the advocates of euthanasia would, if the principle were once admitted, like to carry the removal of useless members of the State even further, and have suggested that capital punishment should be more freely employed, and that it would be advisable that all confirmed criminals, all insane persons, and many others they consider useless or dangerous, should be painlessly removed."[15]

That euthanasia could lead to the legalized killing of those deemed useless or deviant was anticipated, as well, by its advocates. Adolf Jost, discussed in the introduction, proposed medical euthanasia (without using the term) not only for patients who requested it, but also for the mentally ill who were wards of the state. Along with this form of nonvoluntary euthanasia, he derived the right to die from the joint welfare of the individual and society. The one who exercises this right, he argued, "not only rids himself of his suffering, but he also frees human society of a useless burden."[16] This weighing of social interests threatens to convert the right to die into a duty to die. The value of a life becomes subject to a logic of calculation of benefits and burdens, in which that value "cannot only be 0, but also negative."[17] If this "negative life's worth" (*negativen Lebenswerth*) is firstly connected to an experience of suffering that is said to make a life's value negative for the sufferer, this logic of calculation becomes, with seeming inevitability, linked to a social calculation as well that not only justifies but requires the deaths of those whose lives are deemed to have negative value.

In the first part of the twentieth century, various euthanasia laws were proposed, the first of which was in Ohio in 1906.[18] Notably, a 1937 bill considered in the Nebraska state legislature authorized euthanasia for mentally incompetent adults and terminally ill children on the request of a legal guardian.[19] The Nazi "euthanasia" program, however, radicalized such ideas, establishing killing centers beginning in 1939 first for physically and mentally disabled children who were killed by lethal injection or starvation, and subsequently for disabled adults, who were eventually the first victims of prototype gas chambers.[20] "Euthanasia" served as a euphemism for murder, but at the same time indicated the involvement of physicians in an activity that was framed as a medical procedure.[21] As reports of the Nazi killing practices began to circulate in the media outside Germany in 1941, euthanasia was thus given a "bad name" with a long-lasting impact on organizations such as the Voluntary Euthanasia Legalisation Society of England and the Euthanasia

Society of America, both founded in the mid-1930s.[22] What the historian N. D. A. Kemp notes with respect to Britain was valid throughout Europe and North America: "After 1941 the intimate association which was established between the term 'euthanasia' and the Nazi practice of non-voluntary killing for defectives helped obstruct legislative reform well into the second half of the twentieth century."[23]

Beyond the specific comparison of the Nazi T4 program (named for its headquarters at Tiergartenstrasse 4 in Berlin) and later proposals to legalize voluntary euthanasia, euthanasia in the postwar period became increasingly associated with the full scale of Nazi killings, including the death camps.[24] This connection was articulated most forcefully and influentially by the psychiatrist and neurologist Leo Alexander. An Austrian-born Jew who emigrated to the United States in 1933, Alexander served as a medical investigator and aide to counsel at the Nuremberg trials and was an author of the Nuremberg Code of medical ethics, which established the principle of informed consent. In a 1949 article titled "Medical Science under Dictatorship," Alexander formulated what he called a "wedged-in-lever" (now slippery slope) argument: "Whatever proportions these crimes assumed, it became evident to all who investigated them that they had started from small beginnings. The beginnings at first were merely a subtle shift in the attitude of physicians. It started with the acceptance of the attitude, basic in the euthanasia movement, that there is such a thing as a life not worthy of being lived."[25] Alexander alludes here to the infamous notion of "life unworthy of life" advanced by the prominent German jurist Karl Binding together with the psychiatrist Alfred Hoche in their 1920 pamphlet, *Die Freigabe der Vernichtung lebensunwerten Lebens* (*Permission for the Destruction of Life Unworthy of Life*), which endorses Jost's concept of "negative life's worth" even as it expands and refines his arguments. Thus for Alexander, the legalization and regulation even of a limited form of euthanasia—voluntary euthanasia for the terminally ill—would set the medical profession and the law on the path to Auschwitz.

The Politics of Death with Dignity

The Nazi analogy and the slippery slope argument remain deeply contested.[26] For one, conditions in Nazi Germany and in postwar democracies may be too divergent for any reasonable comparison to obtain.[27] There is no reason, right-to-die advocates further suggest, that legal and social institutions cannot adequately regulate physician-assisted death so as to limit it to those who are deemed eligible and who actively request it. Nor must it be the case that the right to die erodes physicians' ethical commitment to healing; instead, honoring patients' requests for help in dying may constitute a form of care.[28] Moreover, legalization can provide transparent protocols for practices that otherwise take place surreptitiously.[29] But even those who argue against the validity of the Nazi analogy acknowledge its power. As the historian Michael Burleigh puts it, contemporary debate on euthanasia "is still haunted—one hesitates to say informed—by events in Nazi Germany over fifty years ago."[30]

In this light, efforts to replace the vocabulary of euthanasia with the new terminology of death with dignity appear not as signs of a definitive break with the past but rather as symptoms of this haunting, of a past that remains unmastered and that bleeds into the present. In England, for instance, the Voluntary Euthanasia Society (formerly the Voluntary Euthanasia Legalisation Society) eliminated the word "euthanasia" from its name in 2006, after more than seventy years of existence, to become Dying with Dignity, so as to "get away from the suggestion that you can only achieve dignity in dying with euthanasia," according to the then chair of the association, John Wiles. In response, anti-legalization groups argued that the organization was simply hiding "euthanasia" behind the new euphemism of dignity.[31]

A similar terminological shift has shaped the history of right-to-die legislation in the United States. In the early 1990s, major right-to-die legalization efforts failed in California and Washington at least in part because they included provisions allowing death by injection, a practice that opponents were able to tie to Nazi killing.[32] "Simply put, introducing euthanasia into the political battles shifted the debate away from passive physician assistance (providing a prescription for a lethal amount of a drug) and concentrated on the feared aggressive physician assistance in hastening death," observes Howard Ball.[33]

Against this background, death with dignity fared better politically. In opinion polls, questions asking voters if they would "vote for or against a law allowing people to choose *euthanasia*" received significantly more negative responses than those concerning "a law allowing people to *die with dignity*."[34] Whereas the failed California and Washington initiatives had been called "Aid-in-Dying" initiatives, and as such had left room for confusion, the subsequent successful referendum in Oregon in 1994 was named the Death with Dignity Act.[35] The shift from "aid-in-dying" and "euthanasia" to "death with dignity" thus enabled the landmark legal event of the passage of the Oregon Death with Dignity Act.[36] As distinct from the non-prosecution policies that had been in place in the Netherlands and Switzerland, from laws that authorize the refusal or withdrawal of life-prolonging treatments, and from the doctrine of double effect permitting medical interventions that might hasten death as long as their primary intention is to alleviate pain, this law marked the first time anywhere (with the exception of an Australian Northern Territory law that was rescinded shortly after its implementation) that a law positively allowed physicians to provide medication to terminally ill patients with the explicit goal of ending a life, albeit under certain conditions.[37] The law can thus be said to have "reversed two thousand years of Western medical ethics and law," as the sociologists Daniel Hillyard and John Dombrink suggest.[38]

Indeed, leading up to the passage of the Oregon law and in the decades since, the notion of death with dignity has been effectively enshrined as the central principle for proponents of the right to die. In 1998, four years after the passage of the Oregon law, a Swiss lawyer, Ludwig Minelli, founded the controversial organization Dignitas, which benefited from a gray area in Swiss law (since formalized) to provide assistance in dying to those who meet its conditions. Major international right-to-die advocacy organizations have similarly placed dignity at the forefront of their missions: the Death with Dignity National Center in the United States, Dignity in Dying in Canada (the counterpart of the British organization with the same name), L'Association de Mourir dans la Dignité in France, Belgium, and Luxembourg, Derecho a Morir Dignamente in Spain, Foreningen Retten til en Verdig Dod in Sweden, the Japan Society for Dying with Dignity, Landsforeningen En Værdig Død in Denmark, La Fundación Pro Derecho a Morir Dignamente in Colombia, and others.

What Hillyard and Dombrink call "the death with dignity movement" (as distinct from earlier "voluntary euthanasia" and "right-to-die" movements) has thus had a material impact on law and social policy.[39] In the United States, laws modeled after Oregon's have been enacted to date in Washington (2008), Vermont (2013), California (2015), Colorado (2016), and the District of Columbia (2017).[40] In the Netherlands, a decades-old policy of non-prosecution was replaced by a formal law in 2002 regulating physician-assisted death. In the same year, Belgium legalized physician-assisted death, followed by Luxembourg. In Québec, after the establishment in 2009 of a "Special Commission on the Right to Die with Dignity," a law closely modeled on the Oregon law was enacted in 2014. Subsequently, the Canadian Supreme Court decided that any blanket prohibition on assisted suicide is unconstitutional, followed by the passage of legislation in June 2016 legalizing medically assisted death for the terminally ill.

And yet even as the concept of death with dignity has come to underwrite a new legitimacy for physician-assisted death, it remains notoriously unclear whether dignity is anything other than a mere "selling slogan" or marketing "catchphrase," as some critics charge.[41] In Oregon's Death with Dignity Act, in exemplary fashion, nowhere is "dignity" defined. Aside from the title of the statute, the term appears solely in adjectival form in the law's repeated (fifteen) references to "medication for the purpose of ending his or her life in a humane and dignified manner." But what is meant by a "dignified manner" remains entirely unspecified. Indeed, in the case of Oregon, one can notice precisely the same shift we saw in the meaning of euthanasia: dignity moves from describing a manner of death (however ambiguously) to the action taken to produce death, since these deaths are no longer recorded as physician-assisted suicides (as they were when the law first came into effect) but instead as "DWDA deaths" (Death with Dignity Act deaths).[42]

The ambiguity of the concept is further evidenced by its history. In its earliest uses, death with dignity refers exclusively to the right to refuse or discontinue life-prolonging treatments and not to active aid in dying. Thus in the Catholic physician John R. Cavanagh's influential 1963 article, "Bene Mori: The Right of the Patient to Die with Dignity," Cavanagh explicitly opposes "euthanasia," which he defines as "the employment of some direct means with the goal of shortening the life of the patient."[43] When the U.S. Senate held hearings in 1973 on "Death with Dignity," it was with Cavanagh's definition in mind: at issue was the right of patients to forgo treatment, not active medical assistance in dying. Similarly, the California Natural Death Act of 1976, which first legalized living wills (see chapter 1), invokes the concept of dignity—it derives the right to issue a living will from "the dignity and privacy which patients have a right to expect"—but stands explicitly against the forms of physician-assisted death that later would come to be represented by the notion of death with dignity. "Nothing in this chapter," the law reads, "shall be construed . . . to permit any affirmative or deliberate act or omission to end life other than to permit the natural process of dying as provided in this chapter."[44]

As death with dignity has come to mean, as in the Oregon law, direct physician aid in dying, those who once advocated death with dignity may therefore find themselves now opposed to what goes under that same term. It is hardly surprising, then, that the notion has come under suspicion from different sides of the debate. For instance, right-to-die activist and founder of the Hemlock Society Derek Humphry uses the term "dignity" extensively in his writings, but nonetheless is critical of its lack of specificity. " 'Death with Dignity' could mean an overdose of lethal drugs to one person, yet to another it could mean dying while thinking of Christ's suffering on the cross," he writes caustically.[45] Across the political divide, Leon Kass, an outspoken critic of physician-assisted death, complains that "dignity" has been co-opted to mean the hastening of death, whereas it might instead mean something like its opposite, living on despite suffering. "Death with dignity," he writes, "is not a matter of pulling plugs or taking poison."[46]

The legislative and political success of death with dignity might, then, seem to indicate an overcoming of the past. Yet the confusion that surrounds dignity, as Distelmans's trip to Auschwitz brings to the surface, indicates a continued haunting of the present by the past. To attend to this haunting, to take it seriously, requires, I suggest, a recasting of the question of the Nazi analogy. The Nazi analogy is not inaccurate due to material differences between past and present conditions, but instead because to judge the analogy according to any standard of accuracy assumes that the past and the present can be clearly distinguished, that the conditions of both can be adequately known and described. Yet to the extent that the present is haunted by the past, such claims are suspect. Instead, it would appear that death with dignity bears witness to an unmastered and persistently enigmatic event in the history of death.

The Claims of Dignity

If death with dignity remains bound to the legacy of euthanasia, this is because the determination of the dignity of any given death remains entangled with structures of social judgment and regulation. To speak of death with dignity, in other words, requires the designation not just of lives not worth living, but also of deaths not worth dying. To further specify this critique of death with dignity—that is, of the ways it reinscribes the category of *lebensunwertes Leben*—requires reflection on the nature of dignity itself, for it is this concept that lends political saliency to the notion of death with dignity. I consider here three interrelated factors that motivate efforts to argue for the right to die in terms of dignity: first, the power of dignity to ground legal, political, and moral claims for recognition, particularly within the framework of human rights; second, the prestige of human dignity as a moral concept; and third, the ethical force of dignity understood as a response to indignity, particularly as indignity is represented by the limit condition of Auschwitz.

Dignity becomes the basis for claims for recognition most prominently within the framework of human rights discourse. This is evidenced most dramatically in the Universal Declaration of Human Rights (UDHR) of 1948, whose preamble states that "recognition of the inherent dignity and of the equal and inalienable rights of all members of the human family is the foundation of freedom, justice, and peace in the world" and whose first article states that "all human beings are born free and equal in dignity and rights."[47] Dignity has also, of course, come to play a crucial role in constitutional law, not only in countries such as postwar Germany where dignity is enshrined as a central legal concept—Article One of the German Basic Law reads, "Human dignity shall be inviolable. To respect and protect it shall be the duty of all state authority"—but also in more nebulous but nonetheless effective ways in U.S. law.

It should be noted that the right to die has never been recognized as a human right within existing institutional frameworks of human rights law. Exemplarily, the "right to life" established in the UDHR as well as in the European Convention on Human Rights has to date not been found to include a corresponding right to die.[48] Notwithstanding this fact, the notion of death with dignity has come to ground claims for recognition of a right to die. This is apparent, for instance, when an organization such as Dignitas in Switzerland sees itself as "work[ing] for the worldwide implementation of 'the last human right.' "[49] We might also recall the case of Diane Pretty, discussed in chapter 1, whose appeal to the European Court of Human Rights, based in part on the claim that her dignity was violated by the British government's refusal to guarantee non-prosecution for her husband were he to assist in her death, allowed Pretty (albeit unsuccessfully) to challenge the jurisdiction of British courts in a higher court of law.

But claims framed in terms of dignity also face the complications that ensue from the structure of recognition to which dignity claims are subject. As Jeremy Waldron notes, such claims involve "the voluntary self-application of norms," in which claimants agree, more or less deliberately, to conform to expected models of comportment.[50] As Katherine Franke observes in a different context, dignity claims "come at a price" in that they require a "convincing portrayal of responsibility and respectability."[51] Thus the one who appeals for the right to assistance in suicide on the basis of a dignity claim must present herself before the law in a way that appears worthy and eligible for such consideration. The one who invokes dignity, then, enters into a necessary and decisive relationship with the authority that sets the terms according to which a dignity claim becomes recognizable, a procedure which necessarily enforces a boundary between what does and what does not qualify for such recognition.

Extrinsic Dignity

Dignity claims thus rely on the moral concept of human dignity, which additionally motivates the discourse of death with dignity and provides the terms by which an appellant qualifies for recognition. This is the case for both of the two primary conceptions of dignity that intersect, and at times compete, in the concept of human dignity. I refer here to the distinction between extrinsic and intrinsic dignity. The first of these understands dignity as a sign of "worthiness, worth, nobleness, excellence," in the words of the *Oxford English Dictionary*, that as such separates certain persons or deeds from others. It is this sense that underlies the term "dignitary," for instance. Intrinsic dignity, by contrast, names an inherent and universal property of the human being. This sense of dignity, which derives from Kant as well as certain religious discourses, does not distinguish some persons (or some modes of behavior) from others, but rather defines the essence and the commonality of the human as such.

In discussions of death with dignity, these two senses are often indiscriminately confused.[52] This is apparent, for instance, in the Ninth Circuit Federal Court of Appeals opinion in the case of *Compassion in Dying v. Washington*, which would eventually reach the Supreme Court as *Washington v Glucksberg*. In the following passage, both senses of dignity appear side by side:

> Like the decision of whether or not to have an abortion, the decision how and when to die is one of "the most intimate and personal choices a person may make in a lifetime," a choice "central to personal dignity and autonomy" [citing *Planned Parenthood v. Casey*]. A competent terminally ill adult, having lived nearly the full measure of his life, has a strong liberty interest in choosing a dignified and humane death rather than being reduced at the end of his existence to

a childlike state of helplessness, diapered, sedated, incontinent. How a person dies not only determines the nature of the final period of his existence, but in many cases, the enduring memories held by those who love him.[53]

In the first usage, where the court quotes *Casey*, dignity is linked to autonomy and appears as an inherently human potentiality. The person is assumed to possess dignity no matter what the conditions of his existence, such that the question for the law becomes how adequately to do justice to this dignity. Dignity in this sense is not dependent on *which* choice a person makes, but instead names the power to choose as such. In the second usage, however, when reference is made to "a dignified and humane death," dignity appears as an extrinsic quality, dependent upon the conditions in which one finds oneself and one's relation to those conditions. With respect to extrinsic dignity, the question arises, in other words, as to whether a manner of dying appears as dignified or undignified. According to this sense of dignity, then, it would appear that if someone were to choose to endure a "state of helplessness, diapered, sedated, incontinent," that person would not be said to possess dignity simply by virtue of having made an autonomous choice, but would instead appear undignified.

The normative dimension of dignity as a moral concept is most evident with respect to extrinsic dignity. We see this, for instance, when the Ninth Circuit opinion reports on a person who, "denied medical assistance, . . . ended his life by jumping from the West Seattle bridge and plummeting to his death." The legalization of death with dignity, the court argues, would save such a patient from being "forced to resort to gruesome alternatives because of the unavailability of physician assistance." Death with dignity is thus understood here to involve dying in a socially sanctioned manner that avoids any suggestion of violence or desperation—that avoids "gruesome," or, we might say, undignified alternatives. This sense of dignity, in fact, is already at issue in Cavanagh's 1963 article, which associates dignity with an image of death reminiscent of the traditional death as described by Ariès. Recalling the "placid look of sleep" on the face of a nun who had just died and the community of nuns and nurses chanting prayers by the bedside, Cavanagh speaks of "the dignity—the beauty—of this deathbed scene." The image of the deceased surrounded by an admiring community as well as the figure of death-as-sleep identify dignity with a thoroughly conventional image of a beautiful death. This traditional image has also come to underwrite the demand for physician-assisted death. The court thus speaks of the need "to *restore* humanity and dignity to the process by which Americans die" and locates the image of this humane and dignified process in the past: "Most Americans used to die at home, in the comfort of familiar surroundings, with their loved ones around them." Dignity in these cases is therefore associated with specific methods and scenes of death, with a certain *style* of dying.

Intrinsic Dignity

In contrast to extrinsically dignified death, the first mention of dignity in the passage cited above from the Ninth Circuit opinion ("personal dignity") introduces what appears to be a radically different and newer conception of dignity in associating it with autonomy. What would make a death dignified in this sense is not its beauty or placidity, not its style, but rather the quality of the decision that brings it about. A more developed version of this notion of death with dignity appears in the amicus curiae brief submitted by a group of American philosophers led by Ronald Dworkin when *Compassion in Dying v. Washington* (as *Washington v. Glucksberg*) reached the U.S. Supreme Court. Employing a nested citation—citing, that is, the Ninth Circuit's citation of *Casey*—they write: "Each individual has a right to make the 'most intimate and personal choices central to personal dignity and autonomy.' That right encompasses the right to exercise some control over the time and manner of one's death."[54] As dignity and autonomy become linked, the dignity of a death resides in the "control" exercised by the one who dies rather than in any particular style of dying.

The court's and the philosophers' association of dignity and autonomy, it should be noted, introduces an additional source of ambiguity. For in one sense, autonomy, and with it "personal dignity," might require simply the exercise of unqualified individual choice, as in the autonomy argument discussed in chapter 1. In another sense, however, the association of dignity and autonomy invokes a Kantian framework in which choice is understood to be free or autonomous only to the extent that it also frees itself from self-interest, that is, to the extent that it is understood as rational and universalizable. A decision is autonomous, in this light, not simply because it is made without coercion, but because it coincides with the choice that any rational being would make. It is this logic that connects autonomy (the "autonomy of reason" rather than merely individual autonomy) and dignity in Kant's thought. For it is precisely because the rational being can act according to generalizable laws, laws that derive not from external coercion but from "freedom of the will," that the human can be said to possess an "inner dignity [*Würde*]" that is "raised above all price."[55] In mainstream bioethics as well as in law, the Kantian conception of intrinsic dignity has thus become a central concept, since according to this conception of human dignity the notion of a human life not worth living would be inconceivable, a contradiction in terms.

But this notion of dignity notoriously runs into problems when associated with assisted suicide, since it is on the basis of this analysis of human dignity that Kant finds suicide morally impermissible, even if it is meant to avoid suffering. This impermissibility stems from what Kant argues is the contradictory nature of suicide. To commit suicide so as to avoid pain would mean "to destroy life itself by means of the same feeling whose destination is to impel towards the furtherance of life."[56] In Kant's *Lectures on Ethics*, suicide appears as "contrary to the supreme self-regarding duty," and as such, like other infractions against self-regarding duties, it "dishonor[s] the dignity of humanity in one's person."[57] As Michael Rosen observes, Kant's secular philosophy here bears the traces of a theological conception of humanity; the individual appears as the steward of humanity in himself rather than as the owner of his self.[58]

Kant's insistence on the incompatibility of dignity and suicide requires finding a rationale for the right to die through a different concept in his thought. In his *Lectures on Ethics*, in fact, Kant posits a situation in which self-destruction would be consistent with human dignity. "If a man can preserve his life no otherwise than by dishonouring his humanity, he ought rather to sacrifice it [*sein Leben aufzuopfern*]. . . . What matters is, that so long as he lives, he should live honourably and not dishonour the dignity of humanity. If he can now no longer live in that fashion, he cannot live at all; his moral life is at an end. But moral life is at an end if it no longer accords with the dignity of humanity."[59] Whereas "suicide" (*Selbstmord*) violates dignity, what Kant calls "sacrifice," which he seeks to distinguish from suicide, preserves the dignity of the human.[60] One could say, in fact, that it is precisely at the moment when disgrace is at hand that something essential about dignity is revealed, that dignity faces its ultimate proof.

But if this is the case, then it also becomes clear that the concept of human dignity requires that the one who seeks to honor that dignity be able to imagine its demise, such that the image of the end of dignity becomes the very foundation of dignity itself. To act according to the demands of human dignity, in other words, the human must be able to conceive of what seemed to be inconceivable, namely a human without dignity. Thus not only extrinsic dignity but intrinsic dignity as well defines itself in relation to what is perceived as the violation of dignity. It must posit a distinction between a life worth living and a life not worth living.

In current efforts to legalize and regulate death with dignity, this distinction encodes itself in the eligibility criteria inscribed in death with dignity laws. Restriction of the right to petition for death with dignity to those with a terminal disease expected to result in death in less than six months (in all U.S. laws), or the incurably ill experiencing constant and unbearable physical or mental suffering (in Canada, Belgium, the Netherlands, and Luxembourg) creates a distinct class of persons. If the state does not thereby independently declare and impose a judgment that these lives are not worth living, it nonetheless requires that the one who seeks the right to die declare her life no longer worth living, that she declare herself better off dead.

The Opposite of Indignity

It is with respect to this dependence of what the UDHR calls "inherent dignity" on the image of the end of dignity that the historic role of the Shoah in motivating and underwriting the politics of dignity comes into view. With several notable exceptions, dignity only begins to enter legal discourse, and particularly constitutional law, in the early twentieth century, when it appears in the constitutions of several countries in Europe and the Americas. But it is only after the Second World War that dignity becomes a prominent and decisive concept.[61] Perhaps most decisively, the UDHR, adopted in 1948, justifies the recognition of dignity as a response to the catastrophe of the Shoah, which is evoked in the second clause of the preamble: "Whereas disregard and contempt for human rights have resulted in barbarous acts which have outraged the conscience of mankind. . . ." In the UDHR, in other words, the recognition of dignity constitutes an immediate and necessary response to Nazi crimes and as such aims to serve as a mode of protection against the recurrence of such crimes.[62] Moreover, even as the central role of dignity in the UDHR is owed in part to dignity's historic moral prestige, at the same time its positive connotations remain essentially, and purposefully, ambiguous in the UDHR and related contexts. Indeed, this purposeful ambiguity belonged to a deliberate strategy that allowed stakeholders with discrepant ideologies to reach an accord. As Jacques Maritain writes, commenting on the process of drafting the Declaration, "we agree on these rights, providing we are not asked why. With the 'why,' the dispute begins."[63] Consequently, the primary significance of dignity in human rights and related legal contexts derives not from its positive content but from its negative determination. As one German legal textbook states: "Ironically, we do not know what human dignity is, but we know exactly whether human dignity is violated or not."[64]

Even as human rights law attempts to imagine a world that respects dignity—that is, a world that recognizes the inherent dignity of the human and that rejects the notion of a life without dignity—it therefore requires constant reference to Auschwitz to the extent that Auschwitz defines the limit, and therefore the very meaning, of the violation of dignity. Auschwitz in turn comes to stand for the life not worth living, life without dignity. This negative determination of dignity in constitutional and human rights law persists in the discourse of death with dignity. As has frequently been noted, it is on the basis less of a positive claim to dignity than of the fear of indignity that the death with dignity movement has often advanced. "Those who invoke dignity in favour of assisted suicide," writes David Albert Jones, "typically characterize a life of dependence and disability as undignified: if the person in this state does not have access to assistance in suicide, then he or she is forced to endure the indignity of what is considered a subhuman condition of life."[65] Hillyard and Dombrink similarly demonstrate that the success of the death with dignity movement has hinged on reframing assisted suicide as what they call the "new good death," where what qualifies this death as good is primarily its opposition to what they variously call, echoing general discourse around the right to die, "the bad death" or a "fate worse than death."[66] To die with dignity, to die so as to avert a subhuman condition, is to die, then, as a witness, wittingly or unwittingly, to a history of catastrophe.

II. Worse Than Death

For Distelmans, death with dignity is the "opposite of Auschwitz" because it represents an exercise of freedom ("He wanted his colleagues to understand his definition of freedom") as opposed to—and, we can now say, defined by—the radical unfreedom represented by Auschwitz. Yet dignity, as the above discussion indicates, marks a site where freedom necessarily, if often imperceptibly, converges with duty. When a rights claim is framed in terms of dignity, when dignity is deployed as a moral concept in either its extrinsic or intrinsic sense, and when dignity is defined with respect to indignity, the one who demands the right to die with dignity inevitably posits her death not simply as possible but also as purposeful and necessary.

Death with dignity is thus subject to a double bind. It seeks to overcome a history in which death was figured as duty for those whose lives were deemed to have negative value and not worth living. It seeks to create the possibility of a legally and socially sanctioned death, a recognized right to die, that would not be informed by the interests or calculations of medico-legal authority but that would wholly respect the dignity of the person—a death that would not be under the shadow of the history of "euthanasia." Yet it overcomes this history only by creating a new obligation: to pursue a death with dignity only so as to prevent falling into an existence not worth living or dying a death not worth dying. It requires that one die not simply *with* but *for the sake of* dignity. Understood as the paradigmatic site of death without dignity and freedom, Auschwitz thus comes to serve as the foundation for the ethical stature of death with dignity. To die with dignity as the opposite of Auschwitz means, in this light, to die so as to salvage an image of humanity from the ruins of Auschwitz, to die so as to assert that Auschwitz is safely in the past. But this comes at a cost, in that the death that seeks to free itself from the past of Auschwitz remains necessarily bound up with it.

What, then, does it mean to relate a decision to die in the present to Holocaust death? In the normative version represented by Distelmans, Auschwitz stands for unfreedom and indignity. But a closer reflection on Holocaust death and its aftermath suggests a different future for death with dignity, a different way in which the Shoah reverberates in the post-Shoah history of death. To explore this question, I turn to a constellation of texts and questions linked to the writing of the Auschwitz survivor Jean Améry, born Hans Meier (or Meyer) in Austria in 1912.[67] In a series of five essays published in 1976 under the title *Hand an sich legen* (literally, *To Lay Hands on Oneself*, but published in English as *On Suicide*), with the subtitle *Diskurs über den Freitod* (*A Discourse on Voluntary Death*), Améry makes a radical case for the "freedom to choose a voluntary death" as "an inalienable human right."[68] Améry does not limit this right to the terminally ill or to those otherwise deemed qualified by a legal or social mechanism of regulation; the book is not, as translator John Barlow notes, "a brief for assisted suicide."[69] Rather than a systematic argument or philosophy, rather than striving to "convince," Améry suggests that his work be considered "testimony," particularly as it insists on a necessary if vexing connection between his experience as a victim and survivor of Nazi violence and his decision to take his own life—a decision that he made in 1974, only to find, emerging from a state of unconsciousness after thirty hours, that he had been hospitalized and revived against his will.[70] Two years after the publication of *Hand an sich legen*, he would succeed in carrying out his plan. Améry's testimony to history, and the consequences he draws from it, opens onto a compelling reconceptualization of the significance of death with dignity in and after Auschwitz.

Whereas the discourse of death with dignity in its normative legal and political forms seeks to make the decision to die comprehensible and "respectable" by contrast with the indignity of Holocaust death, at the heart of Améry's reflection is the suggestion that the experience of voluntary death is linked to the Shoah in ways that both install and expose a permanent and nonnegotiable breach at the heart of the social relation. Auschwitz does not make the decision to die intelligible, but exposes its radical unintelligibility. This, however, does not mean that death is no longer dignified; instead, Améry's writing calls for a reconceptualization of dignity. This is signaled, in the late work *Hand an sich legen*, by his decision to supplement the German *Würde* with the Latinate *Dignität*, a term that estranges the concept of dignity and opens it to a different history. But, as with the barely theorized doubling of *Würde* and *Dignität*, the force and significance of Améry's thought is often contained in what appear to be small details in his writing—details that, as we will see, carry immense weight. It is also the case, as Améry's biographer remarks, that his thought and testimony often inform discourse on Auschwitz and its aftermath in ways that are often unmarked by others.[71] In order to appreciate the relationship of death and *Dignität*—in order to grasp how Améry's thought, as well as his own death, might open a different future for death with dignity after Auschwitz—it will therefore be necessary to set his testimony in relief by considering it in light of both the historical record and the thinking of death in and after Auschwitz by a number of key figures whose writing responds directly or indirectly to Améry, including Theodor Adorno, Hannah Arendt, and Giorgio Agamben.

"Body = Pain = Death"

Améry's testimony to his experience as a victim and survivor of Nazi violence is marked by two moments of radical rupture, the first associated with being tortured in an SS prison in Belgium after being arrested for Resistance activities, and the second with internment as a Jew in the Nazi camps: in Auschwitz-Monowitz from January 1944 until the evacuation of the camp a year later and, after a forced march, in Dora-Mittelbau and Bergen-Belsen, which was liberated by the British army in April 1945. His 1965 essay on

"Torture" was first published in the journal *Merkur* and was broadcast on German radio before its publication a year later in *Jenseits von Schuld und Sühne: Bewältigungsversuche eines Überwältigten*. (The English-language translation instead adopts the title of the first essay in the collection as the title for the entire book, *At the Mind's Limits*.) In this essay, Améry testifies to a radical rupture in his sense of the world, which means also in the human relationship to death. Indeed, what first registers the radical significance of this rupture is the inadequacy of the notion of "human dignity":

> Not much is said when someone who has never been beaten makes the ethical and pathetic statement that upon the first blow the prisoner loses his human dignity. I must confess that I don't know exactly what that is: human dignity [*Menschenwürde*]. One person thinks he loses it when he finds himself in circumstances that make it impossible for him to take a daily bath. Another believes he loses it when he must speak to an official in something other than his native language. In one instance human dignity is bound to a certain physical convenience, in the other to the right of free speech, in still another perhaps to the availability of erotic partners of the same sex. I don't know if the person who is beaten by the police loses human dignity. Yet I am certain that with the very first blow that descends on him he loses something we will perhaps temporarily call "trust in the world."[72]

Under the violence of torture, which inaugurates the history of violence that continues in Améry's deportation to Auschwitz, the conventional sense of human dignity, *die Menschenwürde*, suffers irreparable damage. Dignity, in this light, cannot be anchored to the catastrophic history of torture and of Auschwitz, for these events invalidate human dignity as a moral category. Améry's examples encompass both extrinsic dignity, associated with dignified behavior and appearance, and intrinsic dignity, associated with autonomy. But torture opens a new era for the victim in which neither conception of dignity is valid. The discourse of human dignity, Améry explains, is part of a world in which one can take for granted that "by reason of written or unwritten social contracts the other person will spare me." But the event of torture upends the expectation of eventual aid, of any sort of social contract. Even under a retributive system such as "an eye for an eye, a tooth for a tooth," Améry notes, "you can regulate your life according to that."[73] But torture precludes regulation. If the framework of dignity is thereby invalidated, this is because torture destroys any confidence that the other will respond to one's humanity; it is the demise of any hope for recognition. Thus the collapse of trust in the world, he insists at the end of the essay, is irrevocable; it "cannot be regained."[74] When Améry later seeks to articulate the relationship between dignity and the right to die, he will do so, then, on entirely new grounds, drawing on a sense of dignity scarred by its exposure to the event of torture, and, as mentioned above, proposing even a new word to name "dignity." Correlatively, to grasp the significance of death with dignity as Améry understands it, we will need first to probe the nature and consequences of the survivor's exposure to torture, an exposure that continues and is amplified for Améry in his internment in Auschwitz.

We might recall Améry's account of the impact of pain here. For as torture denies the possibility of being recognized and receiving a response from the other, it also resists communication by its victim:

> It would be totally senseless to try and describe here the pain that was inflicted on me. Was it "like a red-hot iron in my shoulders," and was another "like a dull wooden stake that had been driven into the back of my head"? One comparison would only stand for the other, and in the end we would be hoaxed by turn on the hopeless merry-go-round of figurative speech. The pain was what it was. Beyond that there is nothing to say. Qualities of feeling are as incomparable as they are indescribable. They mark the limit of the capacity of language to communicate. If someone wanted to impart his physical pain, he would be forced to inflict it and thereby become a torturer himself.[75]

The pain of torture, then, invalidates conventional modes of linguistic communication just as it invalidated conventional moral categories. It forces the survivor to enter into a logical contradiction.

Indeed, it is in this sense that the pain of torture can be understood as marking not only a radical loss of trust in the world, not only a radical vulnerability of the body, but also a new relationship to death:

> It is tempting to speculate further. Pain, we said, is the most extreme intensification imaginable of our bodily being. But maybe it is even more, that is: death. No road that can be travelled by logic leads us to death, but perhaps the thought is permissible that through pain a path of feeling and premonition can be paved to it for us. In the end, we would be faced with the equation: Body = Pain = Death, and in our case this could be reduced to the hypothesis that torture, through which we are turned into body by the other, blots out the contradiction of death and allows us to experience it personally. But this is an evasion of the question. We have for it only the excuse of our own experience and must add in explanation that torture has an indelible character. Whoever was tortured, stays tortured.[76]

The mathematical equation ventured by Améry refuses what would be a more expected framing of torture as a near-death or death-like experience. Instead, he insists that he speaks in and through the logical impossibility of his statement, but that this speaking is authorized by the experience he has undergone. Torture, it would therefore seem, requires a mode of testimony that cannot be framed according to referential or logical conventions. It not only allows but requires him to say the impossible, to say that he experienced death, even while acknowledging the unintelligibility of this very statement. Rather than verify an abstract, absolute truth, the mathematical form of Améry's speculation (his equals signs) indexes linguistic failure while at the same time transmitting the experience of pain in a different way. Indeed, it would appear that just as torture consists in subjection not only to pain but also to the radical rupture of the possibility of recognition and communication with the torturer, so Améry's text transmits this experience of incommunicability, exposing its reader to what cannot be said or experienced. "These are pages," writes Primo Levi with respect to Améry's writing, "that we read with an almost physical pain."[77]

Torture, then, cannot be confined to the past not simply due to physical scars or because it burns itself into the memory of the survivor, but because it permanently alters his ability to communicate with others; it produces what Shoshana Felman and Dori Laub call "a crisis of witnessing."[78] For Améry, this extends into the aftermath, leaving him with the ongoing sense of "a foreignness in the world that cannot be compensated by any sort of subsequent communication." What survival comes to mean, then, is not the recovery of a sense of dignity and security. Instead, he remains a "defenseless prisoner of fear."[79]

Fearing Worse Than Death

The event of torture echoes through Améry's account of the camp as the site of a permanent exposure to fear, to a fear that, like the experience of pain, radically exposes him to death—or, more precisely, to dying. As noted in the introduction, Auschwitz for Améry marks the "total collapse of the *aesthetic* view of death," that is, the demise of the philosophical and Romantic image of beautiful death discussed in chapter 2. In Améry's memorable formulation, "No bridge led from death in Auschwitz to *Death in Venice*."[80] But Améry goes on to radicalize this thought, suggesting that linked to the demise of dignity and of the beautiful death is the more essential demise of the ability to think of death at all, to think of "death" (*Tod*) as opposed to "dying" (*Sterben*):

> For all that, if one is free it is possible to entertain thoughts of death that at the same time are not also thoughts of dying, fears of dying. Death in freedom, at least in principle, can be intellectually detached from dying: socially, by infusing it with thoughts of the family that remains behind, of the profession one leaves, and mentally, through the effort, while still being, to feel a whiff of Nothingness. It goes without saying that such an attempt leads nowhere, that death's

contradiction cannot be resolved. Still, the effort contains its own intrinsic dignity: the free person can assume a certain spiritual posture toward death, because for him death (*Tod*) is not totally absorbed into the torment of dying (*Sterben*). The free person can venture to the outmost limit of thought, because within him there is still a space, however tiny, that is without fear.[81]

Under the pressure of a totalizing, permeating fear that leaves no space for detachment, the very thought of death becomes impossible, along with the dignity that served as the condition of possibility for the thought. Fear negates dignity, exposing it as something that depends on external conditions, on a freedom that torture and the camp deny their victim—and, Améry insists, their survivor, who remains the permanent "prisoner of fear."

What does this experience of fear, and the consequent crisis in the thought of death—this ongoing exposure to dying—mean to Améry's readers, to a post-Auschwitz world? In a 1965 lecture delivered at the time he was writing *Negative Dialectics*, Theodor Adorno spoke as one such reader. "Today," states Adorno, "something worse than death is to be feared. Perhaps I might draw your attention in this context to an essay on torture by Jean Améry, an author otherwise unknown to me, in the latest issue of *Merkur*."[82] Adorno does not seem to have been aware of Améry's essay on Auschwitz, which had been broadcast on German radio and published in the Zürich *Weltwoche* the previous year.[83] But his reading of the torture essay, as this develops into a commentary on the consequences of Auschwitz, converges with and illuminates Améry's testimony.[84]

Whereas Améry, perhaps strategically, frames his reflections as intensely personal, as registering the impact of Auschwitz on the survivor, Adorno radicalizes the scope of survival.[85] "In other words," he tells his audience, "it might be said that in view of what we have experienced—and let me say that it is also experienced by those on whom it was not directly perpetrated—there can be no one . . . for whom the world *after* Auschwitz, that is, the world in which Auschwitz was possible, is the same as it was before."[86] Auschwitz thus marks an event in the history of death, and in the history of dignity, that disrupts the conventional significance of these terms not only for the direct victim. It introduces and exposes history to a new kind, even a new era, of fear.

Consider the form this thought takes in *Negative Dialectics*. "In the camps," Adorno writes, this time with no mention of Améry, "death has a novel horror: since Auschwitz, fearing death means fearing worse than death."[87] This formula clarifies the notion that fearing death and fearing the worse than death are not simply two alternatives; one does not now fear the worse than death instead of fearing death. Instead, it redefines, as it were, what the fundamental fear of death might mean—indeed, what fear might mean. For if fear is related, at its limit, to self-preservation, if at its limit fear is the fear of death—as Améry writes elsewhere, "every fear actually goes back to the fear of death"—then fear now transgresses its own limit, or rather, the one who fears is exposed to something beyond the limit of fear.[88] Fear itself, in other words, becomes something worse than fear, in that it does not come to an end with death, but instead survives and exceeds death. Auschwitz thus opens a chasm in the history of death in which the worse than death extends limitlessly into the future, always threatening, according to the asymptotic logic of the "worse," a worse than the worse, and a worse than that.[89] Where fear before Auschwitz acquires meaning with respect to death—to a thought of death that, in Améry's view, requires at least a "tiny space" without fear— fear after Auschwitz is no longer limited by death, but instead by Auschwitz: every fear after Auschwitz, to adopt Améry's phrasing, goes back to the fear of Auschwitz. But the fear of Auschwitz, in turn, is not a fear that comes to a halt with death. It is a vertiginous fear, one that leaves no space, however tiny, untouched.

Death beyond Measure

If the category of human dignity is first invalidated by the event of torture, it is further displaced by the identification of Auschwitz with the "worse than death." This is because the vertiginous fear to which Auschwitz exposes both its victims and survivors, to which it exposes history after Auschwitz, cannot, it would seem, provide a stable ground for an image of death with dignity. Indeed, the corollary of the evacuation of death as the limit of fear, of the advent of a fear without limit, is that death becomes the property of the perpetrator, of the "Master-of-Death from Germany" as Améry writes, alluding to Paul Celan's "Todesfuge."[90] Contrasting the death faced by soldiers in wartime to that of the camp inmate, Améry writes: "The soldier was driven into the fire, and it is true that his life was not worth much. Still the state did not order him to die, but to survive. The final duty of the prisoner, however, was death."[91] This statement sardonically summarizes the duty of the prisoner from the perspective of authority. But the relationship between the authority that condemns the inmate to death and the inmate is not reciprocal. As Jean-François Lyotard observes: "The SS does not have to legitimate for the deportee's benefit the death sentence it apprises him or her of. The deportee does not have to feel obligated by this decree."[92]

But if death can no longer be contemplated in the abstract, if one can no longer "assume a certain spiritual posture" towards death, the question then arises of how one might be able to consider any death, in or after Auschwitz, to be voluntary or "free" (*Freitod*). Améry's remarks on the question of suicide in the camps provide preliminary orientation in addressing this question:

> One was hardly concerned with whether, or that, one had to die, but only with how it would happen. Inmates carried on conversations

about how long it probably takes for the gas in the gas chambers to do its job. One speculated on the painfulness of death by phenol injections. Were you to wish yourself a blow to the skull or a slow death through exhaustion in the infirmary? It was characteristic for the situation of the prisoner in regard to death that only a few decided to "run to the wire," as one said, that is, to commit suicide [*Selbstmord begehen*] through contact with the highly electrified barbed wire. The wire was after all a good and rather certain thing, but it was possible that in the attempt to approach it one would be caught first and thrown into the bunker, and that led to a more difficult and painful dying. Dying [*Sterben*] was omnipresent, death [*Tod*] vanished from sight.[93]

It is telling that Améry refers here to *Selbstmord* and not to *Freitod*. But his testimony as to the omnipresence of dying also raises the question of whether one can even speak of *Selbstmord*, of *self*-killing, in Auschwitz. Can one for whom death is no longer in the future but who is already absorbed by dying, who is subjected to this dying by the law of the camp, be said to commit suicide? In order to grasp the significance of Améry's rethinking of death with dignity after Auschwitz, we will therefore first need to confront the difficult conceptual as well as historical question of suicide in the concentration and death camps, which I consider here through discussion of explicit studies of camp suicide, historical writings and testimony, and reflections on Holocaust death by Arendt and Agamben.

The problems raised by the attempt to understand suicide in the camps are evident in what may be the first study of this question. The French psychopathologist Paul Citrome recognizes in 1952 that to analyze suicide "as a behavior of *concentrationary man living the concentrationary experience*," he must do so "without any preconceived system concerning general conceptions of suicide."[94] To a certain extent, Citrome's effort to confront the enigma of camp suicide without preconceptions falls short. For instance, despite his observation that "testimonies are often contradictory," he nonetheless frames his inquiry with respect to a statistical claim that "suicide seems to have been relatively rare in the camps," as well as to the assumption that the conditions of the camps "should have been particularly generative of suicides."[95] This claim, frequently echoed and rarely questioned, is necessarily tenuous.[96] This is in part due to the sources of the data, drawn from either survivor testimony or Nazi records. In the case of the former, statistical claims by survivors would seem particularly hampered by the fact that "in the inhuman conditions to which they were subjected, the prisoners could barely acquire an overall vision of their universe," as Primo Levi writes; it is telling that when Levi himself mentions the rarity of suicides in the camps, he cites the findings of the "historians of the Lager."[97] Nazi records, for their part, are not only incomplete but inherently biased.[98] Prisoners who decided to die by approaching the electrified fences surrounding Auschwitz-Birkenau, for instance, were commonly recorded as "shot while attempting to escape," not as suicides, while the murders of certain prisoners may have been recorded as suicides.[99] Moreover, prisoners could commit suicide in ways that might not have been immediately recognizable, for instance, by performing deeds that would result in certain death, such as crossing SS guard lines.[100] It has therefore also been claimed that the incidence of suicide was high and even more frequent than "in the outside world."[101] Aside from the problems raised by the quality of the evidence, claims concerning the relative frequency of suicide in the camps face an inherent constraint in that they assume a "normal" suicide rate as a point of comparison. Even if such a norm could be established for the world outside the camps, the question would have to be posed about the validity of any comparison between that hypothetical norm and the *univers concentrationnaire*.[102]

Citrome's attempt to interpret his finding, however, seems to force a confrontation with something more enigmatic than social-scientific methods can explain. Could it be, he asks, that the seemingly low suicide rate is due to the same sociological or psychological factors that had previously been understood to account for decreased suicide rates during wartime? "Some of these explanations remain valid for the concentrationary situation: stronger integration of the individual in the collective that is undergoing a common catastrophe, simplification of the social structure, extreme constriction of vital energy under the pressure of a permanent threat to life, liberation and discharge of the most antisocial aggressive and sado-masochistic tendencies, reversal of traditional values, devaluation of death in general and of suicide in particular." Yet these established explanations, he goes on to remark, are only superficially valid. "But behind these conditions, which are too general, too schematic, and too external, it is necessary to investigate the particular, specific situation of life in the concentration camps."[103] Although the explanations Citrome lists here can be amended and challenged, his underlying point remains valid. What is identified as suicide in the camps does not conform to the expectations of psychological or sociological research, which frame suicide as a symptom determined by diagnosable social or psychological conditions.

What astonishes Citrome, then, is that something that ought to have happened did not happen, or more precisely, did not happen in a recognizable way. In a further attempt to account for the enigma of camp suicide, then, he departs from his disciplinary grounding in psychology and sociology and takes recourse instead to the vocabulary of philosophy: "If suicide is an essentially *human* act . . . and to the extent that it is an act of *freedom* par excellence, as certain philosophers contend, then it is not surprising that it decreases in the concentrationary universe, negator of man and destroyer of liberty."[104] As Citrome moves from viewing camp suicide as a determined, symptomatic behavior to understanding it as an act of freedom, what he continues to refer to as suicide might more accurately, in the philosophical tradition to which he alludes, be aligned with what Kant called sacrifice. The question of suicide in the camps, in this view, might more accurately be rephrased as the question of death with dignity in the camps, since, anticipating Distelmans, Citrome characterizes the camp as essentially the space of unfreedom, with suicide in turn appearing as a form of liberation.

At stake in Citrome's inquiry, then, is no longer simply the question of what particular conditions may have led an individual to react by committing suicide, but rather the question of what suicide in the camps means for the image of the human as such, for the very possibility of performing what he calls an "essentially human act," or, to use Kant's terms, for the possibility of a voluntary death that honors human dignity. Thus in the closing lines of his inquiry, Citrome invokes the words of Gabriel Deshaies's *Psychologie du suicide* (1947): "When the day comes that man no longer commits suicide, on that day man will no longer be human: he will be superhuman, or more probably, subhuman." If suicide appears to Citrome to have been "relatively rare" in the camps, this is not because prisoners did not have good reason to kill themselves and chose not to do so, but because the very conditions for committing suicide as an act of freedom, for dying with dignity, had vanished. In a world divided into the superhuman (who does not have to legitimate the death sentence he issues) and the subhuman (who is excepted even from the capacity to be under obligation), in a world devoid of humanity, suicide ceases to exist. The day feared by Deshaies, in other words, had already arrived. To contest the notion that suicide was rare in the camps, accordingly, is not simply to claim that it was frequent. It is to call attention to the insufficiency of the framework in which such a claim must be made. One cannot simply say that suicide was rare in the camps because, more radically, suicide in the camps becomes unrecognizable.

Hannah Arendt's "We Refugees"

In fact, this radical challenge to the recognizability of suicide is attested to already with respect to suicides that took place prior to deportation to the camps, as Hannah Arendt notices in her essay of January 1943, "We Refugees." Where Citrome confronts the inadequacy of sociological and psychological understandings of suicide, Arendt declares the inadequacy of precisely the sort of philosophical interpretation to which Citrome resorts.

In this essay, Arendt takes the frequent suicides of European Jews prior to deportation as her point of departure.[105] Before turning to the specific and novel meaning of these deaths, she tests a more traditional frame of philosophical explication similar to the one invoked by Citrome: "Perhaps the philosophers are right who teach that suicide is the last and supreme guarantee of human freedom: not being free to create our lives in the world in which we live, we nevertheless are free to throw life away and to leave the world."[106]

But the exercise of this "negative liberty," even if it does not constitute an act of "defiance at life and the world" or an attempt to "kill . . . the whole universe," still implies a commitment to something higher than life—here, freedom—which, when denied, can only be expressed by suicide.[107] Suicide becomes justified in this view, which recalls Kant's ethics, when it serves as a last resort in the event of a threatened deprivation of the conditions for maintaining human dignity. "The man who kills himself asserts that life is not worth living and the world not worth sheltering him," Arendt writes, again invoking the notion of *lebensunwertes Leben.*[108] If Nazi ideology hinges upon the categorization of lives into those deemed worth and not worth living, into those whose dignity is recognized and those whose dignity is eviscerated, then to act autonomously, to assume the place of the legislator, is precisely to decide for oneself when life is or is not worth living.

But this philosophically sanctioned view of suicide, Arendt intimates, was already under siege in 1943: "Brought up in the conviction that life is the highest good and death the greatest dismay, we became witnesses and victims of worse terrors than death—without having been able to discover a higher ideal than life."[109] Anticipating Adorno's claim with respect to Auschwitz at a time when only fragmentary reports of the methods and magnitude of the "final solution" had reached public awareness, Arendt registers the advent of the worse than death and suggests that this new terror transforms what it means to take one's own life. "Unlike other suicides, our friends leave no explanations of their deed, no indictment, no charge against the world. . . . Letters left by them are conventional, meaningless documents. . . . Nobody cares about motives, they seem to be clear to all of us."[110] If the dignified self-sacrifice imagined by Kant is performed in the name of humanity and testifies to freedom and autonomy, if it accuses the world of failing to shelter, to provide the conditions of possibility for, human dignity, these deaths by contrast fail to proclaim their resistance. The traditional philosophical image of suicide and the conventional framework for its interpretation no longer seem adequate.

Indeed, however much Arendt may declare that their motives "seem clear to all of us," the history to which she testifies is one where the very meaning of suicide as an act of freedom—or more precisely, as an act of resistance to its deprivation—is called into question. Thus, for instance, speaking of Shmul Zygielbojm, the representative of the Bund to the Polish government in exile in London, Jan Karski observes: "His suicide, which was to have been a dramatic cry of protest, did not affect the fate of the Polish Jews in any way."[111] An exchange of letters between Mahatma Gandhi and Martin Buber following the events of Kristallnacht in November 1938 similarly registers a newly perceived futility of protest suicide. When Gandhi recommended that the German Jews commit to nonviolent protest even at the price of "the general massacre of the Jews," Buber responded that such an act would remain utterly pointless since it would be only "testimony without acknowledgment, ineffective, unobserved martyrdom" and so would not be meaningful as an act of protest.[112] Arendt herself reports that when interned at Gurs, fellow prisoners proposed to commit mass suicide as "a collective action, apparently some kind of protest to vex the French." But the idea was abandoned when she and others pointed out that "we had been shipped there *'pour crêver'* in any case."[113] Nazi response to a Jewish suicide as early as 1933 seems to confirm Arendt's point. In response to the suicide of Fritz Rosenfelder, a Jew from Bad Cannstatt, Germany, in 1933—a suicide committed, according to Rosenfelder's suicide note "to shock my Christian friends into awareness"—a Nazi publication stated that "we are pleased with him and have no objection if his racial brethren adopt the same method of taking leave."[114]

When the possibility of resistance through suicide, or, otherwise put, the possibility of self-sacrifice, collapses, suicide becomes something that would erase the possibility of registering the historical event at all. It is in this profound sense that such suicides could be said to produce "meaning-less documents." An act that might be committed out of the desire to escape imminent catastrophe, to avert the demise of dignity, would end up only confirming and redoubling that catastrophe: not only would the catastrophe have occurred, but there would be no one remaining to testify.[115]

The End of Suicide

Arendt's 1943 discussion of suicide prior to deportation resonates in a later reference in her writings to suicide in the camps themselves. Along with Citrome and others, she reflects in her 1951 *The Origins of Totalitarianism* on what she takes to be the "astonishing rarity of suicides in the camps."[116] This reference occurs in a footnote to the following analysis of the structure of "total domination" in the concentration and extermination camps:

> For to destroy individuality is to destroy spontaneity, man's power to begin something new out of his own resources, something that cannot be explained on the basis of reactions to environments and events. Nothing then remains but ghastly marionettes with human faces.[117]

In the footnote to this passage, Arendt suggests that the rarity of camp suicides "is of course partly explained by the fact that every attempt was made to prevent suicides which are, after all, spontaneous acts."[118] Although Arendt's claim concerning the rarity of suicide ought to be questioned, as noted above, and although she is perhaps too quick to assume the "fact" of the suppression of suicide by Nazi power, as I will demonstrate shortly, her characterization of suicides as "spontaneous acts," and her analysis of "total domination" as aimed at destroying spontaneity, further illuminates the inadequacy of conventional modes of understanding suicide.

Of course, one way of conceiving of the spontaneity of suicide would be to see it as an act of insurrection. Historians of the Holocaust have sometimes focused on the tension between Jewish suicides, whether completed or attempted, and Nazi efforts to exercise exclusive power over the right to die. "Absolute power cannot brook suicide," writes Wolfgang Sofsky. "The decision to take one's own life is an offense, an insult it cannot permit."[119] This statement is supported by a number of facts and testimonies. Although none of these can underwrite any generalizations, several seem pertinent here. After five women committed suicide in anticipation of deportation from Würzburg, Germany, on August 28, 1942, the Gestapo added "replacements" to the scheduled transport; the community was at least momentarily punished for the suicide of some of its members before it was entirely wiped out.[120] In Theresienstadt, relatives, friends, and physicians who knew of or aided successful suicides were subject to extreme punishments.[121] The Auschwitz-Birkenau *Sonderkommando* survivor Filip Müller reports in his memoirs that after an interrupted attempt to join a group of fellow Czech Jews in the gas chambers, a member of the Gestapo beat him, screaming, "You bloody shit, get it into your stupid head: we decide how long you stay alive and when you die, and not you."[122] It should be remarked that to emphasize the prohibition of suicide is also to place Nazi power in a continuum with other forms of state power, with the traditional structure of sovereignty that reserves for itself the exclusive power to kill. To the extent that the freedom of suicide becomes visible in relation to a prohibition against suicide, it remains within the circuit of traditional meanings of suicide traced earlier (chapter 1), in which the person is figured as a servant or slave whose life and death belongs to a higher authority, whether political or divine.[123]

But Arendt's insight into the insufficiency of conventional understandings of suicide under the Nazis lends significance to another and possibly unprecedented counter-narrative. For it may instead be the case that one of the unique aspects of Nazi power with regard to Jews, particularly in the camps, was *not* to forbid suicide. Official responses to Jewish suicides before deportation begin to suggest this. When the Nazi Ministry of Finance realized that it was not legally entitled to confiscate the property of Jewish suicides, no measures were taken to prevent suicides; instead, a policy was created to treat suicides as deportees so that their property could be forfeited to the state.[124] This indifference, it has also been suggested, extended into the camps. "Like all other types of death in the structure of the camp, suicide of every kind evoked unofficial acceptance on the part of the 'functionals,'" notes the Polish researcher and psychiatrist Zdzisław Ryn.[125] He cites, for instance, a member of the SS in Auschwitz, who wrote in his diaries of incidents where, following suicides by hanging in the barracks, "very thorough interrogations were carried out in order to find out whether the prisoner was not murdered by his companions," suggesting that the murder of another inmate may have been viewed as an infraction of the unstable rules of the

camp, but not suicide.[126] The testimony of Isadore H., a survivor of Treblinka, is relevant for what it does not say. "So many times I got up in the
morning and people right in front of me hang themselves. Quite a few. The
guy I sleep next to—people run out and didn't let him do it. Next guy came
along, don't, don't interrupt him, don't make him hurt, let him do it, we all
gonna be dead. Just right in front of me. I looked at it, I looked at it, I looked
at it."[127] There is no hint here of a fear of reprisal against those who witnessed
without intervening or who assisted this death. We might also recall Bruno
Bettelheim's testimony concerning Dachau: "The stated principle was: the
more prisoners to commit suicide, the better."[128] Indeed, Bettelheim goes on
to describe a practice that contradicts the entire history of criminal treatments
of suicide, namely that "prisoners who attempted suicide but did not succeed
were to receive twenty-five lashes and prolonged solitary confinement."[129]
Whereas the corpses of suicides were once hanged or drawn and quartered in
early modern Europe—subjected to posthumous capital punishment for the
offense of suicide—the law of the camp as attested to by Bettelheim prescribes
punishment not for attempting to kill oneself but rather for failing in that
attempt.[130]

To the extent that suicide no longer appears as a threat to domination,
its recognition as a sign of difference, as a spontaneous act, is called into
question. Extending Arendt's insight into the novel form of suicide that she
witnessed among German Jews prior to deportation to the space and structure of the concentration and death camps means, then, to confront a form
of death that can no longer simply be recognized as suicide.

Can the Muselmann Commit Suicide?

What is worse than death and what, as such, grounds the postwar image of
death with dignity emerges, then, in relation to the unsettling of the traditional link between power and death that seems to define the camps. What
appears to be at the very least an uneven application of the traditional law
of sovereignty and its exclusive hold over the right to kill aligns, to invoke
another frame of reference, with the characterization of the camp as existing
under a "state of exception," a space in which the only law is the suspension
of law.[131] In this light, the end of suicide, its becoming unrecognizable, might
be understood as indicating the definitive displacement of the politics of sovereignty by a biopolitical regime.

To grasp the consequences of Auschwitz for suicide after Auschwitz therefore requires reflection on the camp as the site that most radically exposes
the form and meaning of modern biopolitics. The unwieldy scope that such
a reflection might assume can be brought into focus by considering those
inmates who were called, in the slang of the camps, Muselmänner (or other
synonymous terms)—that is, in Primo Levi's words, "the weak, the inept,
those doomed to selection."[132] For it is the Muselmann who reveals, in Giorgio

Agamben's argument, "the decisive function of the camps in the system of Nazi biopolitics. They are not merely the place of death and destruction; they are also, and above all, the site of the production of the *Muselmann*, the final biopolitical substance to be isolated in the biological continuum."[133] For Agamben, it would also be the figure of the *Muselmann*, then, who would most dramatically demonstrate the consequences of biopolitics for thinking about death and suicide after Auschwitz. Agamben's discussion of the *Muselmann* also allows us to return, through comparison with Améry's testimony, to Améry's reconceptualization of death with dignity.

The *Muselmann* is central to Agamben's reflection on biopolitics because he seems to demonstrate the seemingly inevitable conflation or coincidence of biopolitics and thanatopolitics, that is, of a politics of life that seems to be oriented toward the maintenance of life and a politics that performs this task only through the work of death, that is, through the continual designation, expulsion, and extermination of what is designated as non-life, or not worthy of life, and which is therefore figured as life-threatening—as contamination, illness, invasion, and so on.[134] For Agamben, what perhaps must be called, however awkwardly, bio-thanato-politics begins by dividing (from within) a "people" into a "population," and thus by "transforming an essentially political body into an essentially biological body." It henceforth operates by producing a series of racist and eugenicist caesuras so as to foster the "health" of this population, in each case designating what is included and excluded from life, from the sphere of what is allowed to live.

The *Muselmann*, Agamben suggests, marks the "final limit" of these caesuras.[135] This is because the *Muselmann* is understood to exist in (and to expose) a zone of indistinction between life and death; he cannot be included or excluded from the realm of what is allowed to live because he can neither be said to live or to die. Primo Levi, Agamben notes, writes of the *Muselmann*: "One hesitates to call their death death."[136] Agamben takes this insight of Levi's to be definitive and decisive. For Agamben, the *Muselmann* is thus the "final biopolitical substance" because he is "the being whose life is not truly life" and "whose death"—unhesitatingly, we might note—"cannot be called death, but only the production of a corpse."[137] If bio-thanato-politics assigns for itself the power, in Foucault's well-known formulation, "to make live and to let die," the *Muselmann* marks the limit of this power in that he is, as it were, beyond the question of life and death.

Ryn and Kłodziński, in a study of the *Muselmann* to which Agamben calls special attention, and who are among the few researchers to challenge the orthodoxy concerning the rarity of suicide in the camps, suggest that *Muselmänner* generally did not have the strength to commit suicide, even as they also cite the testimony of a self-described former *Muselmann* who describes contemplating running against the electric fence only to be prevented from doing so by others.[138] Their detailed study characterizes the condition of the *Muselmann* as a form of illness—a diseased condition or state (*stan chorobowy*), even as they recognize that it is "not an illness in the classic sense of the word."[139] Agamben's image of the *Muselmann* as final bio-political substance suggests a different interpretation: not that the inability to commit suicide was a symptom of the condition of the *Muselmann*, but that it constitutes his essential condition: the *Muselmann* could not commit suicide because he was deprived of both life *and* death. Whereas Améry and Arendt testify to conditions that make suicide unrecognizable, in Agamben's image of the *Muselmann*, suicide becomes impossible.

This impossibility, as we will see shortly, has significant consequences for Agamben's reflections on dignity in and after Auschwitz. But before returning to the question of dignity, I wish to contrast the biopolitical definition of the *Muselmann* with Améry's characterization of the *Muselmann* in his essay on Auschwitz. Agamben, in fact, opens the chapter of *Remnants of Auschwitz* devoted to the *Muselmann* with this passage from Améry's writing, but without any comment on Améry's specific way of defining the *Muselmann*.[140] He also enlists Améry at one point as among the several writers who refer to the *Muselmann* as a walking corpse. Thus Améry's image of the *Muselmann* does, to some extent, coincide with that of the Italian philosopher. But it also displays a significantly different understanding, with important consequences. Améry writes:

> The so-called "Muselmann," as the camp language termed the pris-oner who was giving up on himself and was given up on by his comrades [*wie die Lagersprache den sich aufgebenden und von den Kamaraden aufgegebenen Häftling nannte*], no longer had room in his consciousness for the contrasts good or bad, noble or base, intel-lectual or unintellectual. He was a staggering corpse, a bundle of physical functions in its last convulsions. As hard as it may be for us to do so, we must exclude him from our considerations.[141]

As for Agamben, the *Muselmann* appears here as a figure on the threshold of life and death, a "staggering corpse" who was neither fully alive nor fully dead. But Améry's definition also challenges Agamben's. For the latter, the *Muselmann* is produced according to the biopolitical operation that creates caesuras in populations through juridical designation—from non-Aryan, to Jew, to deportee, to prisoner, to *Muselmann*—where each new designation assigns a new juridical status to the designee and thus subjects him to new forms of treatment.[142] John Protevi, in terms that echo the characterization of *Muselmann*-hood as an illness by the Polish researchers Ryn and Kłodziński, cogently notes that the term *Muselmann* does not fit as neatly into this chain of designations as Agamben implies: "'Muselmann' functions like a diag-nosis, an evaluation of a state; it is not a transforming predication but caps what has already happened to a body, rather than opening that body up to what is to come."[143]

Améry's testimony in part confirms Protevi's analysis, for the identity or condition of the *Muselmann* in Améry's definition is in part the function of the acknowledgment by his comrades of the *Muselmann*'s condition, which is attested to in their giving up on him. But Améry's definition also suggests a striking contrast (although not a strict contradiction) with divergent understandings of the *Muselmann* as biopolitical category, as a diagnosis, or as itself a racial category.[144] For in the convergence of *Sich Aufgebenden* and *Aufgegebenen*—of giving up on oneself and the giving up performed by those who nonetheless remain "comrades"—it would seem that a silent transmission takes place, a recognition by the comrades of an abandonment of the self to which the prisoner has a certain right. The *Muselmann* is not simply produced by subjection to or abandonment by others; he also abandons himself and gives that self-abandonment to be recognized and mirrored by his comrades. Thus when Améry excludes the *Muselmann* from his considerations, this gesture should be understood as of a piece with this relation to the *Muselmann*. It does not designate the existence of the *Muselmann* as one not worth living, or dying; it does not create or enforce a biopolitical caesura. Rather, it acknowledges, even as it repeats, the abandonment that the *Muselmann* himself is said to perform. The recognition of the impossibility of bearing witness for the *Muselmann* is, in other words, itself a form of testimony, reflecting the silence of those it excludes.

It is in this light that we might approach Améry's otherwise unexpected and puzzling later suggestion, in *Hand an sich legen*, that, rather than evincing the impossibility of suicide, becoming a *Muselmann* was itself a sort of suicide, albeit a strange sort. Améry makes this suggestion in the course of defining a category of suicides that are "not recorded":

> Then there are those [suicides] who are not recorded [*nicht verzeichnet*] at all . . . . : they let themselves die [*sie lassen sich sterben*], without contradiction, as once did the staggering "*Muselmänner*" in the concentration camps who were much too weak to have the strength to run to the electrified barbed wire.[145]

This passing allusion to the *Muselmänner* extends and in a way radicalizes the definition of the *Muselmann* in *At the Mind's Limits* as prisoners who gave up on themselves. Rather than asking whether the *Muselmann* can commit suicide, Améry provocatively suggests that to become a *Muselmann* is to commit a kind of suicide. The *Muselmänner* do not simply die, or are not simply killed, but "let themselves die," where this "letting" implies a degree of decision, even if it is only the decision to allow something to happen.[146] (We might recall here the argument of the gravedigger in *Hamlet*, discussed in chapter 1, that there is no essential difference between drowning by going out into the sea and waiting at the shoreline to be drowned by the incoming tide.) These suicides, Améry makes clear, are not to be understood in exactly the same way as the voluntary deaths of those who "set the time" of their own deaths and who consequently appear as "deadly earnest real suicides."[147] *Muselmänner* instead let themselves die because they do not have the strength (*Kraft*) to commit the visible and decisive act of running to the fence. But Améry (in another version of the gravedigger's argument) also insists that the distinction often made between "suicides" and "suicidals"—that is, between those with a seemingly clear and serious determination to commit suicide versus those whose suicides or suicide attempts seem to evince ambivalence, uncertainty, or a lack of seriousness—is "quite arbitrary."[148] The *Muselmann*, for Améry, thus does not only occupy a threshold between death and life, but the threshold between two kinds of death, suicide and non-suicide, killing oneself and being killed. Thus where Agamben writes that the death of the *Muselmann* cannot even be called death, Améry locates a space of uncertainty in which the *Muselmann* performs an unrecognizable, unrecorded form of suicide. The figure for whom suicide seemed to be impossible thus comes to open the possibility of recognizing a new form of voluntary death in and after Auschwitz.

III. Dignity without Dignity

Améry's vacillation or hesitation concerning the (non-)suicide of the *Muselmann* has important consequences for the possibility of death with dignity after Auschwitz. For Agamben, Auschwitz, in the figure of the *Muselmann*, marks the "end and ruin of every ethics of dignity and conformity to a norm."[149] This claim is made on the basis of the seemingly inevitable movement within the concept of dignity, which we saw in our analysis of extrinsic and intrinsic dignity, towards the derivation of dignity through reference to a socially regulated norm, even if a negatively determined one. "Both in the case of legal *dignitas* [or extrinsic dignity] and its moral transposition, dignity is autonomous with respect to the existence of its bearer, an interior model or external image to which he must conform and which must be preserved at all costs."[150] The lifeless and deathless existence of the *Muselmann*, in this light, marks the simultaneous delegitimation of both notions of dignity. Just as it would, in Agamben's term, "not be decent" even to ask the question of whether the *Muselmann* could or ought to have acted in a more dignified way, so it would "repeat the gesture of the SS" to declare that the *Muselmann* lost the intrinsic dignity of the human.[151] In the wake of Auschwitz, dignity is thus radically delegitimated for Agamben; to speak of dignity is, in effect, to deny, or at the very least misrecognize, the eventfulness of Auschwitz.

Yet Agamben's analysis, powerful though it is, relies, it must also be noted, on the conflation of extrinsic and intrinsic dignity; the latter for Agamben is simply the "moral transposition" or an "interiorized" version of the former.[152] Indeed, to the extent that intrinsic dignity stabilizes an image of indignity in order to establish itself, transforming that image into a norm, this continuity between the two concepts obtains. But Améry's thought, which insists on the vocabulary of dignity, also poses a challenge to the notion of the absolute collapse of dignity. In *Hand an sich legen*, he will thus insist that dignity is at stake in voluntary death; one of the concepts that will concern him, he writes, "is called 'worth' or 'dignity' ['*Würde*' *oder* '*Dignität*']."[153] The two terms thus appear to be interchangeable at first. But without clearly distinguishing between the two terms, he also writes that *Würde* "can be established by a particular society," while *Dignität*, it seems, involves a rupture with the social. The one who commits suicide, he writes, "doesn't care about society . . . [but] reaffirms one last time its [the subject's] dignity [*Dignität*]."[154] After introducing these two terms as simultaneously synonymous and non-synonymous, Améry then refers throughout the text to *Dignität* only, with the exception of the final paragraph of the book, to which I turn shortly. *Dignität*, then, at once recovers *Würde* and supplants it, installing within Améry's German text, according to Lothar Beier, a term designed "to reflect the French *dignité*."[155] If *Würde* cannot be severed from its historical association with a logic of norms and from the inadequacy of the notion of *Menschenwürde*, of which Améry wrote in his essay on torture, *Dignität* estranges dignity from the social norms to which it is conceptually bound. To speak of dignity after Auschwitz, for Améry, thus does not mean to delegitimate dignity, but to transform it into a new and foreign word within his own language, one that expressly seeks to resist social measurement or relationship to a norm. It names the possibility of a *Dignität* without *Würde*, of a dignity without dignity.

Hovering in the strangeness and opacity of *Dignität*, in the illegibility of a death that may or may not be voluntary, Améry's vacillation on the (non-) suicide of the *Muselmann* captures his own experience as well, the experience of the survivor. For the question of the *Dignität* of a voluntary death, of whether a death after Auschwitz can claim such dignity, would also lead to the interruption of his own 1974 suicide attempt. As Améry notes, the symptomological interpretation of suicide in psychology and sociology—in the disciplines that ground the field of suicidology with which Améry puts himself in reluctant dialogue—employs a circular logic with respect to a failed suicide attempt. The attempt fails, it is said, because the one who attempted to take his own life wanted it to fail, even if unconsciously. Indeed, the same self-justifying logic can be applied to "successful" suicides, which appear from this perspective, as noted earlier, as mistakes. It was this logic to which Améry found himself subjected when he attempted to commit suicide in 1974:

I still know very well how it was when I awoke after what was later reported to me as a thirty-hour coma. Fettered, drilled through with tubes, fitted on both wrists with painful devices for my artificial nourishment. Delivered and surrendered to a couple of nurses who came and went, washed me, cleaned my bed, put thermometers in my mouth, and did everything quite matter-of-factly, as if I were already a thing, *une chose*. . . , I knew better than ever before that I was inclined to die and that the rescue, about which the physician boasted, belonged to the worst that had ever been done to me—and that was not a little. Enough. I will be no more convincing with my private experience than with my circular discussion of death. Besides, I'd rather bear witness than convince.[156]

Améry's comparison of this "rescue" to torture and to Auschwitz, as his biographer notes, "makes difficult reading."[157] Yet one must take seriously the connection he draws between Auschwitz and after, between the "duty to die" imposed on the prisoner in Auschwitz and the duty to live imposed at the hospital. For Améry marks the decision to overrule his decision to take his life as a paradigmatic ethical moment, a moment when an irrevocable crime against humanity is at stake. The rescue opens the vertiginous history of the worse than worse, exposing the survivor to a deprivation of the freedom to die as the seemingly inevitable correlative of the deprivation of the freedom to live. Worse than the fear of death is the fear of not being permitted to die—that is, of an ongoing exposure to the worse than worse.

In opening the possibility of the *Dignität* of the death of the *Muselmann*, whose agency is fundamentally inscrutable, Améry thus proposes an approach towards the dying other that he might have wished had been taken with respect to his dying body. Yet a recognition of the other's right to die, he also insists, cannot be based on a logical judgment. It is not a question of recognizing the other's right to die based on the degree to which it conforms to a norm or manifests a rational intention. Instead, Améry insists on the radical incompatibility of the "logic of life" and the "antilogic of death." He insists that voluntary death cannot be justified according to any logic. Elsewhere, he employs the image of a message. On the one hand, "suicides are also the only ones among far too many who, sending a message into the void, understand the world."[158] On the other hand, however, this message "can't arrive at its destination because it does not have one."[159] This results in an inevitable act of misprision: suicide "delivers me to the other insofar as the latter can now proceed with my terminated life according to whatever seems to be good or bad."[160] What makes a death voluntary, what prevents it from being a murder—its freedom from external determination—can therefore not be ascertained through reference to any socially derived or shared norm (such as a judgment of rationality). Instead, this freedom is both singular and fragile. It cannot be made intelligible to another, it cannot reach its addressee, and as such it can only be mistaken for something other than itself. "As far as I can see," Améry writes, "voluntary death . . . is nowhere recognized for what it is: a precisely *free and voluntary* death and a highly individual matter that, to be sure, is never carried out without social reference, with which however and finally *human beings are alone with themselves, before which society has to be silent*."[161]

In the dense closing paragraphs of his book, Améry again compares the problem of suicide to the situation of the concentration camp. In order to approach what he calls "the threshold of the leap," one must retain, he argues, a feeling of life. Otherwise, those who decide to take their lives "would not find their road to the open and would be like the concentration camp inmate who doesn't dare run against the electrified fence, would still like to gulp down his evening soup and then the hot acorn soup in the morning and again the turnip soup at noon, and on and on."[162] The inmate described here is not quite the *Muselmann*: whereas the *Muselmann* did not run against the fence due to excessive weakness, the inmate pictured here fears failing to die, fears the worse than death that might follow from an unsuccessful suicide attempt. The one who commits suicide, by contrast, necessarily exhibits "a requirement of life." Namely, he issues a "demand to escape a life lacking in dignity [*Würde*], humanity, and freedom," Améry writes—now in the final paragraphs of the book returning to *Würde* rather than *Dignität*.[163] Améry thus seems to associate existence in the camps with a loss of dignity so radical that it suppresses or precludes the possibility of suicide; whereas suicide, even as it responds to a loss of dignity, would seem nonetheless to require a minimum of dignity, for in making a demand to escape a life lacking in dignity, the potential suicide is demonstrating a degree of that very dignity which was felt to be lacking.

But this seeming contradiction within the act of suicide—a contradiction that invalidated suicide for Kant, who suggested that the very conditions of possibility for committing suicide at the same time render suicide unnecessary—leads Améry instead to pry open a space between intrinsic and extrinsic dignity: "But the survivors are right, for what are dignity, humanity, and freedom in preference to smiling, breathing, and striding? What is . . . dignity in opposition to the provision of every form of being dignified [*Würde wider die Voraussetzung jeglichen Würdigseins*]?"[164] In opening a gap between *Würde* and *Würdigsein*, dignity and being dignified, intrinsic and extrinsic dignity, Améry also undermines any basis upon which intrinsic dignity might be legitimated. For if a death is only intrinsically dignified to the extent that it averts the demise or the dishonoring of dignity, to the extent that it safeguards the possibility of a death that averts the worse than death, Améry attests to the possibility, the unrecordable and unwitnessable possibility, of a death with dignity that can only appear undignified, a death that does not produce the survival of dignity but that instead excepts itself from any form of legitimation, and whose dignity therefore consists in precisely its indignity. If this is what dignity means after Auschwitz, it is because Auschwitz resists being established as itself a norm, because it opens the history of the worse than worse, of that which would exceed and rupture every norm, of a fear with no necessary or natural limit, and which for that reason requires a response that can only be arbitrary, can only be spontaneous.

Thus hovering over the death of Améry is necessarily the question of its dignity. If we remain within the normative terms of death with dignity, within the collapse of *Würde* and *würdig*, we confront an impasse between two interpretations of his death. According to the first, it is the sign of a continued and inescapable haunting of the past, of the unbreakable grip that Auschwitz has over the survivor. It is in this way, for instance, that Treblinka survivor Richard Glazar, who would take his own life five years after publishing his testimony, views both Améry's and Primo Levi's deaths. "I am not sure whether the reason [for their suicides] did not lie in the terrible humiliation they had undergone."[165] Glazar thus echoes Primo Levi's own suggestion that Améry's death could be explained by his subjection to torture, a claim that would be made as well, of course, with respect to Levi's own death in 1987.[166] By contrast, Améry's biographer suggests that such an interpretation is itself a denial of freedom, in that it "makes him a victim again and denies him the ability to 'make something else out of what was made of him' for the second time."[167] But despite this risk, or despite the desire to avert it, the question of the survivor's death, and the question of every death after Auschwitz, must remain open. For even if it is clear that Améry staged his death as a fully voluntary one, ensconced in a hotel room and with an unequivocal handwritten note by his side when his body was found, even if it is clear that he did not wish to be "rescued," we must also keep in mind his insistence on the opacity of the final moment. "The second hand trots relentlessly toward the minute of truth. The act is set in motion. Outside the ego, enclosed in itself and perhaps finding its nucleus at the end, no one will be able to assess this act."[168]

If to die today is to die in the wake of Auschwitz, if death after Auschwitz cannot be the same as death before Auschwitz, then hovering over every death, suspended within every death, is the impossible question of its dignity—a dignity about which one can only be silent, that can only go unrecorded. For it is only at the moment when death becomes unrecognizable, when it cannot be legitimated according to any norm, when it withdraws from all regulation and from all obligation, that its enigmatic dignity can take place.

Epilogue

Dead Letters

The practical conditions under which the right to die is exercised will likely have changed between the writing and publication of this book, just as those conditions changed considerably during its research and writing stages. The legalization of medically assisted death in Canada, California, Colorado, and the District of Columbia as this book was in the last stages of the editorial process is but one indication that physician-assisted death may become an increasingly accepted practice. Nor can one predict if, or when, changes in life expectancy may occur; normally incremental increases can undergo unpredictable shifts, as in the dramatic increases associated with the "mortality revolution" (or revolutions) of the past two centuries. Whether there will be another such mortality revolution, or even an immortality revolution, may be less a question of *if* than *when*, although how this will occur, what form it will take, and with what consequences must remain a matter of pure speculation.

One way to pursue such speculation would be to look to utopian or dystopian fictions that imagine possible futures where disease, aging, or violence become subject to regulation or even eradication. José Saramago's startling account of a world, in *Death with Interruptions*, in which death but not aging is arrested, a world of Tithouses in which society therefore comes to resemble a vast nursing home, is as likely as Jorge Luis Borges's vision, in the short tale "A Weary Man's Utopia."[1] In Borges's tale, the end of death also spells the end of history and memory, such that those who are tired of immortality make their own way, oblivious to the legacy they are reenacting, to a "death chamber . . . invented by a philanthropist whose name, I think, was Adolf Hitler."[2] Consonant with the histories of alienation and dehumanization we encounter in the pasts explored in *A Death of One's Own*, such speculative fictions may also remind us of the violent unevenness that has attended the history of technological change. For instance, in Lee Falk's "Time Is Money," a short story from the 1970s that provided the scenario for several dystopian films, extended life is literally the currency of the day, such that the wealthy accumulate time and become immortal at the direct expense of the foreshortened life spans of the destitute.[3] Exclusion from capital accumulation becomes a death sentence. Current correlations between affluence and life expectancy would thus be radicalized. As Kevin T. Keith suggests, the likely expense of life-extension technologies indeed "portends particularly vicious inequities, whereby the advantages of class and clout convey not merely an easier life, but life itself."[4]

But just as history is always the history of the present, just as *A Death of One's Own* has necessarily imagined the past through the prism of the present, any story we can tell of the future is likewise a projection of present preoccupations. If we are solicited, then, to imagine a world without death, and to imagine what the human and what death will mean in such a world, this task can only be undertaken through an excavation of deathlessness in the history we already inhabit, a history that opens onto alternative ways of thinking its own future, which is to say, our present moment. Commenting on the significance of nineteenth-century suicide to his own research a century later, Benjamin claimed that "modernity keeps the raw material for such presentations in readiness," and that such raw material can belatedly be understood as the very "foundation of modernity."[5] At stake in this image is not simply an attempt to explain the past, but to open the present to what has been buried and foreclosed, to imagine different possible futures of the past.[6] Benjamin's image of the storyteller as the dying man, as Moriens, creates, in this light, the possibility, and responsibility, of reading in his face not an already known history, but one that reconfigures the past and casts it in a radically new light. For at the moment of death, Benjamin contends, what becomes transmissible is precisely a history that was previously lost, "views of himself under which he has encountered himself *without being aware of it.*" To claim the right to die, in this light, is to bear witness to an overlooked past and to give it a new future. It is to encounter the ways in which we may all be surrogates of dead letters.

To return to and reread the deaths of some of the main figures that have preoccupied me in this work—Bartleby, Raphaël de Valentin, Jean Améry—has involved opening their histories to a future they (and, in the case of the first two, their authors) may not have anticipated—to debates and to political, legal, cultural, and ethical dilemmas that remained on a distant horizon. It may be, as Benjamin suggests, that precisely such unanticipated futures demand our reading and, in turn, open our present to a new view of itself. The intense politicization of the right to die today fosters hard stances. It requires a posture of certainty on the part of those who call for the right to die as well as those who assist in the exercise of that right, whether directly or indirectly, as physicians, lawmakers, citizens, family, neighbors. The signature on a living will, the petition for life-ending medications, the demand for a death with dignity all depend upon the presumed stability and verifiability of a will that is "voluntary, well-considered, and repeated, and is not the result of any external pressure," as the Belgian law puts it. But the principal arguments used to justify the right to die, as the readings pursued in this book suggest, cannot be so easily secured. They call attention to the uneasy imbrication of freedom and obligation and to the undecidability that confronts the "absolute decision" to die as well as the decision to affirm and assist in another's decision, an undecidability that is perhaps paradigmatic of all decision.[7]

Thus, from within the appeal for the right to die, from within its vacillating claims to autonomy, self-authorship, and dignity, murmurs a more difficult and unsettling attestation to the withdrawal of death and its unheard-of implications. Malte's necropolis, Bartleby's Dead Letter Office, and Raphaël's phantasmagoric antiquities shop describe imagined spaces that resound, however uncomfortably, in the deathless zones to which Améry testifies: the torture chamber, the concentration camp, the hospital where he is "rescued" from his decision to die. If upon first thought these sites seem to be permeated by death, if they seem to threaten the possibility of human life, the appeal for the right to die suggests that these paradigmatic sites of modernity instead expose the individual to an irremissible crisis in the image of death as the limit with respect to which human experience acquires meaning, or as the limit of fear. For it is this deathlessness that elicits the appeal for the right to die. And this appeal, far from confirming an already established or created image of the self and of humanity, and far from conforming to the requirements of the law, instead produces, as we have seen, new legal and ethical questions and configurations and new relations of surrogacy that extend across interpersonal relations, between text and reader, between past and present. It implicates us in each other's suicides and in so doing transforms what suicide has meant and will come to mean. For it may always be the case that what the appeal to "let me die" calls upon us to hear and bear witness to are the ways that a death of one's own is never, in the end, simply one's own.

Introduction

1. Frank Kafka, "A Country Doctor," in *Franz Kafka: The Complete Stories*, trans. Willa Muir and Edwin Muir (New York: Schocken, 1971), 222.

2. "'Yes,' I think blasphemously [*denke ich lästernd*], 'in cases like this, the gods are helpful.'" Ibid. German text in Franz Kafka, *Gesammelte Werke*, ed. Max Brod (New York: Schocken, 1946), 1:148.

3. Ibid., 224.

4. Ibid., 225.

5. Max Brod, *Franz Kafka: A Biography*, 2nd edition, trans. G. Humphrey Roberts and Richard Winston (New York: Schocken, 1960), 212.

6. Kafka, "A Country Doctor," 223.

7. Ruth Macklin, "Dignity Is a Useless Concept," *British Medical Journal* 327, no. 7429 (December 20, 2003): 1419–20.

8. Stevens, concurring, in *Washington v. Glucksberg*, 521 U.S. 702 (1997), 747.

9. See, for example, Macklin, "Dignity Is a Useless Concept."

10. Atul Gawande, *Being Mortal: Medicine and What Matters in the End* (New York: Metropolitan Books, 2015), 128.

11. Ludwig Edelstein, trans. and ed., *Hippocrates: The Oath or the Hippocratic Oath* (Chicago: Ares, 1943), 3.

12. Alan Meisel, Kathy L. Cerminara, and Thaddeus M. Pope, *The Right to Die: The Law of End-of-Life Decisionmaking*, 3rd edition (Frederick, Md.: Wolters Kluwer, 2015), §1.01.

13. See, for example, Breyer, concurring, in *Washington v. Glucksberg*: "The Court describes it as a 'right to commit suicide with another's assistance.' But I would not reject the respondents' claim without considering a different formulation, for which our legal tradition may provide greater support. That formulation would use words roughly like a 'right to die with dignity.'" 521 U.S. 702 at 790.

14. The Conversation Project, www.theconversationproject.org. See also Angelo E. Volandes, *The Conversation: A Revolutionary Plan for End-of-Life Care* (New York: Bloomsbury, 2015).

15. Maurice Blanchot, *L'Entretien infini* (Paris: Gallimard, 1969).

16. J. Hillis Miller, *Versions of Pygmalion* (Cambridge, Mass.: Harvard University Press, 1990), 172. Derrida similarly reminds us that "if there is one word that remains absolutely unassignable or unassigning with respect to its thingness, it is the word 'death.'" Jacques Derrida, *Aporias*, trans. Thomas Dutoit (Stanford, Calif.: Stanford University Press, 1993), 22.

17. Philippe Ariès, *The Hour of Our Death*, trans. Helen Weaver (New York: Oxford University Press, 1981), 559ff.

18. Ibid., 560.

19. Ibid.

20. Ibid., 585.

21. Ibid., 586.

22. Ibid., 587.

23. Ibid., 588.

24. Among other extensions of Ariès's periodization of death, Christina Staudt compellingly suggests that the age of invisible death has been succeeded historically by "a new episteme of death, 'death recognized' or 'death managed.'" "From Concealment to Recognition," in *Speaking of Death: America's New Sense of Mortality,* ed. Michael K. Bartolos (Westport, Conn.: Praeger, 2009), 29.

25. Office of Technology Assessment Task Force, "Life Sustaining Technologies and the Elderly," 41 (1988). Qtd. in Brennan, dissenting, *Cruzan v. Director, Missouri Department of Health,* 497 U.S. 261 (1990), 302.

26. Daniel Callahan, *The Roots of Bioethics: Health, Progress, Technology, Death* (New York: Oxford University Press, 2012), 122.

27. Tad Friend, "The God Pill: Silicon Valley's Quest for Eternal Life," *New Yorker,* April 3, 2017, 54–67. See also Don DeLillo's incisive fictional exploration of ultrawealthy immortalism in *Zero K* (New York: Scribner, 2016). I thank Jennifer Ballengee for calling this novel to my attention.

28. David Boyd Haycock, *Mortal Coil: A Short History of Living Longer* (New Haven, Conn.: Yale University Press, 2008); David Casarett, *Shocked: Adventures in Bringing Back the Recently Dead* (New York: Current/Penguin, 2014).

29. Consider, for instance, the recent use of suspended life (or "emergency preservation and resuscitation") therapies, in which blood is temporarily replaced with a cold saline solution, to extend the life of gunshot and wound victims while surgery is performed. "Gunshot Victims to Be Suspended between Life and Death," *New Scientist,* March 26, 2014, www.newscientist.com. See also the survey of life-extension technologies in Kevin T. Keith, "Life Extension: Proponents, Opponents, and the Social Impact of the Defeat of Death," in Bartolos, *Speaking of Death,* 102–51.

30. Leon Kass, "Mortality," in *Powers That Make Us Human: The Foundations of Medical Ethics,* ed. Kenneth Vaux (Urbana: University of Illinois Press, 1985), 7. See also Kass, *Life, Liberty, and the Defense of Dignity* (San Francisco: Encounter Books, 2002).

31. Kass, "Mortality," 24.

32. *Quill v. Koppell,* 870 F. Supp. 78 (S.D.N.Y. 1994), 84.

33. It is hardly possible here to give a summary, let alone a reading, of Blanchot's essay. For Blanchot, this tension arises from the fact that, on the one hand, literature demands to surpass and negate existing frames of reference, even to negate the materiality of language itself so as to institute a new reality, and on the other hand, cannot escape both existing frames of reference and its own materiality, that is, its radical alterity with respect to what it names. In Blanchot's essay, then, the right to death appears as a right that may not be possible, but that persists despite, or even due to, this impossibility. One might also speculate in this context about the possible difference between "the right to death," *le droit à la mort,* and "the right to die," *le droit de mourir.* Because Blanchot writes before the emergence of a political discourse on *le droit de mourir,* it is not the case that his formulation sets out to register any clear distinction between the two phrases.

To the extent that Blanchot associates this right with the act or process of dying, they appear to be synonymous. Yet Blanchot's thought also opens the possibility of an irreducible difference or discontinuity between dying as human potential or action and death as the end of the potential to act, as radical negation—between, that is, the right to die (*le droit de mourir*) and the right to death (*le droit à la mort*). Death, in this sense, would not be the result of dying, but would remain instead something like the very interruption of dying, or in Blanchot's terms, its impossibility.

34. Maurice Blanchot, *The Space of Literature*, trans. Ann Smock (Lincoln: University of Nebraska Press, 1982), 122ff. Margaret Pabst Battin finds in the *Notebooks* a paradigmatic confrontation with practical issues raised by the standardization of end-of-life care under national versus private health care systems. *The Least Worst Death: Essays in Bioethics on the End of Life* (New York: Oxford University Press, 1994), 80–98.

35. For Anglophone readers, the title may also justifiably evoke Virginia Woolf's *A Room of One's Own*. While the central concerns of Woolf's essay are quite removed from the focus of the present study, it is not entirely inappropriate if her title resonates here. One might recall, for one, the relationship between literature and death suggested in her story of Judith Shakespeare, whose imagined suicide becomes the foundational event in the (re)construction of a genealogy of women's literature—which would also mean, for Woolf, more radically, of the possibility of literature as such. More resonant with the thought of Blanchot, one might also invoke Woolf's suggestion that the writer must undergo a sort of death or anonymization in order for literature to take place. To become an author, in other words, means to undergo a death of one's own (as woman or as man).

36. Rainer Maria Rilke, *The Notebooks of Malte Laurids Brigge*, trans. Michael Hulse (New York: Penguin, 2009), 3. Translations are modified occasionally. Rainer Maria Rilke, *Die Aufzeichnungen des Malte Laurids Brigge* (Frankfurt am Main: Insel, 1982).

37. Derrida, *Aporias*, 25.

38. Rilke, *Notebooks*, 6.

39. Avner Ben-Amos, "The Sacred Center of Power: Paris and Republican State Funerals," *Journal of Interdisciplinary History* 22, no. 1 (summer 1991): 30. Ben-Amos notes that the coffin of ex-President Raymond Poincaré in 1934 was laid in state precisely atop the bronze slab marking the symbolic geographic center of the nation (38).

40. Rilke, *Notebooks*, 6.

41. Ibid.

42. Ibid.

43. Blanchot, *The Space of Literature*, 147–48.

44. Ibid., 148.

45. Ibid., 149.

46. Ibid., 130.

47. It is interesting to note that Rilke drafted but rejected a different ending for *Malte* in which Tolstoy appears.

48. Leo Tolstoy, "The Death of Ivan Ilych" (1886), in *Ivan Ilych and Hadji Murad and Other Stories*, trans. Louise and Aylmer Maude (London: Oxford University Press, 1957), 73.

49. I borrow here Ross Chambers's association of "writerly suicide" with the production of semantic indeterminacy. *The Writing of Melancholy: Modes of Opposition in Early French Modernism* (Chicago: University of Chicago Press, 1993), 83ff.

50. Rilke, *Notebooks*, 6.

51. Ibid., 7.

52. Ibid., 6–7.

53. Rainer Maria Rilke, *Gedichte* (Frankfurt am Main: Insel, 1955), 1:342.

54. With different emphasis, Walter Sokel notes that the *Notebooks* does not sustain and confirm the possession of one's death, but rather that the death of the Chamberlain, who is said to die his own death, turns out to be at odds with the self, such that "his maturing death usurps the self's place." "The Devolution of the Self in *The Notebooks of Malte Laurids Brigge*," in *Rilke: The Alchemy of Alienation,* ed. Frank Baron, Ernst S. Dick, and Warren R. Maurer (Lawrence: Regents Press of Kansas, 1980), 188.

55. Rilke, *Notebooks*, 6.

56. On the importance of simile in Rilke's poetry, see Patrick Greaney, *Untimely Beggar: Power and Poverty from Baudelaire to Benjamin* (Minneapolis: University of Minnesota Press, 2008), 102–8. The permeation of simile and its denaturalization of the "proper death" also problematize the frequent accusation that Rilke aestheticizes death, a charge that tends to derive from the "prayer" for a death of one's own in "The Book of Poverty and Death." Theodor Adorno, most consequentially, complains that "Rilke's prayer for 'a death of one's own' is a piteous attempt to conceal the fact that nowadays people merely snuff out." *Minima Moralia: Reflections on a Damaged Life,* trans. E. F. N. Jephcott (London: Verso, 2005), 233. As Greaney points out, Blanchot also finds fault with the Rilke of "The Book of Poverty and Death," dividing the poet into a "good, later Rilke [who] denies the possibility of a death that can be mastered, while the bad, early Rilke insists on such a death," even as Blanchot goes on to undo this very distinction (*Untimely Beggar*, 142).

57. Blanchot, *The Space of Literature*, 122.

58. Ulrich Baer, *Remnants of Song: Trauma and the Experience of Modernity in Charles Baudelaire and Paul Celan* (Stanford, Calif.: Stanford University Press, 2000), 172.

59. Giorgio Agamben, *Remnants of Auschwitz: The Witness and the Archive,* trans. Daniel Heller-Roazen (New York: Zone Books, 2002), 62. See also Eric Santner, *On Creaturely Life: Rilke, Benjamin, Sebald* (Chicago: University of Chicago Press, 2006), vxi–xvii.

60. Sandra M. Gilbert, *Death's Door: Modern Dying and the Ways We Grieve* (New York: W.W. Norton, 2006), 167.

61. Agamben, *Remnants of Auschwitz*, 71–72.

62. Hannah Arendt, *The Origins of Totalitarianism* (New York: Harcourt Brace, 1976), 454n150.

63. See, for instance, the testimony of Motke Zaïdl and Itzhak Dugin in Claude Lanzmann, *Shoah: The Complete Text of the Acclaimed Holocaust Film* (New York: Da Capo, 1995), 9.

64. Jean Améry, *At the Mind's Limits: Contemplations by a Survivor on Auschwitz and Its Realities,* trans. Sidney Rosenfeld and Stella P. Rosenfeld (Bloomington: Indiana University Press, 1980), 16.

65. Maurice Blanchot, *The Writing of the Disaster*, trans. Ann Smock (Lincoln: University of Nebraska Press, 1986), 143.

66. See especially Shai J. Lavi, *The Modern Art of Dying: A History of Euthanasia in the United States* (Princeton, N.J.: Princeton University Press, 2005); Raymond Whiting, *A Natural Right to Die: Twenty-Three Centuries of Debate* (Westport, Conn.: Greenwood, 2002); N. D. A. Kemp, *"Merciful Release": The History of the British Euthanasia Movement* (Manchester: Manchester University Press, 2002); and Walter Schmuhl, *Rassenhygiene, Nationalsozialismus, Euthanasie: Von der Verhütung zur Vernichtung "lebensunwerten Lebens" 1890–1945* (Göttingen: Vandenhoeck & Ruprecht, 1987).

67. Drucilla Cornell, "Who Bears the Right to Die?" *Graduate Faculty Philosophy Journal* 26, no. 1 (2005): 183–84.

68. Alexander García Düttmann, *Between Cultures: Tensions in the Struggle for Recognition*, trans. Kenneth B. Woodgate (London: Verso, 2000), 48.

69. Lavi, *The Modern Art of Dying*, 166.

70. Judith Jarvis Thomson, "Physician-Assisted Suicide: Two Moral Arguments," *Ethics* 109, no. 3 (April 1999): 497.

71. I owe this formulation to my last conversation with Geoffrey Hartman in the months before his death.

72. Heilbrun's guest column, "From Reading to Reading," as well as a prefatory "Editor's Note" by Marianne Hirsch and a forum of responses including my own appeared in *PMLA* 119, no. 2 (March 2004): 209–17 and 317–44.

73. The method of Heilbrun's death resembled that recommended by Hemlock Society founder Derek Humphry in, among other books, *Let Me Die before I Wake: Hemlock's Book of Self-Deliverance for the Dying* (New York: Dell, 1984), 149–52.

74. Carolyn Heilbrun, "Taking a U-Turn: The Aging Woman as Explorer of New Territory," *The Women's Review of Books* 20, nos. 10/11 (July 2003): 18.

75. Katha Politt, "Choosing Death," *New York Times*, December 28, 2003.

76. Ibid.

77. Ibid.

78. Lisa Lieberman, *Leaving You: The Cultural Meaning of Suicide* (Chicago: Ivan R. Dee, 2003), 7. Lieberman's argument aligns with a number of major studies in the history of suicide. See, especially, Georges Minois, *History of Suicide: Voluntary Death in Western Culture*, trans. Lydia Cochrane (Baltimore: Johns Hopkins University Press, 1999); and A. Alvarez, *The Savage God* (New York: W. W. Norton, 1971).

79. Amanda Cross [pseudonym of Carolyn Heilbrun], *Death in a Tenured Position* (New York: Ballantine, 1986), 175.

80. Ibid., 184–85.

81. Ibid., 187.

82. Ibid., 102. For important critiques of the conventional melodramatic framing of female suicide, see Margaret Higonnet, "Suicide: Representations of the Feminine in the Nineteenth-Century," *Poetics Today* 6, nos. 1/2 (1985): 103–18; and Barbara T. Gates, *Victorian Suicide: Mad Crimes and Sad Histories* (Princeton, N.J.: Princeton University Press, 1988), 125–50. On the connection between women's writing and women's suicide, see Elisabeth Bronfen, *Over Her Dead Body: Death, Femininity, and the Aesthetic* (New York: Routledge, 1992),

142–43. Highly relevant here as well is Gayatri Spivak's analysis of the vacillation and mutual interruption of culturally and politically determined readings of female suicide in "Can the Subaltern Speak?" in *Marxism and the Interpretation of Culture*, ed. Cary Nelson and Lawrence Grossberg (Chicago: University of Illinois Press, 1988), 271–313, esp. 297–308. See also my "Wharton's Suicides," *The Edith Wharton Review* 18, no. 2 (fall 2002): 12–25.

83. Cross [Heilbrun], *Death in a Tenured Position*, 186.

84. Heilbrun, "Taking a U-Turn," 18.

85. Hans Jonas, "The Right to Die," *The Hastings Center Report* 8, no. 4 (August 1978): 31–36.

86. Michael Burleigh, *Death and Deliverance: "Euthanasia" in Germany c. 1900–1945* (Cambridge: Cambridge University Press, 1994), 12–13.

87. Adolf Jost, *Das Recht auf den Tod* (Göttingen, 1895), 1.

88. Ibid., 37.

89. Ramón Sampedro, "¿Y cómo hablo de amor si estoy muerto?" in *Cartas desde el infierno* (Barcelona: Planeta, 2005), 23–24.

90. Ibid., lines 17–29.

Chapter 1

1. Leon Kass, for instance, argues that "with court-appointed proxy consentors, we will quickly erase the distinction between the right to choose one's death and the right to request someone else's." "Why Doctors Must Not Kill," *Commonweal* 118 (August 1991): 473. Ian McEwan exploits the potential of such a scenario for crime fiction in his novel *Amsterdam*.

2. "Convention for the Protection of Human Rights and Dignity with Regard to the Application of Biology and Medicine: European Convention on Human Rights and Biomedicine," *Counsel of Europe/Conseil de l'Europe*, April 4, 1997. See especially articles 5 and 9.

3. "The Natural Death Act," California Health and Safety Code §§ 7185–7195 (West Supp. 1977). The law has since been amended, with the corresponding passage found at California Probate Code 4656.

4. Alan Meisel, Kathy L. Cerminara, and Thaddeus M. Pope, *The Right to Die: The Law of End-of-Life Decisionmaking*, 3rd edition (Frederick, Md.: Wolters Kluwer, 2015), §12.04.

5. *Cruzan v. Director, Missouri Department of Health*, 497 U.S. 261 (1990), 262.

6. For instance, the majority opinion in *Washington v. Glucksberg* devotes nine pages (of thirty-five) to rehearsing the history of laws concerning suicide and assisted suicide. 521 U.S. 702 (1997), 710–719.

7. See, among others, James Rachels's now-classic critique of this distinction in "Active and Passive Euthanasia," *New England Journal of Medicine* 292, no. 2 (January 1975): 78–80.

8. Neil M. Gorsuch, *The Future of Assisted Suicide and Euthanasia* (Princeton, N.J.: Princeton University Press, 2006), 69.

9. Such a case is described by Timothy Quill in his *Death and Dignity: Making Choices and Taking Charge* (New York: W. W. Norton, 1993), 93–96, 105, 109.

10. Ibid., 136.

11. Ibid., 144.

12. *Pittsburgh Post-Gazette*, April 1, 2005, A10.

13. Denise Grady, "The Best Way to Keep Control Is to Leave Instructions," *New York Times*, March 29, 2005.

14. *Larry King Live*, March 21, 2005.

15. Anne E. Kornblut, "First Lady Says She and President Have Living Wills," *New York Times*, March 30, 2005.

16. For the history of the *Quinlan* and *Cruzan* cases, see especially Peter G. Filene, *In the Arms of Others: A Cultural History of the Right-to-Die in America* (Chicago: Ivan R. Dee, 1998).

17. *Cruzan*, 497 U.S. 261 at 261.

18. M. L. Tina Stevens, *Bioethics in America: Origins and Cultural Politics* (Baltimore: Johns Hopkins University Press, 2000), 128–29.

19. Qtd. in Filene, *In the Arms of Others*, 104.

20. In Re Quinlan, 70 N.J. 10 (1976) 355 A.2d 647, 40.

21. Ibid., 41.

22. Ibid.

23. *Cruzan*, 497 U.S. 261 at 277.

24. Ibid., 279.

25. Tamar Lewin, "Nancy Cruzan Dies, Outlived by a Debate over the Right to Die," *New York Times*, December 27, 1990.

26. Filene, *In the Arms of Others*, 182.

27. Susan Adler Channick, "The Myth of Autonomy at the End-of-Life: Questioning the Paradigm of Rights," *Villanova Law Review* 44, no. 4 (1999): 577–642, esp. 585ff.

28. Filene, *In the Arms of Others*, 159.

29. Kenneth W. Goodman, "Terri Schiavo and the Culture Wars: Ethics vs. Politics," in *The Case of Terri Schiavo: Ethics, Politics, and Death in the 21st Century*, ed. Kenneth W. Goodman (New York: Oxford University Press, 2010), 1.

30. "Instruction Directive (Living Will)," New Jersey Commission on Legal and Ethical Problems in the Delivery of Health Care, www.nj.gov/health/advance directive/forms_faqs.shtml.

31. In most U.S. states one may also, in the wake of *Quinlan* and *Cruzan*, appoint a health care surrogate or proxy—a family member or friend who is authorized to make health care decisions on one's behalf. At the same time, the power of the surrogate is normally limited when it comes to the decision to forgo or withdraw life-prolonging treatments. In the United States, legal protocols vary by state, but in many jurisdictions a health care surrogate cannot request the withdrawal or withholding of artificial nutrition or hydration unless there is an explicit advance directive from the patient.

32. Jon B. Eisenberg, "The Continuing Assault on Personal Autonomy in the Wake of the Schiavo Case," in Goodman, *The Case of Terri Schiavo*, 109.

33. One study reports that "unauthorized CPR was delivered to 11% of patients who died with advance directives." M. D. Goodman, M. Tarnoff, and G. J. Slotman, "Effect of Advance Directives on the Management of Elderly Critically Ill Patients," *Critical Care Medicine* 26, no. 4 (April 1998): 701–4. Another study shows that only 70 percent of living wills in their sample were consulted at the appropriate time. Howard B. Degenholtz, YongJoo Rhee, and Robert M. Arnold, "The Relationship between Having a Living Will and Dying in Place," *Annals of Internal Medicine* 141, no. 2 (July 20, 2004): 113–17. A more recent

study, however, suggests higher rates of correlation between living wills and outcomes. Maria J. Silveira, Scott Y. H. Kim, and Kenneth M. Langa, "Advance Directives and Outcomes of Surrogate Decision Making before Death," *New England Journal of Medicine* 362, no. 13 (April 2010): 1211–18.

34. Atul Gawande, *Being Mortal: Medicine and What Matters in the End* (New York: Metropolitan Books, 2015), 252.

35. Grady, "The Best Way to Keep Control."

36. Meta Calder, "Chapter 765 Revisited: Florida's New Advance Directives Law," *Florida State University Law Review* 20, no. 2 (fall 1992): 291–365.

37. Jay Wolfson, "The Basis for Decisions to End Life: The Schiavo Dilemma: An Essay by the Special Guardian Ad Litem," *Clinical Interventions in Aging* 1, no. 1 (March 2006): 3–6.

38. Justin Waddell, "Dead Letters: Protecting the Intentions of a Living Will Declarant with a Dedicated Advocate," *Georgetown Journal of Legal Ethics* 25, no. 3 (summer 2012): 801.

39. Nadia N. Sawicki, "A New Life for Wrongful Living," *New York Law School Law Review* 58, no. 2 (2013/14): 279–302. See also Arthur S. Berger, "Last Rights: The Views from a U.S. Courthouse," in *To Die or Not to Die?: Cross-Disciplinary, Cultural, and Legal Perspectives on the Right to Choose Death*, ed. Arthur S. Berger and Joyce Berger (New York: Praeger, 1990): 140–41.

40. Luis Kutner, "Due Process of Euthanasia: The Living Will, a Proposal," *Indiana Law Journal* 44, no. 4 (July 1, 1969): 553.

41. The living will template provided by Eileen P. Flynn exemplifies the checklist format. It outlines four different medical scenarios and for each one provides a list of ten medical treatments (cardiopulmonary resuscitation, mechanical breathing, tube-feeding, kidney dialysis, etc.) along with three options—"perform," "do not perform," "I do not want to make a decision about this matter now; I direct my attending physician to follow my Proxy's instructions"—among which the author of the living will simply selects. Eileen P. Flynn, *Your Living Will: Why, When and How to Write One* (New York: Citadel, 1992): 59–78. See also Shai Lavi's cogent critique of patient autonomy as "bounded and constructed" in *The Modern Art of Dying: A History of Euthanasia in the United States* (Princeton, N.J.: Princeton University Press, 2005), 166–68.

42. The signature on a living will, we might say, thus lays bare the structural conditions of all acts of signature, whose "repeatable, iterable, imitatable form" necessarily allows the signature "to be detached from the singular present and singular intention of its production," as Jacques Derrida observes. "Signature Event Context," trans. Samuel Weber and Jeffrey Mehlman, *Glyph* 1 (1977): 194.

43. Angela Fagerlin and Carl E. Schnieder, "Enough: The Failure of the Living Will," *Hastings Center Report* 34, no. 2 (2004): 34.

44. Ronald Dworkin, *Life's Dominion: An Argument about Abortion, Euthanasia, and Individual Freedom* (New York: Alfred A. Knopf, 1993), 231.

45. Kutner, "Due Process of Euthanasia," 540. It should be noted that other legal traditions do at times view something like the "impulse of mercy" as an exonerating factor in assisted suicide, most notably Switzerland.

46. Ibid., 550.

47. Ibid., 553.

48. Frederic W. Maitland and Francis C. Montague, *A Sketch of English Legal History* (New York: G. P. Putnam's Sons, 1915), 123.

49. Henry Hansmann and Ugo Mattei, "The Functions of Trust Law: A Comparative Legal and Economic Analysis," *New York University Law Review* 73, no. 434 (May 1998): 439.

50. Sarah Worthington, *Equity* (Oxford: Oxford University Press, 2006), 62–63.

51. St. Thomas Aquinas, *The "Summa Theologica" of St. Thomas Aquinas*, trans. Fathers of the English Dominican Province (London: Burns Oates and Washburn, 1929), 10:204.

52. John Locke, *Second Treatise of Government* (1690), ed. C. B. Macpherson (Indianapolis, Ind.: Hackett, 1980), 9.

53. William Shakespeare, *Hamlet*, 5.1.15–23.

54. Ibid., 5.1.26.

55. *Cruzan*, 497 U.S. 261 at 296.

56. Shakespeare, *Hamlet*, 5.1.120–32.

57. Qtd. in *Glucksberg*, 521 U.S. 702 at 714.

58. "Suicide," *Dictionnaire des sciences médicales* (Paris: C.L.F. Pancoucke, 1812–22), v. 53 (1821), 213–83.

59. The earliest text cited by Durkheim is Gustave Étoc-Demazy's *Recherches statistiques sur le suicide*, published in Paris in 1844, though several important studies preceded Etoc-Demazy's work, including J. P. Falret, *Du suicide et de l'hypochondrie* (Paris, 1822), A. M. Guerry, *Essai sur la statistique morale de la France* (Paris, 1833), and M. Brouc, "Considerations sur les suicides de notre époque," *Annales d'hygiene publique et de medicine légale* 16 (1836). Such studies proliferated after the middle of the century. Durkheim's principal sources include Enrico Morselli's *Il suicidio* (Milan, 1879), Alexander Von Oettingen's *Ueber akuten und chronishen Selbstmord* (Dorpat, 1881), William Ogle's "Suicides in England and Wales in Relation to Age, Sex, Season, and Occupation" (1886), and Thomas Masaryk's *Selbstmord als sociale Massenerscheinung* (Vienna, 1881).

60. A. Alvarez, *The Savage God* (New York: W. W. Norton, 1971), 99.

61. Edwin Shneidman, "Suicide Notes Reconsidered" (1976), in *Lives and Deaths: Selections from the Works of Edwin S. Shneidman,* ed. Antoon A. Leenaars (Taylor and Francis, 1999), 264. Shneidman reaffirms this argument in a later work as well, *Voices of Death* (New York: HarperCollins, 1980).

62. See, for instance, the French right-to-die organization, *Ultime Liberté.*

63. Antje Pedain, "The Human Rights Dimension of the Diane Pretty Case," *Cambridge Law Journal* 62, no. 1 (March 2003): 187.

64. European Court of Human Rights, *Pretty v. United Kingdom*, no 2346/02, Judgment of April 29, 2002. Pretty filed suit under articles 2 (the right to life), 3 (concerning torture or inhuman or degrading treatment or punishment), 8 (right to respect for private and family life), 9 (freedom of thought, conscience, and religion), and 14 (freedom from discrimination) of the European Convention of Human Rights. Neither the British House of Lords nor the Court found that Pretty's rights were engaged with respect to articles 2, 3, or 9, and 14. Article 2, the Court ruled, does not confer a right to die (27). Although she was clearly suffering, the Court found with respect to article 3 that "it is beyond dispute that the respondent State has not, itself, inflicted any ill-treatment on the applicant" (31).

With respect to article 9, it found that "her claims do not involve a manifestation of a religion or belief" (38). With respect to Article 14, the Court found that "there is . . . objective and reasonable justification for not distinguishing between those who are and those who are not physically capable of committing suicide" (40).

65. Ibid., 32.

66. *R. (Pretty) v. Director of Public Prosecutions (Secretary of State for the Home Department intervening)*, [2001] UKHL 61; [2002] 1 A.C. 800, [61].

67. ECtHR, *Pretty v. United Kingdom*, 33.

68. *R. (Pretty) v. Director of Public Prosecutions*, [100].

69. Pedain, "The Human Rights Dimension of the Diane Pretty Case."

70. ECtHR, *Pretty v. United Kingdom*, 34.

71. Ibid., 32.

72. "Please Help Me Die," *Panorama*, BBC-1, transmission May 12, 2002, news.bbc.co.uk/2/hi/programmes/panorama/.

73. European Court of Human Rights, *Sanles v. Spain* 48335/99, decision of October 26, 2000.

74. "Please Help Me Die," *Panorama*.

75. ECtHR, *Pretty v. United Kingdom*, 36.

76. Ibid., 16.

77. "Please Help Me Die," *Panorama*.

78. ECtHR, *Pretty v. United Kingdom*, 3.

79. "The Dutch Termination of Life on Request and Assisted Suicide (Review Procedures) Act," rpt. in *Assisted Death in Europe and America: Four Regimes and Their Lessons*, ed. Guenter Lewy (Oxford: Oxford University Press, 2011), 162.

80. "The Belgian Act on Euthanasia of 28 May 2002," rpt. in Lewy, *Assisted Death in Europe and America*, 173.

81. The Oregon Death with Dignity Act, 127.810, www.oregonlaws.org; The Washington Death with Dignity Act, Chapter 70.245 RCW, app.leg.wa.gov/; Vermont S.77 (ACT 0039) "An Act relating to Patient Choice and Control at End of Life," www.leg.state.vt.us.

82. The Oregon and Washington versions of the law specify that this request should state that "I make this request voluntarily and without reservation, and I accept full moral responsibility for my actions." See Oregon 127.897 and Washington RCW 70.245.220.

83. It is telling that Pretty's name itself becomes appropriated as a common adjective in several scholarly studies, for example, Emily Wada, "A Pretty Picture: The Margin of Appreciation and the Right to Assisted Suicide," *Loyola of Los Angeles International and Comparative Law Review* 27, no. 2 (2005): 275–89; Hazel Biggs, "A Pretty Fine Line: Life, Death, Autonomy and Letting It B" (which also puns on a case involving "Mrs. B"), *Feminist Legal Studies* 11, no. 3 (2003): 291–301.

84. "Please Help Me Die," *Panorama*.

85. Timothy J. Deines, "Bartleby the Scrivener, Immanence and the Resistance of Community," *Culture Machine* 8 (2006), www.culturemachine.net.

86. Herman Melville, "Bartleby, the Scrivener: A Story of Wall-Street," in *The Piazza Tales and Other Prose Pieces 1839–1860*, ed. Harrison Hayford, Hershel

Parker, and G. Thomas Tanselle, vol. 9 of *The Writings of Herman Melville: The Northwestern-Newberry Edition* (Evanston, Ill.: Northwestern University Press, 1987), 19. Page references to "Bartleby" refer to this edition.

87. As J. Hillis Miller notes, then, at the heart of the lawyer's storytelling enterprise is an ethical question: "I cannot determine what my ethical obligation to my neighbor is, and then act on that obligation, unless I can identify him by telling his story." At the same time, because this story remains incomplete, because what the lawyer knows of Bartleby's past is limited to hearsay, "'Bartleby the Scrivener' is the story of the failure of the narrator to tell the complete story of Bartleby." *Versions of Pygmalion* (Cambridge, Mass.: Harvard University Press, 1990), 142.

88. Johannes Dietrich Bergmann, "'Bartleby' and *The Lawyer's Story*," *American Literature* 47, no. 3 (November 1975): 432–36.

89. Rosemarie Garland-Thomson, "The Cultural Logic of Euthanasia: 'Sad Fancyings' in Herman Melville's 'Bartleby,'" *American Literature* 76, no. 4 (December 2004): 777–806.

90. Ibid., 782–83.

91. Ibid., 796.

92. Ibid., 800.

93. Ibid., 783.

94. T. H. Giddings, "Melville, the Colt-Adams Murder, and 'Bartleby,'" *Studies in American Fiction* 2 (1974): 123–32.

95. Tom Cohen purses a different but compelling reading of this moment, linking the "bar" in bar-tender to Bartleby's name and, "read here in the barest[!] possible way," to the disruption of representation and referentiality. *Antimimesis from Plato to Hitchcock* (Cambridge: Cambridge University Press, 1994), 170.

96. Naomi C. Reed, "The Specter of Wall Street: 'Bartleby, the Scrivener' and the Language of Commodities," *American Literature* 76, no. 2 (June 2004): 261.

97. Ibid., 261–62.

98. Ibid., 266.

99. Gilles Deleuze, "Bartleby; or The Formula," in *Essays Critical and Clinical*, trans. Daniel W. Smith and Michael A. Greco (Minneapolis: University of Minnesota Press, 1997), 73. Deleuze takes pains to list the "ten principal circumstances" in which Bartleby "prefers not to," with the tenth of these being when he is forced out of the law office (69–70). Puzzlingly, then, Deleuze leaves off Bartleby's final "prefer not to" in the prison, "I prefer not to dine to-day," which implies his possible preferring not to live. One might speculate that this last instance may be overlooked because it does not easily align with Deleuze's affirmative reading of Bartleby as "the new Christ or the brother to us all"—unless, that is, Christ is himself considered a suicide (90).

100. The relevance of Melville's "Tale of Wall-Street" to the Occupy Wall Street action was widely noticed by media commentators from its early weeks. See, for example, Nina Martyris, "A Patron Saint for Occupy Wall Street," *New Republic*, October 15, 2011.

101. "He has been turned into a human machine . . . . But by degrees, Bartleby becomes the embodiment of a gigantic protest against this waste, the degradation of human life. At the end he looms up as a man of epic stature. With all the strength of his ill-fed, ill-clad, ill-housed body, he protested." C. L. R. James,

Marines, Renegades and Castaways: The Story of Herman Melville and the World We Live In (1953; Hanover, N.H.: University Press of New England, 2001), 107.

102. Charles Z. Lincoln, *The Constitutional History of New York State from the Beginning of the Colonial Period to the Year 1905* (Lawyers Co-operative, 1906), 2:152.

103. Maurice Blanchot, *The Writing of the Disaster*, trans. Ann Smock (Lincoln: University of Nebraska Press, 1986), 17.

104. For a compelling elaboration of Lot's wife as a figure of the witness, see Martin Harries, *Forgetting Lot's Wife: On Destructive Spectatorship* (New York: Fordham University Press, 2007).

105. Job 3:11–14 (KJV).

106. On the lawyer-narrator as a Judas figure, see, for instance, William Bysshe Stein, "Bartleby: The Christian Conscience," in *"Bartleby the Scrivener": A Symposium*, ed. Howard P. Vincent (Kent, Ohio: Kent State University Press, 1966), 107; as a Pontius Pilate figure, Alexander Eliot, "Melville and Bartleby," *Furioso* 3 (1947): 11; and as a "prudent Samaritan," Steven Doloff, "The Prudent Samaritan: Melville's 'Bartleby the Scrivener' as a Parody of Christ's Parable to the Lawyer," *Studies in Short Fiction* 34 (1997): 357–61.

107. See, for instance, H. Bruce Franklin, *The Wake of the Gods: Melville's Mythology* (Stanford, Calif.: Stanford University Press, 1963), 126–36; Donald M. Feine, "Bartleby the Christ," *American Transcendental Quarterly* 7 (1970): 18–23; and Deleuze, "Bartleby, or the Formula." The identification of Bartleby with humanity, as J. Hillis Miller notes, is characteristic of a large class of interpretations that "claim in one way or another to have identified Bartleby and accounted for him," whether by "making him an example of some universal type" or by seeing him as representative of some historical or cultural context. Miller argues that Bartleby disrupts such identifications; he is "neither general nor particular: he is neutral." *Versions of Pygmalion*, 173–74.

108. To Nathaniel Hawthorne, June 1?, 1851, in *The Letters of Herman Melville,* ed. Merrell R. Davis and William H. Gilman (New Haven, Conn.: Yale University Press, 1960), 128. Leo Marx associates this "banned" writing with Bartleby, joining a series of critics who see the copyist as a figure for the author. "Melville's Parable of the Walls," *Sewanee Review* 61, no. 4 (autumn 1953): 602.

Chapter 2

1. Katha Politt, "Choosing Death," *New York Times*, December 28, 2003.

2. Stevens, concurring, *Washington v. Glucksberg*, 521 U.S. 702 (1997), 747.

3. Atul Gawande, *Being Mortal: Medicine and What Matters in the End* (New York: Metropolitan Books, 2015), 140, 249.

4. Walter Benjamin, "The Storyteller: Observations on the Works of Nikolai Leskov," trans. Harry Zohn, in *Selected Writings: Volume 3, 1935–1938*, ed. Howard Eiland and Michael W. Jennings (Cambridge, Mass.: Belknap Press of Harvard University Press, 2002), 156.

5. Ronald Dworkin, *Life's Dominion: An Argument about Abortion, Euthanasia, and Individual Freedom* (New York: Alfred A. Knopf, 1993), 197. Dworkin's observation is bolstered by the fact, noted earlier, that claims for "wrongful living" have not been recognized, to date, as the basis for tort claims (see chapter 1, note 39).

6. Ibid., 199.

7. Ibid., 209.

8. Ibid., 213.

9. Ibid.

10. Richard K. Sanderson interestingly observes that similar narrative conventions and expectations seem to structure memoirs published by those who have assisted the suicide of a family member or loved one. "Memoirs of Assisted Suicide," *a/b: Auto/Biography Studies* 18, no. 1 (2003): 23–44.

11. Dworkin, *Life's Dominion*, 205.

12. E. S. Burt, *Regard for the Other: Autothanatography in Rousseau, De Quincey, Baudelaire, and Wilde* (New York: Fordham University Press, 2009), 6.

13. See Peter Brooks, *Reading for the Plot: Design and Intention in Narrative* (Cambridge, Mass.: Harvard University Press, 1984), 283ff.

14. Jonathan Strauss, *Human Remains: Medicine, Death, and Desire in Nineteenth-Century Paris* (New York: Fordham University Press, 2012), 11.

15. Ibid., 35.

16. Ibid., 36–37.

17. Ibid., 60–61.

18. Michel Vovelle, *La Mort et l'Occident de 1300 à nos jours* (Paris: Gallimard, 2000), 455. George Behlmer, "Grave Doubts: Victorian Medicine, Moral Panic, and the Signs of Death," *Journal of British Studies* 42, no. 2 (April 2003): 222.

19. Edgar Allan Poe, "The Premature Burial" (1844), in *Poetry and Tales* (New York: Library of America, 1984), 666.

20. Edgar Allan Poe, "The Facts in the Case of M. Valdemar" (1845), in *Poetry and Tales*, 841.

21. This fear of being buried alive resurfaces in Rilke's novel, in Malte's account of the puncturing of his father's heart upon his death: "And at that moment I grasped that what he wanted was certainty. . . . Now he was to get it." Rainer Maria Rilke, *The Notebooks of Malte Laurids Brigge*, trans. Michael Hulse (New York: Penguin, 2009), 101.

22. Charles Baudelaire, "De l'héroisme de la vie moderne," in *Oeuvres complètes*, ed. Claude Pichois, 2 vols. (Paris: Gallimard, 1976), 2:494.

23. Charles Baudelaire, "Le Peintre de la vie moderne," in *Oeuvres completes*, 2:684. See Paul de Man, "Literary History and Literary Modernity," in *Blindness and Insight: Essays in the Rhetoric of Contemporary Criticism*, 2nd edition (Minneapolis: University of Minnesota Press, 1983), 142–65.

24. Baudelaire, "De l'héroisme," 2:494.

25. Walter Benjamin, "The Paris of the Second Empire in Baudelaire," trans. Harry Zohn, in *Selected Writings, Volume 2, Part 2: 1931–1934*, ed. Michael W. Jennings, Howard Eiland, and Gary Smith (Cambridge, Mass.: Belknap Press of Harvard University Press, 1999), 45.

26. Madame de Stael, *Lettres sur l'ouvrage et le caractère de J. J. Rousseau* (Paris: Au Temple de la Vertu, 1789), 108. Olivier de Corancez, *De Jean-Jacques Rousseau: Extrait du Journal de Paris, des Nos. 251, 256, 258, 259, 260 & 261, de l'an VI* (Paris, 1798), 59–65.

27. V. de Musset-Pathay, *La Vie et les ouvrages de J. J. Rousseau* (1823), new edition (Paris: P. Dupont, 1827), 433.

28. Baudelaire, "De l'héroisme," 2:494.

29. One could speculate here about Baudelaire's reference to Rousseau, for at least Musset-Pathay's version could be seen as disrupting a traditional image of how a philosopher should commit suicide. Whereas Socrates is presented as dying calmly after drinking the hemlock, Rousseau is depicted as suffering in pain after ingesting the poison, and then resorting to the pistol, as if rejecting the conventional image of a philosopher's death. A similar representation of Rousseau's death can be found in a slightly later text, Gerard de Nerval's 1850 *Les Faux saulniers*, where the poison Rousseau imbibes is specifically said to be hemlock and a scene of calm demise—the philosopher drinks his poisoned draught while stroking the hair of his child—is succeeded by an image of Rousseau wracked with pain until he shoots himself (enacting Musset-Pathay's account of Rousseau's double suicide). Gerard de Nerval, *Les Faux saulniers,* in *Oeuvres completes de Gerard de Nerval*, vol. 4 (Paris: Michel Lévy Frères, 1869), 405–6.

30. This consequence of the figure of metempsychosis, where a future is imagined in which the contingent attributes of former life will have been wiped away, a future that is severed from the past, is dramatized in the final stanza of the poem "La Vie antérieure" ("A Former Life") from *Les Fleurs du mal*, in which the speaker recalls a life surrounded by:

> . . . des esclaves nus, tout imprégnés d'odeurs,
>
> Qui me rafraîchissaient le front avec des palmes,
> Et dont l'unique soin était d'approfondir
> Le secret douloureux qui me faisait languir. (248)
>
> . . . many a naked, perfumed slave,
>
> Who fanned my languid brow with waving palms.
> They were my slaves—the only care they had
> To know what secret grief had made me sad. (20; trans. F. P. Sturm)

Rather than present a clear image or identity, the past life appears here as a secret. The figure of metempsychosis, then, does not describe a movement from one positive identity to another, but rather a movement of continual lack, in which the self is predicated on what it does not or cannot know about its past or, consequently, its future. Charles Baudelaire, *The Flowers of Evil*, ed. Marthiel Mathews and Jackson Mathews (New York: New Directions, 1989).

31. Baudelaire, "Le Peintre de la vie moderne," 2:692.

32. Samuel Weber, *Unwrapping Balzac: A Reading of "La Peau de chagrin"* (Toronto: University of Toronto Press, 1979).

33. Nancy Lee Beaty, *The Craft of Dying Well: A Study in the Literary Tradition of the Ars Moriendi in England* (New Haven, Conn.: Yale University Press, 1970), 6, 197.

34. Frances M. M. Comper, ed., *The Book of the Craft of Dying and Other Early English Tracts concerning Death* (London: Longman, Greens, 1917), 27.

35. Ibid.

36. Ibid., 7–8.

37. James W. Green, *Beyond the Good Death: The Anthropology of Modern Dying* (Philadelphia: University of Pennsylvania Press, 2008), 8–10, 203n2.

38. Ibid., 14.

39. Ibid., 11.

40. Derek Humphry, *Let Me Die before I Wake: Hemlock's Book of Self-Deliverance for the Dying* (New York: Dell, 1984), 12.

41. Claude Gillon and Yves Le Bonniec, *Suicide mode d'emploi: Histoire, technique, actualité* (Paris: Alain Moreau, 1982), 11, 209–40.

42. Derek Humphry, "Farewell to Hemlock: Killed by Its Name" (February 21, 2005), www.assistedsuicide.org/farewell-to-hemlock.html.

43. Page numbers for *La Peau de chagrin* refer first to the French—Balzac, *La Comedie humaine, Vol X: Études philosophiques* (Paris: Gallimard, 1979)—followed by the English translation, *The Wild Ass's Skin*, trans. Herbert J. Hunt (London: Penguin, 1977). Translations are modified throughout.

44. C.-A. Sainte-Beuve. *Causeries du lundi*, 3rd edition, vol. 1. (Paris: Garnier Frères, 1857), 19.

45. Lisa Lieberman, *Leaving You: The Cultural Meaning of Suicide* (Chicago: Ivan R. Dee, 2003), 104. See also Weber, who claims that the suicide in this passage "precisely by putting an end to *her* life, conserves it in its enigmatic integrity as a meaningful mystery, the aura of which survives in the newspaper report." *Unwrapping Balzac*, 31.

46. The genesis of the novel underscores this point. The first published fragment, which appeared in *La Caricature* on December 16, 1830, under the title "Le Dernier Napoléon," recounted the anonymous young man's loss at the casino and walk to the Pont Royal, concluding with him on the brink of suicide ("son regard plongea jusqu'au fond de la Seine . . ."). *La Comédie humaine*, 10:1232–34; ellipses in original. In relation to this first fragment, the novel thus appears in its entirety as a response to the mystery of the ellipses with which "Le Dernier Napoléon" concludes.

47. François Jost, "Littérature et suicide: De Werther à Madame Bovary," *Revue de littérature comparée* 42 (1968): 161–98. The deep association of Goethe's *Werther* with imitative suicide is evidenced by the sociological concept of "the Werther effect" coined by the sociologist David Phillips in 1974, based on observations that a publicized suicide seems to lead to a spike or increase in the suicide rate. See David P. Phillips, "The Influence of Suggestion on Suicide: Substantive and Theoretical Implications of the Werther Effect," *American Sociological Review* 39, no. 3 (June 1974): 340–54.

48. See Eric Blackall, *Goethe and the Novel* (Ithaca, N.Y.: Cornell University Press, 1976), 52–53; Benjamin Bennett, "Goethe's *Werther*: Double Perspective and the Game of Life," *The German Quarterly* 53, no. 1 (1980): 64–81; and Caroline Wellbery, "Sentimental Paradigms in Goethe's *Werther*," *Studies in Romanticism* 25, no. 2 (summer 1986): 231–49.

49. It is worth recalling here the role of Rastignac elsewhere in *La Comédie humaine*. Of course, it would not be until the writing of *Le Père Goriot* four years later that Balzac would initiate his system of recurring characters, placing the figure of Rastignac, a minor character in the already published *La Peau de chagrin*, at the center of the later novel. However, with respect to historical setting, *Le Père Goriot* takes place before *La Peau de chagrin*, and so the Rastignac we meet in the latter novel has, within the overall world of *La Comédie humaine*, already undergone the experiences recounted in *Le Père Goriot*. That is to say, he has already realized the impossibility of remaining an outsider to society and has

decided to enter into what is at once a truce and a battle with the social world of Paris, as emblematized in the final declaration he makes to the city in *Le Père Goriot*: "A nous deux!"

50. Benjamin, "The Storyteller," 150–51.

51. Ibid.

52. Benjamin, "The Paris of the Second Empire in Baudelaire," 45; translation modified. Benjamin's "die Moderne," like Baudelaire's "modernité," might be translated as either "modernity" or "modernism." In a letter to Adorno concerning this text, Benjamin states that his use of the term "die Moderne" is synonymous with Baudelaire's *modernité*, and that his text "could not go beyond the limits imposed on the word in Baudelaire's usage." Theodor W. Adorno and Walter Benjamin, *The Complete Correspondence 1928–1940*, ed. Henri Lonitz, trans. Nicholas Walter (Cambridge: Polity, 1999), 291.

53. Without mentioning this discussion of suicide by Benjamin, Shoshana Felman (uncannily) echoes Benjamin's language in a description of his own death: "By asserting his own choice of death and by taking his own life, Benjamin repeats . . . the posthumous, mute message of the suicide as a symbolic gesture of protest against the war and as the autonomous assertion of an uncoerced and uncoercible will in the face of the overpowering spread of world violence." *The Juridical Unconscious* (Cambridge, Mass.: Harvard University Press, 2002), 49.

54. I adapt this formulation from Cathy Caruth, *Literature in the Ashes of History* (Baltimore: Johns Hopkins University Press, 2013).

55. Benjamin, "The Paris of the Second Empire in Baudelaire," 45.

56. Benjamin describes purchasing an early edition of Balzac's novel at auction in "Unpacking My Library," in *Selected Writings, Volume 2, Part 2: 1931–1934*, ed. Michael W. Jennings, Howard Eiland, and Gary Smith (Cambridge, Mass.: Belknap Press of Harvard University Press, 1999), 490.

57. Qtd. in Benjamin, "The Paris of the Second Empire in Baudelaire," 43.

58. On the association of Romantic or heroic suicide with an aristocratic elite, see Georges Minois, *History of Suicide: Voluntary Death in Western Culture*, trans. Lydia Cochrane (Baltimore: Johns Hopkins University Press, 1999), 248–77.

59. Benjamin, "The Paris of the Second Empire in Baudelaire," 45–46. Benjamin quotes here from Charles Benoist, "L'Homme de 1848," *Revue des deux mondes*, February 1, 1914, 667.

60. Patrice Higonnet makes a related observation on the ways that pre-Revolutionary conventions surrounding sentimental suicide in France are "recycled" in the form of exemplary political suicides after the Revolution. "Du suicide sentimental au suicide politique," in *La Revolution et la mort*, ed. Elizabeth Liris and Jean Maurice Biziere (Toulouse: Presses Universitaires de Mirail, 1991), 137–49.

61. On Castlereagh and the publicity surrounding his death, see Barbara T. Gates, *Victorian Suicide: Mad Crimes and Sad Histories* (Princeton, N.J.: Princeton University Press, 1998), 3–5.

62. Fréderic Caille, *La Figure du sauveteur: Naissance du citoyen secoureur en France (1780–1914)* (Rennes: Presses Universitaires de Rennes, 2006), 197–98.

63. *Galignani's New Paris Guide* (Paris: A. & W. Galignani, 1830), 48. Galignani's guide specifies rewards of twenty-five francs for rescuing someone still alive

and fifteen francs for the dead. In the 1852 edition, while the rewards remain the same, the number of first-aid stations increases to eighty.

64. *Paris; ou Le Livre des cent-et-un*, 15 vols. (Paris: Ladvocat, 1831–35), 1:vi. Launched by Ladvocat in an attempt to rescue his failing publishing business, *Le Livre des cent-et-un* styled itself as a comprehensive portrait of modern Paris featuring articles by 101 well-known writers of the time. In the front matter to the first volume, among the list of writers said to have signed on to contribute two articles each, is the name of Balzac; but the novelist does not seem to have made good on his supposed pledge, as none of the articles in the collection bear his name.

65. Léon Gozlan, "La Morgue," in *Paris; ou Le Livre des cent-et-un*, 1:324–25. The translation given here is modified from a two-volume abridged version of this anthology published in Boston in 1833 as *Paris, or the Book of the Hundred-and-One* (Boston: Lilly, Wait, Colman and Holden, 1833), 2:248.

66. Although the period covered in Cobb's *Death in Paris, 1795–1801* pre-dates the system of monetary rewards described here, he describes the dense legal, administrative, and social network that surrounded suicide by drowning in late eighteenth-century Paris and that created the conditions for the later system. Richard Cobb, *Death in Paris: The Records of the Basse-Geôle de la Seine, October 1795–September 1801, Vendémaire Year IV–Fructidor Year IX* (Oxford: Oxford University Press, 1978).

67. Cobb, *Death in Paris*, 27.

68. The single most detailed and rigorous reading of the novel, Weber's *Unwrapping Balzac*, surprisingly does not explore the Faustian intertext. For sustained discussions of Faustian intertexts in later novels by Balzac, see Mireille Labourers, "Méphistophélès et l'androgyne: Les Figures du pacte dans *Illusions perdues*," *Année Balzacienne* 17 (1996): 211–30; and, focusing on *Le Père Goriot*, Dan Edelstein, "The Modernization of Myth: From Balzac to Sorel," *Yale French Studies*, no. 111, "Myth and Modernity" (2007): 32–44. Edelstein notes in passing the Faustian intertext in *La Peau de chagrin*, but argues that it "does not break in any way with the Romantic mythical paradigm, since . . . the supernatural and ancient features of the myth are preserved" (36). I suggest instead that the novel situates itself and the Faust allusion in a self-consciously belated relation to the Faust myth.

69. The allusion continues as Raphaël's diverted suicide attempt recalls an early scene in Goethe's drama where Faust turns away from suicide under the influence of the Easter bells he hears echoing outside his study. Raphaël, as he leaves the Pont Royal, encounters a similar religiously toned message just as he leaves the Pont Royal. "We will pray to God to keep you in long life," call out some mendicants after Raphaël offers them a few copper coins he discovers lurking in his coat pocket (67; 69). Later in the novel, when Raphaël gives an autobiographical account of the events leading up to his encounter with the talisman, we learn that, also like Faust, he was a scholar frustrated with the limits of knowledge: despite "completing the researches of Mesmer, Lavater, Gall, and Bichat by blazing a new trail in human science," he nonetheless laments that "my life was one cruel antithesis, a perpetual falsehood" (111–12). When he tells the antiquarian, "I had decided to give my life to study and thought, but they had not even provided me with food" (87; 54), we therefore understand that the food in question is not

merely comestible but spiritual, as in Faust's lament, in Goethe's version, that despite his learning, "I've neither goods nor gold, / No worldly honour, or splendour hold: / Not even a dog would play this part!" (lines 374–76). The novel's reworking of *Faust* continues in its descriptions of the ancient merchant, whose face appears as "the jeering mask of Mephistopheles" (78; 44), and who invokes the Faust tradition himself when he declares that "You've signed the pact, all is said" (88; 55)—despite the fact that Raphaël is not said to have signed anything. The particular evocation of Goethe's *Faust*, the first part of which had been published in three different French translations by 1831, is confirmed in an allusion to the Walpurgisnacht scene of Goethe's text, an element of Goethe's version not borrowed from the existing Faust tradition. Raphaël perceives the shop itself as "a weird witches' sabbath worthy of the fantasies glimpsed by Dr. Faustus on the Brocken" (76; 42). Finally, Raphaël himself belatedly acknowledges his precursor when he crosses paths again with the antiquarian later in the novel. First, the latter's "bloodless lips . . . suggested to Raphaël's vivid imagination a striking analogy with the hypothetical face of Goethe's Mephistopheles, as painters have portrayed it" (222; 207). Then, momentarily, Raphaël fantasizes that he, too, has entered into a pact with the devil: "Recoiling in dread from the prospect of meeting the fate of Faust, he impulsively invoked Heaven" (222; 207).

70. Richard Halpern, "Marlowe's Theater of Night: Doctor Faustus and Capital," *ELH* 71, no. 2 (summer 2004): 461.

71. György Lukács, *Goethe and His Age*, trans. Robert Anchor (London: Merlin, 1968), 198–200.

72. Marshall Berman, *All That Is Solid Melts into Air: The Experience of Modernity* (New York: Penguin, 1982), 49.

73. Ibid., 51–52.

74. Weber, *Unwrapping Balzac*, 48. As mentioned above, Weber does not explore the relation to *Faust*.

75. Indeed, it is perhaps best compared to that proto-photographic institution of early nineteenth-century Paris, the diorama, invented and operated by Daguerre. The illusionistic display of the diorama was created by manipulating light projections onto screens to create three-dimensional effects.

76. See, for instance, Peter Osborne, "Marx and the Philosophy of Time," *Radical Philosophy* 147 (January/February 2008): 20.

77. Karl Marx, *Capital: A Critique of Political Economy, Vol. 1*, trans. Samuel Moore and Edward Aveling (New York: International Publishers, 1967), 77; translation modified.

78. Ibid., 50.

79. Victor Brombert, *The Hidden Reader: Stendhal, Balzac, Hugo, Baudelaire, Flaubert* (Cambridge, Mass.: Harvard University Press, 1988), 47.

80. Alois Richard Nykl, "The Talisman in Balzac's *La peau de chagrin*," *Modern Language Notes* 34, no. 8 (December 1919): 479–81.

81. An early, rejected scheme for what would become *La Peau de chagrin* heightens this ambiguity: it seems that Balzac initially imagined a tale in which an old man (eventually, the antiquarian) deceives a young man (eventually, Raphaël) into falsely believing that a skin whose sole power is to shrink in fact has talismanic powers and will take the life of its owner. When the young man dies, the old man declares, "This skin only shrank in your pocket because that was one

of its properties. Die, then, shameful of your ignorance and stupid credulity." Pierres-Georges Castex et al., "La peau de chagrin: Histoire du texte," in Balzac, *La Comédie humaine,* vol. 10 (Paris: Gallimard, 1979), 1221.

82. Strauss compellingly demonstrates that nineteenth-century French medicine produced and exploited an image of death as enigma in order to establish and shore up its own authority. In this light, Raphaël could be said perhaps to appropriate the medical authority over death for himself. *Human Remains,* 67–79.

83. In fact, at one point this exact wish is attributed to him, but of course it remains apparently unfulfilled: "He wanted to live forever" (255; 242).

84. I thank Michael Levine for pointing out the pun on *verge* (penis) in the servant's malapropism.

85. Félix Nadar, *Quand j'étais photographe* (New York: Arno, 1979), 6.

86. For a fuller consideration of the relationship between suicide and photography, see my "Overexposures: Notes on Suicide and Photography," *Connect: art. politics.theory. practice* 3, "Corpus" (December 2001): 83–88.

87. Benjamin, "The Storyteller," 146.

88. Felman powerfully suggests that Benjamin's own suicide might be understood as this sort of communication. See above, note 53.

89. This resistance to resolution, we might note, also spills over into Balzac's *La Comedie humaine* in general, in which each novel, beginning (retroactively) with *La Peau de chagrin*, continues or is continued by others.

90. I allude here to Frank Kermode, *The Sense of an Ending: Studies in the Theory of Fiction* (Oxford: Oxford University Press, 1967).

Chapter 3

1. Whereas recent legislation in the United States, Canada, and elsewhere has tended to focus on limiting the physician's role to prescribing medications to be taken orally by the patient (physician-assisted suicide), Belgium and Luxembourg have taken a different path in which the only form of legal physician-assisted death is where lethal drugs are administered directly by a doctor. In addition, Belgium does not limit eligibility to the terminally ill (defined in most jurisdictions as having six months or less to live according to medical diagnosis). Distelmans has been controversial in part due to several highly publicized cases in which he agreed to grant euthanasia requests to the non-terminally ill. On Distelmans, see Rachel Aviv, "The Death Treatment," *The New Yorker,* June 22, 2015.

2. Wim Distelmans, *In Pursuit of a Dignified Life's End: The Belgian Model,* trans. Jacqueline Balfour (London: Hartfield, 2015), 197.

3. Shirli Sitbon, "Doctor Plans 'Inspiring' Auschwitz Tour to Talk about Euthanasia," *TheJC.com,* May 23, 2014, www.thejc.com.

4. Johathan Petre, "Outrage as 'Dr. Death' Offers Euthanasia Tours of 'Inspiring' Auschwitz," *Daily Mail Online,* July 12, 2014, www.dailymail.co.uk.

5. Katrin Kuntz, "Euthanasia Doctors Seek Existential Answers at Auschwitz," *Der Spiegel Online,* November 21, 2014, www.spiegel.de.

6. Kevin Fitzpatrick and Tom Mortier, "Why Would a Euthanasia Practitioner Tour Auschwitz?" *Careful: A Blog about End of Life Issues,* May 20, 2014, www .mercatornet.com. See also, on Mortier's history and his opposition to Distelmans, Aviv, "The Death Treatment."

7. Qtd. in Guido Joris, "Zware kritiek op 'euthanasie-seminarie' in Auschwitz," *Joods Actueel* digital edition, September 29, 2014, www.joodsactueel .be. Translated with the assistance of Gabry Kuijten. (It bears noting that this text regrettably conflates the name of Konzentrationslager Auschwitz with that of the Polish city of Oświęcim.) Several commentators criticized Distelmans for calling Auschwitz an "inspiring" site. For instance, in the British *Daily Mail*, Labor MP Sir Gerald Kaufman is quoted as saying: "Whatever one's views on euthanasia— and I am against—it is abominable to describe Auschwitz as an 'inspiring venue.'" Petre, "Outrage." This criticism derives from a partial translation of the Flemish word "*inspirerend*," which does not necessarily carry the positive connotations of the English term "inspiring." Distelmans also characterizes Auschwitz-Birkenau as "the place that perfectly symbolizes a degrading (undignified) end of life" in his *In Pursuit of a Dignified Life's End*, 26.

8. Qtd. in Kuntz, "Euthanasia Doctors."

9. Ibid. Distelmans also contends that "several sensation-seeking journalists published articles about the trip without any respect for or understanding of its purpose" (*In Pursuit of a Dignified Life's End*, 26).

10. Paul Celan, "Speech on the Occasion of Receiving the Literature Prize of the Free Hanseatic City of Bremen," in *Selected Poems and Prose of Paul Celan*, trans. John Felstiner (New York: W.W. Norton, 2001), 395.

11. Shai J. Lavi, *The Modern Art of Dying: A History of Euthanasia in the United States* (Princeton, N.J.: Princeton University Press, 2005), 5.

12. Ibid., 3, 41.

13. Ibid., 6.

14. "The Moral Side of Euthanasia," *Journal of the American Medical Association* 5, no. 4 (October 3, 1885): 382. Qtd. in Ezekiel J. Emanuel, "The History of Euthanasia Debates in the United States and Britain," *Annals of Internal Medicine* 121, no. 10 (1994): 798.

15. S. Russell Wells, "Is 'Euthanasia' Ever Justifiable?" *Transactions of the Medico-Legal Society for the Year 1906–1907* (London: Baillière, Tindall and Cox, 1907), 5.

16. Adolf Jost, *Das Recht auf den Tod* (Göttingen, 1895), 37. Translated with the assistance of John Benjamin.

17. Ibid., 26.

18. Lavi, *Modern Art of Dying*, 93–95.

19. Ibid., 115–16.

20. See Michael Burleigh, *Death and Deliverance: "Euthanasia" in Nazi Germany c. 1900 to 1945* (Cambridge: Cambridge University Press, 1995); and Henry Friedlander, *The Origins of Nazi Genocide: From Euthanasia to the Final Solution* (Chapel Hill: University of North Carolina Press, 1995).

21. Among the considerable literature on the role of physicians in implementing Nazi killing programs, see Robert Jay Lifton, *Medical Killing and the Psychology of Genocide* (New York: Basic Books, 1986); and Roberto Esposito, *Bios: Biopolitics and Philosophy*, trans. Timothy Campbell (Minneapolis: University of Minnesota Press, 2008).

22. Lavi, *The Modern Art of Dying*, 122. See also N. D. A. Kemp, "*Merciful Release*": *The History of the British Euthanasia Movement* (Manchester: Manchester University Press, 2002), 123.

23. Kemp, *"Merciful Release,"* 143. Henry R. Glick makes a similar observation with respect to American legalization efforts: "Nazi *involuntary* euthanasia and extermination programs discredited political organizations and proposals that employed the term euthanasia in any form." *The Right to Die: Policy Innovation and Its Consequences* (New York: Columbia University Press, 1992), 58.

24. See Friedlander, *The Origins of Nazi Genocide.*

25. Leo Alexander, "Medical Science under Dictatorship," *New England Journal of Medicine* 241, no. 2 (July 1949): 44. On Alexander's life and work, see Ulf Schmidt, *Judgment at Nuremberg: Leo Alexander and the Nazi Doctors' Trial* (New York: Palgrave Macmillan, 2004).

26. See, among others, Daniel Callahan et al., "Biomedical Ethics and the Shadow of Nazism: A Conference on the Proper Use of the Nazi Analogy in Ethical Debate, April 8, 1976," *The Hastings Center Report* 6, no. 4 (August 1976): 1–19; Nat Hentoff et al., "Contested Terrain: The Nazi Analogy in Bioethics," *The Hastings Center Report* 18, no. 4 (August-September 1988): 29–33; Michael Burleigh, "The Nazi Analogy and Contemporary Debates on Euthanasia," in *Ethics and Extermination: Reflections on Nazi Genocide* (Cambridge: Cambridge University Press, 1997), 142–52; Arthur L. Caplan, "The Doctor's Trial and Analogies to the Holocaust in Contemporary Bioethical Debates," in *The Nazi Doctors and the Nuremberg Code: Human Rights in Human Experimentation,* ed. George J. Annas and Michael A. Grodin (New York: Oxford University Press, 1992), 258–75; and the cluster of essays included in Leslie E. Gerber, ed., "Euthanasia Symposium," *Issues in Integrative Studies* 18 (2000).

27. See, for instance, Henry Friedlander, who asserts that "whatever one's position on abortion or assisted suicide, comparisons with Nazi killing operations do not illuminate today's discussion." Yet the fragility of such an assertion is apparent in the sentences that immediately follow, in which Friedlander does in fact derive a "general lesson" from the Nazi era that he applies to contemporary debates: "It seems to me, however, that one general lesson can be applied. Government programs launched by the Nazi regime to exclude and kill clearly show that there are private spheres of human life where no state interest is sufficiently compelling to justify intervention. Only the individual directly affected, and perhaps his or her closest relatives, should make such intimate decisions." *The Origins of Nazi Genocide,* xxii.

28. See, for example, Timothy Quill, *Death and Dignity: Making Choices and Taking Charge* (New York: W.W. Norton, 1993).

29. Sarah Ferber, *Bioethics in Historical Perspective* (New York: Palgrave Macmillan, 2013), 67.

30. Burleigh, "The Nazi Analogy," 143.

31. "New Pro-Euthanasia Group Name Row," *BBC News,* January 23, 2006, www.bbc.co.uk.

32. The defeated California aid-in-dying bill included the provision that "'aid in dying' means a medical procedure that will terminate the life of the qualified patient in a painless, humane, dignified manner, whether administered by the physician at the patient's choice or direction or whether the physician provides means to the patient for self-administration." Qtd. in Howard Ball, *At Liberty to Die: The Battle for Death with Dignity in America* (New York: New York University Press, 2012), 112.

33. Ball, *At Liberty to Die*, 113. See also Hillyard and Dombrink, *Dying Right: The Death with Dignity Movement* (New York: Routledge, 2001), 24.

34. Derek Humphry and Mary Clement, *Freedom to Die: People, Politics, and the Right-to-Die Movement* (New York: St. Martin's Griffin, 2000), 246.

35. Hillyard and Dombrink, *Dying Right*, 36–7, 94. The historian Shai Lavi suggests that the Oregon law alludes to Nazi crimes in its specific provision that "no person shall qualify for the provisions of [the Act] solely because of age or disability" (*The Modern Art of Dying*, 166). Moreover, it deliberately disallows the direct administration of a life-shortening drug by a physician (death by injection), and instead authorizes only a form of physician-assisted suicide in which a doctor prescribes oral medications to end life.

36. The Belgian context presents a partial exception in continuing to employ the term "euthanasia." At the same time, this requires a continuing effort to circumscribe the meaning of this term, to distinguish between "correct" and "incorrect" usages. See Distelmans, *In Pursuit of a Dignified Life's End*, 8–9 and 197. Yet Distelmans also notes the difficulty of limiting the meaning and connotations of "euthanasia": "The word 'euthanasia' has bad historical and emotional connotations because it is frequently associated with the Nazis' so-called 'Euthanasieprogramm' during which those considered inferior by the Nazis were killed (this was, however, *not at their request*). In addition, it is often used by the media and opponents to indicate other end-of-life decisions. Nonetheless, the term is now established and there is no alternative that describes *self-determined* death as succinctly" (*In Pursuit of a Dignified Life's End*, 197). It is telling that despite this defense of "euthanasia," the title of his book draws instead on the vocabulary of dignity.

37. On the Australian Northern Territory law, see Ferber, *Bioethics in Historical Perspective*, 56–59.

38. Hillyard and Dombrink, *Dying Right*, 98.

39. As noted in the introduction, Hillyard and Dombrink, in *Dying Right*, identify three phases in the history of efforts to legalize physician-assisted death, a "voluntary euthanasia movement," which begins early in the twentieth century (9), a "right-to-die movement," with the Quinlan case in 1976 as its "starting point" (13), and a "death with dignity movement," which they confusingly also associate with the Quinlan case (14).

40. In Montana, a 2009 court decision ruled that physician-assisted suicide is not illegal, and that physicians who assist a patient's suicide upon request cannot be prosecuted. At the same time, the ruling did not provide any method for regulating the practice, and it has since been a matter of significant and, at the time of writing, unresolved legislative debate.

41. Herbert Hendin, "Selling Death and Dignity," *IAETF Update* (May-June 1995): 5–9, www.patientsrightscouncil.org; Elizabeth Atwood Gailey, *Write to Death: News Framing of the Right to Die Conflict from Quinlan's Coma to Kevorkian's Conviction* (Westport, Conn.: Praeger, 2003), 1.

42. For the text of the Oregon law, see the Oregon Death with Dignity Act, 127.810, www.oregonlaws.org. For reporting methods, see "Death with Dignity Annual Reports," public.health.oregon.gov.

43. John R. Cavanagh, "Bene Mori: The Right of the Patient to Die with Dignity," *Linacre Quarterly* 30 (May 1963): 66.

44. "The California Natural Death Act: State of California, 1976," in *Sourcebook in Bioethics: A Documentary History,* ed. Albert R. Jonsen et al. (Washington, D.C.: Georgetown University Press, 1998), 149–52, section 7195.

45. Derek Humphry, "What Do You Call an Assisted Death?" November 9, 2006, www.assistedsuicide.org. Thomas R. McCormick makes a similar observation with reference to various patient scenarios in "Human Dignity in End-of-Life Issues: From Palliative Care to Euthanasia," in *Human Dignity in Bioethics: From Worldviews to the Public Square,* ed. Stephen Dilley and Nathan J. Palpant (New York: Routledge, 2013), 264.

46. Leon Kass, *Life, Liberty, and the Defense of Dignity: The Challenge for Bioethics* (San Francisco: Encounter Books), 249. See also Somerville, *Death Talk,* who notes that "the language of a right to a dignified death is often, although it need not be, used as a euphemism for euthanasia." *Death Talk: The Case against Euthanasia and Physician-Assisted Suicide* (Montreal: McGill-Queen's University Press, 2001), 43.

47. "The Universal Declaration of Human Rights," www.un.org.

48. The European Court of Human Rights—which enforces not the UDHR but rather the similar European Convention on Human Rights, whose second article, like that of the UDHR, guarantees a "right to life"—found, in the case of Diane Pretty (discussed in chapter 1), that "Article 2 cannot, without a distortion of language, be interpreted as conferring the diametrically opposite right, namely a right to die." See Douwe Korff, *The Right to Life: A Guide to the Implementation of Article 2 of the European Convention on Human Rights* (Strasbourg: Council of Europe, 2006), 15–22. Neither of the other two international institutions for the enforcement of human rights law, the United Nations Human Rights Council and the Inter-American Human Rights Court, have issued decisions on right-to-die cases.

49. Dignitas, www.dignitas.ch/.

50. Qtd. in Katherine Franke, "Dignifying Rights: A Comment on Jeremy Waldron's *Dignity, Rights, and Responsibility,*" *Arizona State Law Journal* 43 (2012): 1178.

51. Ibid., 1178, 1183.

52. For a related and compelling analysis of the discourse of dignity, and particularly of the common structures of supposedly competing definitions of dignity, see Scott Cutler Shershow, *Deconstructing Dignity: A Critique of the Right-to-Die Debate* (Chicago: University of Chicago Press, 2014), published during the final stages of the preparation of this book. Aside from the significant methodological differences between Shershow's primarily philosophical work and my own, *Deconstructing Dignity* does not broach the central question of this book concerning the significance of the right to die in the time of *postnatural* death.

53. *Compassion in Dying v. Washington,* 79 F. 3d 790, 9th Cir. (1996). Qtd. in part in Hillyard and Dombrink, *Dying Right,* 258.

54. Ronald Dworkin, Thomas Nagel, Robert Nozick, John Rawls, Thomas Scanlon, and Judith Jarvis Thompson, "Assisted Suicide: The Philosopher's Brief," *New York Review of Books,* March 27, 1997.

55. Immanuel Kant, *Groundwork of the Metaphysics of Morals,* trans. and ed. Mary Gregor (Cambridge: Cambridge University Press, 1998), 42.

56. Ibid., 32.

57. Immanuel Kant, *Lectures on Ethics*, ed. Peter Heath and J. B. Schneewind, trans. Peter Heath (Cambridge: Cambridge University Press, 1997), 145, 150.

58. Michael Rosen, *Dignity: Its History and Meaning* (Cambridge, Mass.: Harvard University Press, 2012), 149.

59. Kant, *Lectures on Ethics*, 150; Kant, *Vorlesung zur Moralphilosophie*, ed. Werner Stark (Berlin: Walter de Gruyter, 2004), 228.

60. "For to risk one's life against one's foes, and to observe the duty towards oneself, and even to sacrifice one's life, is not suicide." Kant, *Lectures on Ethics*, 146.

61. Christopher McCrudden, "Human Dignity and Judicial Interpretation of Human Rights," *European Journal of International Law* 19, no. 4 (2008): 664ff.

62. David Hollenbach, "Human Dignity: Experience and History, Practical Reason and Faith," in *Understanding Human Dignity*, ed. Christopher McCrudden (Oxford: Oxford University Press, 2013). The historical role of the Shoah in motivating the turn to "dignity" in postwar constitutional law (especially German Basic Law) and the UDHR has been the subject of compelling disagreement. Christoph Goos, for instance, argues that it is neither theological nor Kantian conceptions of dignity that led to its central role in German law, but that it was defined as precisely the "inner freedom" that had been suppressed by Nazism. Samuel Moyn, by contrast, argues compellingly for a reevaluation of dignity's Catholic theological legacy and the implications thereof. See Goos, "Würde des Menschen: Restoring Human Dignity in Post-Nazi Germany"; and Moyn, "The Secret History of Constitutional Dignity," in McCrudden, *Understanding Human Dignity*.

63. Qtd. in Naomi Rao, "Three Concepts of Dignity in Constitutional Law," *Notre Dame Law Review* 86, no. 1 (2011): 194n36. As Rao observes: "Although modern constitutions and constitutional courts often treat the equality of human dignity with the highest moral overtones, in practice, the concept often serves as an open-ended legal term that can be filled with prevailing moral preferences. Courts invoking human dignity have generally allowed its meaning to rest on intuition." Naomi Rao, "On the Use and Abuse of Dignity in Constitutional Law," *Columbia Journal of European Law* 14, no. 2 (spring 2008): 220. See also Lois Shepherd, "Dignity and Autonomy after *Washington v. Glucksberg*: An Essay about Abortion, Death, and Crime," *Cornell Journal of Law and Public Policy* 7, no. 2 (winter 1988): 431–66.

64. Qtd. in Goos, "Würde des Menschen."

65. David Albert Jones, "Is Dignity Language Useful in Bioethical Discussion of Assisted Suicide and Abortion?" in McCrudden, *Understanding Human Dignity*.

66. Hillyard and Dombrink, *Dying Right*, 257.

67. On the variations in Améry's name, see Irène Heidelberger-Leonard, *The Philosopher of Auschwitz: Jean Améry and Living with the Holocaust* (London: I.B. Tauris, 2010), 1–3.

68. Jean Améry, *On Suicide: A Discourse on Voluntary Death*, trans. John D. Barlow (Bloomington: Indiana University Press, 1999), 53. Quotations from the German edition refer to Jean Améry, *Hand an sich legen: Diskurs über den Freitod*, in *Werke*, vol. 3 (Stuttgart: Klett-Cotta, 2005), 173–344.

69. John D. Barlow, "Translator's Introduction," in Améry, *On Suicide*, xi.

70. Améry, *On Suicide*, 78–79.

71. "It is also certain that Primo Levi still lives on through discourse on Auschwitz today, while Améry's works, which created the opportunity for that discourse

in the first place, went into it so deeply that we no longer feel it necessary to relate the discourse to Améry's name." Heidelberger-Leonard, *The Philosopher of Auschwitz*, 71.

72. Jean Améry, *At the Mind's Limits: Contemplations by a Survivor on Auschwitz and Its Realities*, trans. Sidney Rosenfeld and Stella P. Rosenfeld (Bloomington: Indiana University Press, 1980), 27–28. Originally published as Jean Améry, *Jenseits von Schuld und Sühne: Bewältigungsversuche eines Überwältigten* (Stuttgart: Klett-Cotta, 1977).

73. Ibid., 28.

74. Ibid., 40.

75. Ibid., 34.

76. Ibid., 33–34.

77. Primo Levi, "Jean Améry, Philosopher and Suicide" (*La Stampa*, December 7, 1978), in *The Black Hole of Auschwitz* (Cambridge: Polity, 2005), 48–49.

78. Shoshana Felman and Dori Laub, *Testimony: Crises of Witnessing in Literature, Psychoanalysis, and History* (New York: Routledge, 1992).

79. Améry, *At the Mind's Limits*, 39, 40.

80. Ibid., 16.

81. Ibid., 17–18.

82. Theodor Adorno, "Lecture Fourteen: 'The Liquidation of the Self' (July 15, 1965)," trans. Edmund Jephcott, in *Can One Live after Auschwitz?: A Philosophical Reader*, ed. Rolf Tiedemann (Stanford, Calif.: Stanford University Press, 2003), 430.

83. Heidelberger-Leonard, *The Philosopher of Auschwitz*, 142. On Améry's views of Adorno, see ibid., 154–56.

84. While I focus on the convergence of Améry's and Adorno's thought here, it should be noted that they each openly acknowledged differences in philosophical temperament. See Adorno, "Lecture Fourteen: 'The Liquidation of the Self,'" 430; Jean Améry, "Jargon der Dialektik," *Merkur* 236 (November 1967); and Heidelberger-Leonard, *The Philosopher of Auschwitz*, 154–56.

85. On the "strategic" dimension of Améry's rhetorical stance in *At the Mind's Limits*, see Magdalena Zolkos, "Forgiveness, Theologies of Justice, and Jean Améry's Resenting Subject," in *Declensions of the Self: A Bestiary of Modernity*, ed. Jean-Jacques Defert, Trevor Tchir, and Dan Webb (Newcastle upon Tyne: Cambridge Scholars, 2008), 154–69.

86. Adorno, "Lecture Fourteen: 'The Liquidation of the Self,'" 428.

87. Theodor Adorno, *Negative Dialectics* (1966), trans. E. B. Ashton (London: Routledge, 1973), 371.

88. "Can't we conclude that not only the fear of dying but every fear actually goes back to the fear of death?" Jean Améry, *On Aging: Revolt and Resignation*, trans. John D. Barlow (Bloomington: Indiana University Press, 1994), 120.

89. See Derrida's statement that "traumatism is produced by the future, by the to come, by the threat of the worst to come, rather than by an aggression that is 'over and done with.'" Jacques Derrida and Giovanna Borradori, "Autoimmunity: Real and Symbolic Suicides; A Dialogue with Jacques Derrida," trans. Pascale-Anne Brault and Michael Naas, in Giovanna Borradori, *Philosophy in a Time of Terror: Dialogues with Jürgen Habermas and Jacques Derrida* (Chicago: University of Chicago Press, 2003), 97.

90. Jean Améry, *Radical Humanism: Selected Essays*, trans. Sidney Rosenfeld and Stella P. Rosenfeld (Bloomington: Indiana University Press, 1984), 17.

91. Améry, *At the Mind's Limits*, 16.

92. Jean-François Lyotard, *The Differend: Phrases in Dispute*, trans. Georges Van Den Abbeele (Minneapolis: University of Minnesota Press, 1988), 101. Along with Adorno's *Negative Dialectics*, to which the relevant section of Lyotard's book responds, *The Differend* may also be enlisted as evidence of Heidelberger-Leonard's observation on the absence of Améry's name from reflections deeply indebted to his thought. One might compare, in particular, Améry's testimony about the collapse of the "aesthetic view of death" in Auschwitz to Lyotard's dictum that "'Auschwitz' is the forbiddance of the beautiful death" (*The Differend*, 100).

93. Améry, *At the Mind's Limits*, 17. Primo Levi contrasts his recollections with Améry's, but comes to a similar conclusion: "Precisely because of the constant imminence of death there was no time to concentrate on the idea of death." *The Drowned and the Saved*, trans. Raymond Rosenthal (New York: Vintage, 1988), 76.

94. Paul Citrome, "Conclusions d'un enquête sur le suicide dans les camps de concentration," *Cahiers internationaux de sociologie* 12 (1952): 147.

95. Ibid.

96. See, for example, Levi, *The Drowned and the Saved*, 76; Bruno Bettelheim, *The Informed Heart: Autonomy in a Mass Age* (Glencoe, Ill.: The Free Press, 1960), 121, 126, 144; Améry, *At the Mind's Limits*, 17; Viktor Frankl, *Man's Search for Meaning*, 4th edition (Boston: Beacon, 1992), 31; Hannah Arendt, "Social Science Techniques and the Study of Concentration Camps," in *Essays in Understanding, 1930–1954*, ed. Jerome Kohn (New York: Harcourt Brace, 1994); and *The Origins of Totalitarianism* (San Diego: Harcourt Brace, 1973), 455n. References to a low suicide rate in studies devoted specifically to the Nazi camps include Thomas Bronisch, "Suicidality in German Concentration Camps," *Archives of Suicide Research* 2 (1996): 129–44; and Konrad Kweit, "The Ultimate Refuge: Suicide in the Jewish Community under the Nazis," *Leo Baeck Institute Yearbook*, vol. 29 (London: Secker and Warburg, 1984): 135–67.

97. Levi, *The Drowned and the Saved*, 17, 76.

98. Kweit, "The Ultimate Refuge," 161.

99. Danuta Czech, *Auschwitz Chronicle: 1939–1945* (New York: Henry Holt, 1990), 46 and passim; and Benedykt Kautsky, *Teufel und Verdammte: Erfahrungen und Erkenntnisse aus sieben Jahren in deutschen Konzentrationslagern*, cited in Zdisław Ryn, "Suicides in the Nazi Concentration Camps," *Suicide and Life-Threatening Behavior* 16, no. 4 (winter 1986): 421.

100. Ryn, "Suicides in the Nazi Concentration Camps," 420. For an expanded version of this study, see Zdzisław Ryn and Stanisław Kłodziński, "Z problematyki samobójstw w hitlerowskich obozach koncentracyjnych," *Przelgląd Lekarski* 33, no. 1 (1976): 25–45.

101. Ryn, "Suicides in the Nazi Concentration Camps," 420–21. See also David Lester, "The Suicide Rate in the Concentration Camps Was Extraordinarily High: A Comment on Bronisch and Lester," *Archives of Suicide Research* 8, no. 2 (2004): 199–201.

102. For a salient critique of the use of statistics in the study of suicide in general, see Jack Douglas, *The Social Meaning of Suicide* (Princeton, N.J.: Princeton University Press, 1967), esp. 163–234. On the problem of comparison, see Lester, "The Suicide Rate in the Concentration Camps Was Extraordinarily High."

103. Citrome, "Conclusions," 148. This point is more recently confirmed by Ryn: "In the whole literature dealing with suicide, it would be difficult to find any analogies to many factors typical of suicide in the concentration camp" ("Suicides in the Nazi Concentration Camps," 432). For an attempt to apply a sociological framework to suicides during and after the Holocaust, see Jack Nussan Porter, "Holocaust Suicides," in *Problems Unique to the Holocaust*, ed. Harry Cargas (Lexington: University of Kentucky Press, 1999), 51–56.

104. Citrome, "Conclusions," 149.

105. See Kweit, "The Ultimate Refuge," for a detailed discussion of Jewish suicides in Germany during the war. In an essay based on personal experience as well as archival research, Charlotte Opfermann suggests that many such suicides might also be considered as (indirect) murders. "Suicides or Murders?" in *Problems Unique to the Holocaust*, ed. Cargas, 43–50.

106. Hannah Arendt, "We Refugees," in *The Jew as Pariah: Jewish Identity and Politics in the Modern Age*, ed. Ron H. Feldman (New York: Grove, 1978), 61.

107. Ibid., 61–62.

108. Ibid., 62.

109. Ibid., 57–58.

110. Ibid., 58.

111. Interview with Jan Karski by Maciej Kozłowski published as Maciej Kozłowski, "The Mission That Failed: A Polish Courier Who Tried to Help the Jews," in *My Brother's Keeper?: Recent Polish Debates on the Holocaust*, ed. Anthony Polonsky (London: Routledge, 1990), 92. I thank Ulrich Baer for alerting me to this episode as well as to the Buber-Gandhi exchange.

112. Mahatma Gandhi, Harijan, November 26, 1938, included in Martin Buber and J. L. Manges, "Two Letters to Gandhi," in *The Bond* (Jerusalem: Ruben Mass, 1939), 42. Martin Buber, open letter to Mahatma Gandhi, in Buber and Manges, "Two Letters to Gandhi," 5.

113. Arendt, "We Refugees," 59.

114. Kweit, "The Ultimate Refuge," 148.

115. In her pathbreaking essay on Claude Lanzmann's *Shoah*, Shoshana Felman makes a related point in relation to the suicides of Adam Czerniakow, the head of the Warsaw *Judenrat*, and Freddy Hirsch, the leader of the so-called "Family Camp" at Auschwitz who committed suicide when he learned that the inmates in the camp, including the children, would be gassed. "Both suicides are elected as the desperate solutions to the impossibility of witnessing, whose double bind and dead end they materialize. To kill oneself is, in effect, at once to kill the witness and to remain, by means of one's own death, outside the witnessing. Both suicides are thus motivated by the desire not to be inside." It then becomes the task of *Shoah* to "testify from inside . . . the suicide of the witness" (Felman and Laub, *Testimony*, 228; emphasis in the original). Felman does not, however, address the question of whether such suicides can themselves be considered acts of witness.

116. Arendt, *The Origins of Totalitarianism*, 455.

117. Ibid.

118. Ibid.

119. Wolfgang Sofsky, *The Order of Terror: The Concentration Camp*, trans. William Templer (Princeton, N.J.: Princeton University Press, 1997), 23.

120. Kweit, "The Ultimate Refuge," 152.

121. Ibid., 163.

122. Filip Müller, *Eyewitness Auschwitz: Three Years in the Gas Chambers* (New York: Stein and Day, 1979), 114.

123. Paradigmatically, Thomas Aquinas, as quoted in chapter 1: "Whoever takes his own life, sins against God, even as he who kills another's slave, sins against that slave's master." *The "Summa Theologica" of St. Thomas Aquinas*, trans. Fathers of the English Dominican Province, 22 vols. (London: Burns Oates and Washburn, 1929), 10:204.

124. Kweit, "The Ultimate Refuge," 158. See also Raul Hilberg, *The Destruction of the European Jews*, revised edition, 3 vols. (New York: Holmes and Meier, 1985), 2:457.

125. Ryn, "Suicides in the Nazi Concentration Camps," 432. See also Jean Baechler, *Suicides*, trans. Barry Cooper (New York: Basic Books, 1979), 27; and Hilberg's observation that "'accounting for the life of an inmate' (even a German inmate) was defined as a complete and accurate report of his death . . . . When a Jew died, no special report had to be made; a death list sufficed. Whether an individual Jew lived or died did not matter at all." *The Destruction of the European Jews*, 3:908.

126. Cited in Ryn, "Suicides in the Nazi Concentration Camps," 421.

127. Isadore H. Holocaust Testimony (HVT-413), Fortunoff Video Archive for Holocaust Testimonies, Yale University Library. By permission of the Yale University Library.

128. Bettelheim, *The Informed Heart*, 150–51.

129. Ibid.

130. It should be noted that Bettelheim's own retrospective interpretation of this phenomenon differs from the one presented here. He writes: "Supposedly this was to punish them for their failure to do away with themselves, but I am convinced it was much more to punish them for the act of self-determination." Ibid. Bettelheim's personal interpretation of the motives for Nazi actions retroactively makes suicide recognizable as a sign of autonomy and opposition, perhaps because it seems unthinkable to accept at face value the seemingly paradoxical notion of punishment for failing to kill oneself. On Bettelheim's own death, see below, note 167.

131. Giorgio Agamben, *Homo Sacer: Sovereign Power and Bare Life*, trans. Daniel Heller-Roazen (Stanford, Calif.: Stanford University Press, 1998).

132. Levi, *The Drowned and the Saved*, 88.

133. Giorgio Agamben, *Remnants of Auschwitz: The Witness and the Archive*, trans. Daniel Heller-Roazen (New York: Zone Books, 2002), 85.

134. Among the vast literature on biopolitics, and on Agamben in particular, see Esposito's contrasting analysis of the possible relation between biopolitics and thanatopolitics. For a provocative critique of Esposito's notion of affirmative biopolitics, see Stuart J. Murray, "Affirming the Human? The Question of Biopolitics," *Law, Culture, and the Humanities* (June 2014, online before print): 1–11.

135. Agamben, *Remnants of Auschwitz*, 84–85.

136. Ibid., 70.

137. Ibid., 81.

138. Zdzisław Ryn and Stanisław Kłodziński, "Na granicy życia i śmierci: Studium obowozowego 'muzulmaństwa,'" *Przelgląd Lekarski* 40, no. 1 (1983): 65. Agamben refers to the German translation of this study without acknowledging its prior publication in Polish. I am grateful to Agnieszka Makles for her assistance with this and other texts in Polish. In a separate study, as noted earlier, Ryn unequivocally states that *Muselmänner* did indeed commit suicide. Ryn, "Suicides in the Nazi Concentration Camps," 420.

139. Ryn and Kłodziński, "Na granicy życia i śmierci," 41.

140. Agamben's only comment after quoting this passage is to remark that it gives further evidence of the "lacuna in testimony, one which is now consciously affirmed" (*Remnants of Auschwitz*, 41).

141. Améry, *At the Mind's Limits*, 9; trans. modified (from Améry, *Jenseits*, 21).

142. Agamben, *Remnants of Auschwitz*, 85.

143. John Protevi, *Political Affect: Connecting the Social and the Somatic* (Minneapolis: University of Minnesota Press, 2009), 123.

144. Protevi critiques Agamben's conceptualization of the *Muselmann* by pointing out that rather than a juridical designation, the name *Muselmann* seems to have been a "diagnosis" referring to a complex of physical and other symptoms. Alexander G. Weheliye insightfully questions Agamben's positioning of the *Muselmann* as a figure who "transcends race" (Agamben, *Remnants of Auschwitz*, 85) and argues instead that the *Muselmann* itself "represents an intense and excessive instantiation thereof, penetrating every crevice of political racialization." Weheliye's critique is based in part on the possibility that the designation of the *Muselmänner* encodes a racial slur. Weheliye, *Habeas Viscus: Racializing Assemblages, Biopolitics, and Black Feminist Theories of the Human* (Durham, N.C.: Duke University Press, 2014), 55. For an extended consideration of the politico-theological implications of this term, also with respect to Agamben, see Gil Anidjar, *The Jew, the Arab: A History of the Enemy* (Stanford, Calif.: Stanford University Press, 2003), 138–49.

145. Améry, *On Suicide*, 82; trans. modified.

146. Améry's testimony here might usefully illuminate what seems like an aside on the question of suicide by Foucault at the center of his brief but influential discussion of the shift from sovereignty to biopower in the first volume of *The History of Sexuality*. "Now it is over life, throughout its unfolding, that power established its dominion; death is power's limit, the moment that escapes it; death becomes the most secret aspect of existence, the most 'private.' It is not surprising that suicide—once a crime, since it was a way to usurp the power over death which the sovereign alone, whether the one here below or the Lord above, had the right to exercise—became, in the course of the nineteenth century, one of the first conducts to enter the sphere of sociological analysis; it testified to the individual and private right to die, at the border and in the interstices of power that was exercised over life. This determination to die . . . was one of the first astonishments of a society in which political power had assigned itself the task of administering life." What Foucault calls here "the right to die" exposes a rift, and

thus a possible space of resistance, within the biopolitical regime. The one who commits suicide, in this light, would not simply be "biopolitical substance" but would instead expose a limit to biopower. Michel Foucault, *The History of Sexuality: An Introduction*, trans. Robert Hurley (New York: Vintage, 1990), 138–39.

147. Améry, *On Suicide*, 85, 81.

148. Ibid., 81.

149. Agamben, *Remnants of Auschwitz*, 69.

150. Ibid., 68–69.

151. Ibid., 60, 63.

152. Ibid., 67.

153. Améry, *On Suicide*, 44; *Hand an sich legen*, 228.

154. Améry, *On Suicide*, 44–45.

155. Lothar Beier, "Échec und Dignität: Jean Amérys Nachdenken über den Freitod," in *Jean Améry: Der Schriftsteller*, ed. Irène Heidelberger-Leonard and Hans Höller (Stuttgart: Han-Dieter Heinz, 2000), 118. Translated with the assistance of John Benjamin.

156. Améry, *On Suicide*, 78–79; trans. modified.

157. Heidelberger-Leonard, *The Philosopher of Auschwitz*, 212.

158. Améry, *On Suicide*, 111.

159. Ibid., 121.

160. Ibid., 147.

161. Ibid., 97.

162. Ibid., 152.

163. Ibid.

164. Ibid., 153.

165. Qtd. in Beier, "Échec und Dignität," 107. Perhaps the strangest and least defensible interpretation of the connection between Améry's Holocaust survival and his death is that of Wolfgang Treitler, who proposes a parallel between Améry's suicide, which he sees as enacting a form of self-glorification, and the "self-glorification of a people" that led to Auschwitz. Wolfgang Treitler, "Saying No and Fleeing Nowhere: Jean Améry's Introspection of Voluntary Death," in *On Jean Améry: Philosophy of Catastrophe*, ed. Magdalena Zolkos (Lanham, Md.: Lexington Books, 2011), 274.

166. Primo Levi, "Jean Améry, Philosopher and Suicide." In this short text, published in *La Stampa* two months after Améry's death, Levi suggests that while, in general, there is a "kernel of incomprehensibility" in suicide, Améry's death is "on the contrary, absolutely comprehensible," and that the torture he suffered "weighed down on him right to his death, indeed was an interminable death." However, in a later essay on Améry, "The Intellectual in Auschwitz," in *The Drowned and the Saved*, Levi seems less certain as to the reasons for Améry's death. On the problem of interpreting Primo Levi's death, see my "Suicide after Auschwitz," *Yale Journal of Criticism* 14, no. 1 (2001): 101–4.

167. Heidelberger-Leonard, *The Philosopher of Auschwitz*, 239. See also Elaine G. Caruth's compelling interpretation of Bruno Bettelheim's death not as the belated enactment of the Nazi death sentence but rather as a determined refusal to be returned by illness to conditions resembling those of the camp: "This act was the final autonomous act of a man who freely chose to end his life while he had that freedom, rather than to continue to an end that could only be a

recreation of the concentration camps . . . ." "Bruno Bettelheim's Death: Further Considerations," *Psychologist-Psychoanalyst* 9, no. 1 (winter 1991), 7. I thank Cathy Caruth for bringing this text to my attention.

168. Améry, *On Suicide*, 92.

Epilogue

1. José Saramago, *Death with Interruptions*, trans. Margaret Juli Costa (New York: Mariner, 2009). When the goddess Eos requests that Zeus grant immortality to her lover, Tithonus, she neglects to request his eternal youth.

2. Jorge Luis Borges, "A Weary Man's Utopia" (1975), in *Collected Fictions*, trans. Andrew Hurley (New York: Penguin, 1998), 460–65.

3. Lee Falk, "Time Is Money," *Playboy* (December 1975). Films that adapt the basic scenario of Falk's story include *The Price of Life* (1987) and *In Time* (2011).

4. Kevin T. Keith, "Life Extension: Proponents, Opponents, and the Social Impact of the Defeat of Death," in *Speaking of Death: America's New Sense of Mortality*, ed. Michael K. Bartolos (Westport, Conn.: Praeger, 2009), 123. See also Don DeLillo, *Zero K* (New York: Scribner, 2016).

5. Walter Benjamin, "The Paris of the Second Empire in Baudelaire," trans. Harry Zohn, in *Selected Writings, Volume 2, Part 2: 1931–1934*, ed. Michael W. Jennings, Howard Eiland, and Gary Smith (Cambridge, Mass.: Belknap Press of Harvard University Press, 1999), 45.

6. On the temporality of "a time to come" in Benjamin, see Michael G. Levine, *A Weak Messianic Power: Figures of a Time to Come in Benjamin, Derrida, and Celan* (New York: Fordham University Press, 2014).

7. Jacques Derrida writes, with reference to Abraham: "He decides, but his absolute decision is neither guided nor controlled by knowledge. Such, in fact, is the paradoxical condition of every decision: it cannot be deduced from a form of knowledge of which it would simply be the effect, conclusion, or explicitation." *The Gift of Death*, trans. David Wills (Chicago: University of Chicago Press, 1995), 77.